History of Computing

T0143020

The *History of Computing* series publishes high-quality books which address the history of computing, with an emphasis on the 'externalist' view of this history, more accessible to a wider audience. The series examines content and history from four main quadrants: the history of relevant technologies, the history of the core science, the history of relevant business and economic developments, and the history of computing as it pertains to social history and societal developments.

Titles can span a variety of product types, including but not exclusively, themed volumes, biographies, 'profile' books (with brief biographies of a number of key people), expansions of workshop proceedings, general readers, scholarly expositions, titles used as ancillary textbooks, revivals and new editions of previous worthy titles.

These books will appeal, varyingly, to academics and students in computer science, history, mathematics, business and technology studies. Some titles will also directly appeal to professionals and practitioners of different backgrounds.

Author guidelines: springer.com > Authors > Author Guidelines

For other titles published in this series, go to www.springer.com/series/8442

David L. Stearns

Electronic Value Exchange

Origins of the VISA Electronic Payment System

 Springer

Dr. David L. Stearns
Seattle Pacific University
3307 Third Avenue West
Seattle, WA, 98119
USA
dave.stearns@gmail.com

ISSN 2190-6831   e-ISSN 2190-684X
ISBN 978-1-4471-2623-2   ISBN 978-1-84996-139-4 (eBook)
DOI 10.1007/978-1-84996-139-4
Springer London Dordrecht Heidelberg New York

British Library Cataloguing in Publication Data
A catalogue record for this book is available from the British Library

Cover design: eStudio Calamar S.L.

Printed on acid-free paper

Springer is part of Springer Science+Business Media (www.springer.com)

For Chuck Russell, the operational brains and second CEO of Visa, who died in a tragic motorcycle accident on 1 September 2008. He was 78 years old, and still riding a Harley.

Preface

Most anywhere in the developed world, I can use a small rectangular piece of plastic, issued to me by a bank I have never visited, to obtain local currency or purchase goods and services directly from a merchant. The cashier and I may not even speak a common language, and the face of my card may look quite different from those carried by locals, but the cashier will nevertheless recognize my card as an acceptable form of payment. My account may be measured in a different currency unit from the merchant's, but no haggling over foreign exchange rates needs to take place. Although my bank may be on the opposite side of the world and closed for the night, the cashier can insert my card into a small, relatively inexpensive terminal and in a few seconds receive what amounts to a guarantee of payment. Even if our respective banks participate in entirely different banking systems, that merchant will have access to those funds, converted to local currency, generally within a day.

It is perhaps a sign of the increasing rate of technological change that we, after a relatively short period of time, have ceased to find this surprising. Fifty years ago, paying for goods and services outside your local area typically required the use of pre-purchased local currency or travelers cheques, and if you ran out, your options for obtaining more funds away from home were limited. Today, we hardly think twice about leaving home with nothing but a payment card, and rarely reflect on how these little bits of plastic, as well as the systems they access, have fundamentally changed the ways in which we exchange monetary value. As with countless other technological innovations, we have come to regard these electronic payment networks as "normal" or even "natural."

But there is nothing "natural" about electronic payment systems. Although those born after the 1990s might never have known a time without them, payment cards and the electronic networks they activate went through an explicit process of creation and adoption, a process which actively shaped these systems into what they are today. If one wants to understand why these systems ended up the way they did, one first needs to understand their origins, and how decisions made in their early years fundamentally shaped the way they evolved.

This book recaptures the origins of one of these systems in particular: the electronic payment network known as "VISA."[1] It traces in detail how this system was designed, built and actively adopted from the mid-1960s through the early 1980s. This period encompasses not only the system's foundational years, but also its most prolific period of innovation. It was during this period that the system transformed from a collection of disintegrated, localized, paper-based bank credit card programs into the cooperative, global, electronic value exchange network we know today.

What is Visa?

Before we discuss why Visa might be an interesting and important subject, we first must understand a bit about what Visa is. Unless you have worked in or studied the banking industry, Visa is probably not what you assume it to be. Many readers may be surprised to learn that Visa itself does not actually issue cards. Visa is not a bank, nor is it a public utility or a governmental institution. Visa does not extend credit to consumers, nor maintain their accounts. It does not recruit business to accept the cards bearing its name, nor does it maintain their accounts either. It does not even build nor sell those little point-of-sale terminals used to read the cards. So what *is* Visa, and what does it actually *do*?

Visa is in essence an *enabling organization*. For most of its history, it has been an effectively not-for-profit cooperative membership association, owned and governed by the same set of financial institutions it serves.[2] Visa provides an infrastructure, both technical and organizational, in which multiple competing financial institutions can cooperate, just enough, to provide a service that none could have realistically provided alone. In short, Visa makes money *move*.

Today, the Visa system makes a rather significant amount of that money move—about $4.8 *trillion* (USD) each year and rising.[3] Close to 16,000 financial institutions from 200 countries and territories now participate in the system, either by

---

[1] As we shall see, VISA is technically a recursive acronym for Visa International Services Association, but it is typically referred to simply as "Visa" after first use.

[2] Visa was legally organized as a for-profit, non-stock membership association but since it did not issue stock and was solely owned by the same institutions that provided its operational funding, it effectively operated as a non-profit. Any accumulated net revenue amassed by the organization was either put back into operations, or was used as a settlement reserve in compliance with the Basel accords.

[3] For current statistics on Visa, see http://corporate.visa.com/about-visa/our-business/global-presence.shtml (accessed 3 August 2010). For comparison, MasterCard's sales volume for 2009 was $2.5 trillion, and American Express's volume was $620 billion. Volume figures come from each company's respective annual report to shareholders. In America, checks still account for the majority of non-cash payments in terms of dollar volume (nearly ten times Visa's dollar volume in the US), but only 30 percent of the total number of payments. See *The 2007 Federal Reserve Payments Study*, available at http://www.frbservices.org/files/communications/pdf/research/2007_payments_study.pdf (accessed 5 August 2010). The use of checks has been steadily falling for the last decade, so cards may soon surpass checks in dollar volume as well.

issuing some of the 1.8 billion cards in circulation, or by representing merchants that accept those cards. Visa's technical infrastructure now processes around 66 billion transactions a year, nearly 2,000 per second, making it the largest payment card network in the world.[4]

Why Visa?

The critical role that Visa presently plays in facilitating global commerce is certainly one important reason for us to study its origins, but there is another, perhaps more significant, reason as well. Visa, more than any other organization at the time, *defined* the electronically-processed credit and debit cards we know today. Visa's founder and his staff changed the way bankers and consumers thought about the card, transforming it from a vehicle for automating consumer credit to an access device for a global electronic value exchange network.

Although the organization that would eventually be known as Visa was created ostensibly to fix a broken domestic credit card system, we shall see that from the beginning its founder had far larger aspirations. Even before the organization was formed, he had come to the conclusion that money had become nothing more than "guaranteed alphanumeric data," and that computers and telecommunications would soon enable the near-instant transfer of those monetary data anywhere in the world.[5] The implications for banking and payments were enormous: any organization that was adept to data processing could easily become a "bank"; and any organization that could facilitate and guarantee transmission of these data would effectively create, and sit at the nexus of, a new global currency.

He also realized that the term "credit card" was a misnomer, a historically-contingent label that limited how people thought about what this kind of card could do. The card, he argued, was simply an access device, something that identified an account holder to a value exchange system. There was no reason why the account in question had to be a line of credit; it could just as easily be a deposit account, an investment account, or any other pool of value the consumer might possess. In fact, there was little reason why the access device needed to be a rectangular plastic card; it could just as easily be something else typically carried by a consumer.

From these insights, Visa's founder articulated a vision for a global electronic value exchange network that set the agenda for the organization's formative years. He surrounded himself with a highly-innovative technical staff, who created some of the first nationwide, and eventually international, computerized authorization and clearing systems. He also used his position to change the way his member bankers

---

[4]Throughout the period discussed in this book, Visa remained an effectively not-for-profit membership association, but it is worth noting that in 2008, most of the system restructured into a for-profit, publicly-traded corporation. The European region decided to remain a separate membership association and continues to participate in the overall payment system, but in the rest of the world, the core organization now more closely resembles a typical stock-issuing corporation.

[5]Hock (2005), pp. 95–96.

thought about the card, challenging their existing conceptual boundaries by introducing the first wide-scale debit card and the first payment card to access an investment account. Through national advertising, Visa attempted to change the way consumers thought about the card as well, telling them to "think of it as money," and use the card for routine purchases as well as those that required financing.

In short, what that little rectangular plastic card was "good for" was not something that was immediately obvious to those at the time. Instead, the very meaning and purpose of the card had to be actively constructed, and Visa in particular played perhaps the most significant role in that process.

Purpose of the Book

Despite Visa's importance to the global economy and our everyday lives, there are surprisingly few examinations of Visa's early history, and none that adequately deal with the technological infrastructure that underpins the system.[6] As a historian of technology and former information systems engineer, I found this surprising, as I wanted to understand on a technical level how my own Visa card worked. At the very least, this book should fill this gap, providing a deep and comprehensive history of Visa's transaction processing systems.

But as an interdisciplinary researcher trained in Science and Technology Studies, I also knew that making a system like Visa "work" requires much more than an array of computers, software programs, and telecommunication networks. Coordinating the work several thousand independent organizations, establishing the proper incentives for participation, and balancing out the participants' respective interests requires "engineering" of the social relations as well. Both the technological and the social infrastructures are necessary for the system to operate, but neither alone are sufficient to explain how the system works, nor account for its survival, growth, and current success. This book weaves together these two threads to provide the first sociotechnical account of Visa's history, one that I think will provide a deeper understanding of, as well as new insights into, this system that many of us rely upon everyday.[7]

As a detailed case study, this book also gives us the chance to interact with two grand themes that have been increasingly developed in the history of technology literature. The first is the mutual shaping of technology and social relations, which

---

[6]For an excellent economic analysis of the payment card industry with some specific history of Visa, see Evans and Schmalensee (2005). For an early financial history of credit cards in general, see Mandell (1990). For an impressive journalistic history of the American post-war financial services industry, with significant sections on Visa, see Nocera (1994). For an autobiography written by Visa's founder, see Hock (2005). For Visa's own corporate autobiography see Chutkow (2001).

[7]For the concept of sociotechnical systems history, see Hughes (1983). For a review of this perspective in *Technology and Culture* articles, see Staudenmaier (1985). I will also make use of concepts from the related Actor-Network Theory (ANT) approach, which is described in Callon (1986a), Latour (1987), and more recently, Latour (2005).

examines the ways in which artifacts are often profoundly shaped by social dynamics in addition to technical ones, and how those social relations are then reshaped in return as those artifacts are widely adopted.[8] The second grand theme concerns the influence that earlier information processing practices often have on the way firms adopt electronic computers and telecommunications.[9] As we shall see, the Visa case offers a substantial number of examples that help us deepen our understanding of both these themes.

In addition to informing these grand themes, I also develop two new dynamics that I think may be found in the history of other payment systems, or transactional networks in general. The first concerns how participants in a payment system establish trust in new payment devices, and how that trust can overcome the risks endemic to economic exchange. The second concerns how "gateways" in transactional networks can either reinforce or undermine established social boundaries. I will discuss these new dynamics in detail in Chap. 10, and show how they apply not only to the case of Visa, but also more generally.

This book also contributes to a growing body of literature on the history of money, payment systems, and financial services in general. Historians of money have traced the origins of earlier monetary artifacts such as coins, paper money, and written transfer orders (e.g., bills of exchange and modern checks), and a few have begun to include payment cards and their electronic processing systems into their narratives.[10] Historians of business and finance are increasingly studying the adoption of computers and telecommunication by banks and securities trading organizations, as well as the electronic services those systems enabled for consumers such as Automated Teller Machines (ATMs) and Giro payments.[11] Economists have done several analyses of credit cards, debit cards, and ATMs.[12] Sociologists have examined the history of consumer credit, credit scoring, as well as the ways in which social networks influence the adoption of new payment systems.[13] And legal scholars have recently concentrated on the regulatory and legal aspects of the credit card industry, arguing for reforms.[14]

In addition to these core contributions, the case study that makes up this book will likely be of interest to scholars in a few other fields as well. Visa's international

---

[8]For an introduction to this theme, see MacKenzie and Wajcman (1999). For an overview of the ways in which artifacts are often shaped during their adoption, see Mackay and Gillespie (1992), and Hartmann et al. (2005). For other similar approaches, see Pinch and Bijker (1984), Law (1987), and Callon (1986a).

[9]Yates (2005).

[10]Davies (1994), Chown (1994), Einzig (1966), Robertson (2005), and Weatherford (1997).

[11]For a recent and broad collection of such works, see Bátiz-Lazo et al. (2011). See also Richardson (1970), Humphrey (1995), Fry et al. (1999), Howells and Hine (1993), Kirkman (1987), Frazer (1985), and Wonglimpiyarat (2004).

[12]Evans and Schmalensee (2005), Russell (1975), McLeod (1979), and Hayashi et al. (2003).

[13]For consumer credit, see Calder (1999). For credit scoring, see Poon's chapter in Bátiz-Lazo et al. (2011), and for social networks, see Guseva (2008).

[14]Mann (2006).

cooperative network of competing financial institutions should be a valuable example to those who study organizations and joint-ventures. Visa's rise from a minor player in the payments industry to the world's largest payment card network will no doubt interest business historians. And the international expansion of the Visa system and its role in facilitating global commerce will also be interesting to those who study economic history and globalization.

Finally, this book was also written with an eye toward the generally-curious reader who simply wants a deeper understanding of this system and its history. Academic jargon will be kept to a minimum, and where specific concepts from Science and Technology Studies would be useful, I will explain them briefly so that those without a background in this field can follow the argument.

What This Book is Not

I should also note at this point what this book is not. It is not a critical examination of the evils of consumer credit, or the predatory lending practices of the individual banks—that has been already been accomplished by several authors, and their points are well taken.[15] Instead, this book concentrates on the central organization and its transaction processing system, which, as we shall see, was consciously moved *away* from its historical association with credit and debt, toward an electronic system for the exchange of any kind of value. In fact, I will argue that it would be incorrect to assume that the interests of the central Visa organization and its member banks were always aligned during these formative years; in several cases, including the early debit card, they simply were not.[16]

This book is also not a comparative examination of the development of payment card systems in several countries. That would no doubt be interesting and fruitful, but it is nevertheless outside the scope of this book. Instead, this book concentrates on the origins of the Visa organization and its electronic processing systems, which were primarily created and developed in the United States. I do discuss the expansion of the system internationally, and some of the processing challenges this created (such as settling transactions in multiple currencies), but I do not compare the existing national systems in other countries to those in the United States. This book captures Visa's origins in detail so that future work can make an informed comparative study.

Lastly, this book also focused more on the central Visa organization and the motivations its staff than it does on the individual member banks. This is a weakness, but a somewhat unavoidable one at this stage of my research. Even when the original Visa organization formed, there were already hundreds of member banks spread across the country. Although I did interview a few of those who worked in these early member banks, and collected comments others made in the trade press, their

---

[15]For example, see Manning (2000). For a more balanced view, see Mann (2006).

[16]See Chaps. 8 and 9.

perspectives are nevertheless relatively underrepresented in this book. I hope to improve this in future publications on this subject.

Sources and Methods

The historical narrative in this book is based upon research I conducted over a six year period, and my sources fall into roughly three categories. The first was news and trade publications from period (1970–1984), which not only provided me with a basic timeline of the events, but also revealed the issues that were most contentious at the time. To gain a mix of perspectives, I consulted not only banking-oriented news sources, but also merchant and consumer-oriented ones as well.[17]

The second group of sources included the autobiography of Visa's founder, and interviews I conducted with those who designed, built, and participated in the Visa payment system. Autobiographies and oral histories have obvious dangers that have been discussed at length elsewhere, but they complemented the news sources in a few important ways.[18] First, they helped uncover *why* certain decisions reported in the news accounts were made, what other options were discussed, and what their motivations were at the time. Second, they uncovered new information that was never reported publicly, and many times, never written down at all. Third, they often provided a less-guarded perspective on the events of this period, as all the informants had already retired or no longer worked for Visa. A full list of interviewees is provided after the table of contents.

The third set of sources consisted of a selection of documents from personal collections that were created by some of the key actors near the time of the events. These included reprints of speeches given by Visa's founder and other executives, project reports, statistics, brochures produced for the member banks, consumer survey results, as well as artifacts such as old sample cards. These sources enabled me not only to corroborate statements made by the interviewees, but also to discover new, detailed information that did not appear elsewhere. The speeches were especially useful for validating that the philosophical ideas Visa's founder discusses retrospectively in his autobiography did actually play a significant role in his decision making at the time.

While constructing the narrative, I continually combined information from all three types of sources, cross-checking them against one another, and asking follow-up questions of the informants when necessary. Wherever possible, exact dates, statistics, or factual claims came from printed sources created near the time of the events. Reflections upon the *meaning* of those events came from a mixture of quotes

---

[17]Banking-oriented sources included *The American Banker* newspaper, the *ABA Banking Journal*, *The Nilson Report* and the *Payment Systems Newsletter*. Merchant-oriented publications included *Business Week*, and *Forbes*. Consumer publications included *Life*, *Newsweek* and *Time*.

[18]Thompson (2000), Perks and Thomson (1998), Vansina (1965), Smith and Watson (1996, 2001).

from those printed sources, comments made during interviews, and my own analysis. Disagreement between sources was surprisingly infrequent, but when it did occur, I noted the various accounts or opinions and left the question open.

Although the methods discussed in this section should, I hope, lead to a narrative that is as accurate as possible, no method will produce a true and accurate description of the time period "as it really was." This is widely recognized as a chimera in historiography, and I only claim that what follows is *a* history of the Visa payment system's origins, not *the* history.[19] Like any history, this history is told from my own perspective, which is highly influenced by my academic training in Science and Technology Studies, and my technical training in information systems and software engineering.

Structure of the Book

The chapters of this book are organized mostly in chronological order, and each builds upon the previous ones. Chapter 1 sets the context for the story, describing the early history of merchant-specific charge cards, travel and entertainment cards, and the first bank-issued credit cards. Chapter 2 then analyzes the national network built around one of these cards in particular, the BankAmericard licensed by Bank of America, pointing out its various operational and organizational problems. I then introduce Visa's founder and first CEO, Dee Ward Hock, and describe how his philosophical ideas shaped the structure for his new organization, initially known as National BankAmericard Incorporated (NBI).

Chapter 3 then takes a bit of a sociological detour to discuss the role of the operating regulations in a cooperative network like NBI/Visa. Establishing the operating regulations was one of the first steps taken by the new organization, and I liken it to crafting the social dynamics of the system. I argue that these regulations are a key part of what makes the Visa system "work" at the inter-organizational level, and how Visa's role in adjudicating these rules helps establish just enough trust between the competing participants for the system to function and grow.

Chapters 4 and 5 return to the technological aspects of the system, describing in detail NBI's first computerized authorization and clearing systems, known mostly by their acronyms BASE I and II. NBI was of course not the only organization building such systems in the early 1970s, and these chapters put their systems in the context of other similar efforts by individual banks, independent processors, and bank service organizations. Chapter 5 also discusses NBI's first significant technical failure, a program intended to run within the member banks' processing centers, known as BASE III.

Chapter 6 charts the various ways in which the system was expanded throughout the 1970s, both technically and organizationally. On the organizational side, I discusses the formation of the international version of the organization, antitrust battles

---

[19]For a classic statement of this historiographic point, see Carr (1961). For a recent continuation of this theme, see Gaddis (2002).

and the institution of "duality," and the name change to "Visa." On the technical side, I discuss the shift of BASE I to the Airline Control Program (ACP) running on IBM hardware, the creation of a second cooperative data center, the expansion of the electronic authorization network internationally, and multi-currency settlement.

Chapter 7 returns to the technological aspects of authorization, describing how Visa helped fully-automated the point-of-sale. It discusses the various debates surrounding how to make the cards machine readable, and Visa's role in stimulating the development and widespread adoption of inexpensive merchant dial terminals.

Chapters 8 and 9 examine the ways in which the role of the central organization had to be worked out through a series of power struggles with the member banks. Chapter 8 chronicles the history of Visa's debit card, first introduced in 1975, but not widely issued until several decades later. This chapter argues that this delay had more to do with the ways in which the debit card clashed with the member banks' existing electronic funds transfer (EFT) plans, and disputes about Visa's role in the deposit side of the banks. Chapter 9 continues this theme of role negotiation by discussing other controversial moves by the central organization: the creation of a Visa-branded travelers cheque; the direct signing of the national retail giant JC Penney by Visa USA; and various signs of empire building that eventually resulted in Hock being forced out of the organization.

Chapter 10 concludes the book by summarizing the narrative and its contributions to the grand themes discussed earlier, and offering two new dynamics that I think may apply to the study of other payment systems, or cooperative transactional networks in general.

Acknowledgements

This book would have never come to fruition without the gracious help of several people. First and foremost, I wish to thank the many former Visa employees who graciously gave of their time to educate me on their experiences with the organization and its technical systems. A full list of interviewees is included at the beginning of the book, but the following people gave even more of their time over the years to read and make comments on my narrative: Tom Cleveland, Walt Conway, Win Derman, Frank Fojtik, Scott Harrison, Tom Honey, Roger Peirce, Bill Powar, Chuck Russell, Ron Schmidt, and B Ray Traweek. Special thanks must also be extended to Ingrid Kollmann, the coordinator of Visa's unofficial alumni network, who connected me with most everybody.

The research for this book began with my PhD dissertation at the University of Edinburgh, and many thanks must be extended to my supervisor, Donald MacKenzie, for shepherding me through that process and providing me with quick and valuable feedback along the way.

I am also deeply indebted to Martin Campbell-Kelley and everyone at Springer for giving me a chance to revise, expand, and publish this work. Martin's encouragement gave me the impetus to dive back into this topic with new vigor, and Springer's Wayne Wheeler and Simon Rees have patiently helped me navigate the entire publication process.

Much of the research for this book was conducted while I was a visiting researcher at the University of California, Berkeley, and many thanks must be extended to Cathryn Carson, the director of their Office for the History of Science and Technology for hosting me. My time at Berkeley was also greatly enriched by my conversations with Elihu Gerson, who kindly took the time not only to interact with my ideas, but also to encourage me during the most difficult times.

Another colleague who has helped me tremendously over the years is Bernardo Bátiz-Lazo. Many thanks are due him for including me in his recent edited collection, *Technological Innovation in Retail Finance*, and for encouraging me to embark on publishing this book. Bernardo was also kind enough to read various bits of the manuscript and provide helpful feedback, for which I am most grateful.

Donna Messner, a fellow graduate of Edinburgh and general science studies maven, also deserves special credit for reading and commenting upon several iterations of the introduction.

Many thanks must also be made to Sue Peterson, who took the time not only to explain to me several arcane aspects of high finance, but also to copy-edit the bulk of my original dissertation chapters, in between the thousands of other things she does each day. Her talents, precision, and limitless energy never cease to amaze me.

Last, but certainly not least, I wish to thank my amazing wife Chelle, without whom I would have never attempted this, much less finished it.

Contents

List of Interviewees

All interviews were conducted by the author. Dates and locations of the interviews follow each name. All subjects were previous employees of Visa, except where noted. Job titles and departmental affiliations meant very little during this period, as the company was small, project-oriented, and subject to constant reorganization. In the early days, Hock allowed his employees to create their own job titles, and although they were eventually standardized, they followed the conventions of banking, where nearly all key players are given a variant of the title "Vice President."

Terry Abrams. 29 March 2006, telephone.

Anonymous. 21 April 2006, telephone.

Elaine Baum. 8 June 2007, telephone.

Carol Coye Benson. 13 December 2005, telephone.

Greg Bjorndahl. 22 November 2005, telephone.

Brad Boston. 24 January 2006 and 6 March 2006, telephone.

Victor Chinn. IBM Systems Engineer assigned to Visa 1985–1989. 20 September 2005, telephone.

Walter Conway. 17 May 2006, San Francisco, CA.

Tom Cleveland. 8 November 2005 and 7 December 2005, telephone.

Irwin (Win) Derman. 28 September 2005, 21 October 2005, and 11 January 2006, Milbrae, CA.

Denny Dumler. Although he eventually became a Visa employee, Dumler was previously with Colorado National Bank and the PLUS ATM association. 9 December 2005 and 6 January 2006, telephone.

Linda Elliott. 3 November 2004, Denver, CO.

Frank Fojtik. 23 May 2006, Dublin, CA.

Jeff von Gillern. 23 February 2006, telephone.

George Glasser. McKinsey consultant hired for the BASE I project. Spring 2005, telephone.

Dave Goldsmith. 28 March 2006, telephone.

Scott Harrison. 16 May 2006, telephone.

H Robert (Bob) Heller. 10 October 2005, Tiburon, CA.

Tom Honey. 26 June 2006 and 18 July 2006, San Francisco, CA.

Mick Hosken. 6 April 2006, telephone.

Perry Hudson. Chase Manhattan Bank and the American Bankers Association's card standardization committee. 12 March 2007, telephone.

Denver Huff. Involved with the BankAmericard program at First National Bank of Oregon (formerly First National Bank of Portland). 8 May 2006, Grants Pass, OR.

Mike Jones. 4 April 2006, telephone.

Don Jutilla. Managed the BankAmericard program at Puget Sound National Bank in Tacoma, Washington. 10 March 2006, telephone.

Bennett Katz. 26 October 2005, San Francisco, CA.

Ingrid Kollmann. 18 May 2006, telephone.

Scott Loftesness. 13 October 2005, Palo Alto, CA.

Lewis Mandell. Historian of Finance and Professor at the SUNY, Buffalo. 1 March 2006, telephone.

Richard Martin. 19 April 2006, Orinda, CA.

David Nordemann. 5 June 2006, San Mateo, CA.

Ron Olive. 26 January 2006, telephone.

Roger Peirce. 25 October 2005 and 14 Dec 2005, telephone.

Paul Pittenger. Worked for CompuServe during the Point of Sale Dial Terminal trials. 17 July 2006, San Mateo, CA.

Bill Powar. 11 November 2005, 16 November 2005, and 23 January 2006, Palo Alto, CA.

Bill Reid. 3 November 2004 and 5 November 2004, Denver, CO.

Brian Ruder. 16 May 2006, telephone.

Chuck Russell. 14 October 2005, telephone.

Ron Schmidt. 30 May 2006, Walnut Creek, CA.

Diderik Schonheyder. 17 October 2006, telephone.

Tom Schramm. 13 January 2006 and 1 February 2006, Crow Canyon, CA.

Jean Stewart. 9 November 2005, San Mateo, CA.

Dawn Tindal. 12 May 2006 and 24 May 2006, telephone.

Aram Tootelian. 6 March 2006, telephone.

John Totten. 2 March 2006 and 3 March 2006, telephone.

B Ray Traweek. 12 May 2006 and 24 May 2006, Roseville, CA.

Pete Yeatrakas. President of WesPay, formerly the California Automated Clearinghouse Association. 19 December 2006, telephone.

Acronyms

ABA	American Bankers Association, the professional organization that represents the interests of bankers in America.
ACH	Automated Clearing House (or Automated Clearinghouse). A computerized system for clearing transactions submitted in electronic form.
ACP	Airline Control Program, the IBM operating system and database originally created for the Sabre system, and used for Visa's authorization system since 1977. Now known as Transaction Processing Facility.
ANSI	American National Standards Institute.
BASC	BankAmericard Service Corporation, a subsidiary of Bank of America created to administer the BankAmericard licensing program in 1966. This organization was replaced for the domestic members in 1970 by NBI, and for the international members in 1974 by IBANCO.
BASE	Originally BankAmericard Authorization System Experimental, later changed to BankAmericard Service Exchange, and today treated simply as a title for Visa's electronic authorization and clearing and settlement systems (BASE I and II respectively).
BWG	Blue-White-and-Gold, often used to describe the bands design that was part of the Visa mark until recently.
CMA	Cash Management Account, a hybrid between an investment and demand deposit account featuring a money market fund attached to an investment portfolio.
CNBT	City National Bank and Trust of Columbus, Ohio.
CSI	Credit Systems Incorporated, the organization that built and operated the first authorization system for the Interbank system.
DEC	Digital Equipment Corporation, suppliers of the PDP line of computers used for NBI's first authorization system.
DOJ	The US Department of Justice.
ECR	Electronic Cash Register.
EFT	Electronic Funds Transfer.
EFTS	Electronic Funds Transfer System, a system capable of transferring funds in electronic form.

EIRF	Electronic Interchange Reimbursement Fee, a discounted fee available for transactions authorized electronically and posted within three days.
ESBA	Eastern States Bankcard Association, the processor for several Interbank members on the East Coast.
FNCB	First National City Bank, known today as Citibank.
IATA	International Air Transport Association.
IBANCO	International Bankcard Company, the original name for the international version of NBI, later changed to Visa International.
INAS	Interbank National Authorization System.
ISO	International Organization for Standardization. Technically ISO is not an acronym, but a word derived from the Greek *isos*, meaning equal. See http://www.iso.org/iso/en/networking/pr/isoname/isoname.html.
MAPS	The ABA Monetary and Payments System planning committee.
MICR	Magnetic Ink Character Recognition, a technique for encoding the issuing bank, account, and amount on a paper draft, which can be read by both humans and machines.
NBI	National BankAmericard Incorporated, the original name of the organization now known as Visa. The name was formally changed to Visa in 1977.
NDC	National Data Corporation, a large processor for both Interbank and BankAmericard members in the 1970s.
OCR	Optical Character Recognition, a technique for machine-reading printed or hand-written characters.
PARS	Programmed Airline Reservation System, the commercial name for the repackaged Sabre system.
PERT	The Program Evaluation and Review Technique, a project management technique used to understand dependencies between tasks.
POS	Point of Sale. This is commonly used as a modifier for "terminal" when the terminal is designed to be used at the point of sale.
RFP	Request for Proposal, a document sent to potential contractors describing the system desired by the client.
SRI	Originally Stanford Research Institute, but this organization formally changed their name SRI International in 1977.
TIRF	Terminal Interchange Reimbursement Fee, the discounted fee paid by acquirers to issuers for transactions authorized through a point of sale terminal.
TPF	Transaction Processing Facility, the current name for Airline Control Program.
TTI	Transaction Technology Incorporated, a subsidiary of Citicorp that developed electronic transaction processing technologies.
TTU	Tape Transmission Unit, the name given to the DEC computers and magnetic tape readers installed in NBI member processing locations for use with the BASE II system.
UATP	Universal Air Travel Plan, a credit card program run by the airlines.

VISA   Visa International Services Association. This is the formal name of the Visa organization, though it is commonly referred to simply as "Visa" after first use.

WATS   Wide Area Telephone Service, a fee structure that allows organizations to provide toll-free numbers to consumers (IN-WATS), or make long distance calls for discounted rates (OUT-WATS).

WSBA   Western States Bankcard Association. The processor for several Interbank members on the West Coast.

Chapter 1
Setting the Stage: Money, Credit, and Payments in America

In the weeks leading up to September 18, 1958, some 65,000 households in the relatively obscure town of Fresno, California found a curious, thick envelope in their mailboxes. The envelope contained a small plastic card, about the size of a businessman's calling card and slightly larger than the charga-plates issued by the big department stores in San Francisco. It had the name "BankAmericard" emblazoned across the front with a series of embossed numbers below. In smaller letters at the bottom, it described itself as the "Bank of America charge account plan." The letter accompanying it explained that this card could be used to purchase goods and services at hundreds of different shops around the Fresno area. But, as the commercials often say, there was more: you would receive a consolidated bill each month, but if you did not want to pay it all, that was just fine with the Bank of America. You could simply pay a minimum amount, and turn the rest into an instant personal loan, paid back slowly, at your convenience, over several months.[1]

No doubt, some residents of Fresno must have been surprised to receive these cards and their attached lines of credit, but most would have seen or at least heard of something like them before. Although the BankAmericard program was a significant watershed event in the history of Visa, very little about it was entirely novel. Gasoline stations and department stores had been issuing charge cards since the 1920s, and some had even begun to offer revolving credit lines with minimum payments. The Diners Club card had already established a model where one card could be used a several different establishments, and the American Express company had begun issuing a plastic card a few weeks prior. The Bank of America (commonly abbreviated BofA) was not even the first bank to issue a credit card—many banks had attempted to start card programs in the late 1940s and early 1950s, and the rival banks that would soon rally to form the Master Charge network were already planing similar programs in the major urban centers of California.

All this is to say that the BankAmericard program did not materialize out of thin air or drop upon the residents of California like a revolutionary gift from the heavens. It was not a radical break from everything that came before it. As with all

---

[1]Chutkow (2001), pp. 64–66.

D.L. Stearns, *Electronic Value Exchange*, History of Computing,
DOI 10.1007/978-1-84996-139-4_1, © Springer-Verlag London Limited 2011

technological systems, the basic idea as well as the design details of the BankAmericard were based on ideas and influenced by events that preceded it. This purpose of this chapter is to review these antecedents in order to establish a historical context in which we can better understand the story presented throughout the rest of this book.

The Federal Reserve System and National Check Clearing

The events that directly influenced the formation and design of Visa stretch back to the beginning of the twentieth century with the formation of the Federal Reserve System in 1913 and its national check clearing network in 1915. The entire American banking system was radically altered by the formation of the Federal Reserve System (commonly abbreviated as the Fed), but our chief concern here is with the way it altered the clearing and settlement of checks. These changes created the economic conditions that would subsequently make checks the predominant method of payment in America throughout the rest of the twentieth century, and eventually a thorn in the side of debit card transaction pricing. To understand this development fully, we first need to understand a bit about how checks operated in the American payment system before the creation of the Fed.

A check is a different kind of payment instrument from cash. A check is an instruction, to the bank upon which it is drawn, to pay the bearer the specified amount upon presentment. As opposed to cash, a check does not directly represent value. Rather it is a *tentative claim* on value, and in order for the holder of a check to receive actual funds, the check must go through a logistical process of clearing and settlement.

Clearing a check means routing it to the bank upon which it is drawn in order for that bank to ascertain if the check is valid and if the account has sufficient funds for payment. This sounds simple enough, but check clearing in the nineteenth and early twentieth centuries was an amazingly complicated process due to the laws that governed how checks were paid. In order to receive the full value written on the check, the holder (or an agent of the holder) had to present the physical piece of paper to the bank upon which it was drawn; the paying bank was then required to clear the check *at par*, meaning that they paid the full value of the check to the bearer. If the check was presented through the mail or by a third-party courier, the paying bank was allowed to *discount* the check, meaning that it would pay something less than the full face value. This discount ostensibly helped cover the costs and risks to the paying bank but it was also an attractive source of additional revenue. The presenting bank would typically pass on these discount fees to the depositor, which might be a significant portion of the check's value. Thus there was little incentive for payees to accept checks drawn on banks other than their own, unless their bank had a way to avoid paying the discounts.[2]

---

[2]Evans and Schmalensee (2005), p. 38.

One way in which banks avoided paying discounts on local checks was to send messengers to each bank to present their checks in person. In areas where multiple banks operated, the banks typically formed cooperative *clearinghouses* in order to make the process more efficient. Instead of each bank sending messengers to every other bank, all the messengers assembled at one location and simply exchanged each other's checks.[3] Although the messengers were no longer technically presenting the checks at the bank itself, the banks saw no value in charging discounts on each other, as they would only tend to cancel each other out. Thus it was common that checks presented to clearinghouses were cleared at par.

The way in which banks avoided paying discounts on out-of-town checks has more to do with the way these checks were *settled*, which is the process of transferring "good and final funds" to the presenter.[4] Instead of shipping gold or notes around the country, most banks by the early 1900s had established *correspondent relationships* with banks in other cities in order simplify the process of long distance funds transfer. Correspondent banks make deposits with each other, and then debit or credit those deposits when they need to transfer funds. For example, a bank in Boston might deposit funds with a bank in New York, and vice versa. When the Boston bank needed to transfer funds to the New York bank (perhaps to settle a batch of checks), the New York bank would simply debit the Boston bank's account and credit the account of the payee. Thus, transferring funds became a simple bookkeeping entry instead of a physical movement of currency. Because the transfer was relatively easy, and because correspondent banks wanted to maintain a congenial relationship, they would settle each other's checks at par, even if they were sent via a third-party courier.

The combination of correspondent relationships and clearinghouses created a complex, web-like network of banks willing to clear checks at par, and not surprisingly, banks went to great strides to leverage this network to avoid incurring discounts. There are legendary stories from the time of checks traveling ridiculous distances over circuitous routes to get to a paying bank that was relatively close to the originating bank. One story described a check that had traveled 1,500 miles over 11 days to get to a paying bank that was only 100 miles away.[5] Another story told of a check that traveled 4,500 miles over two weeks to get to a competing bank that was only 4 miles away, only to find that there were insufficient funds, resulting in its return via the same route.[6]

The cases were no doubt atypical, but the more-typical delays were actually welcomed by those who wrote the checks and their issuing banks, as it allowed them to hold onto the funds for a longer period of time. This delay between the time a check is deposited and the time funds are finally settled is called *float*. This is an important concept in payment systems, and something that will recur throughout the story of

---

[3]This was by no means a new idea. The Bankers' Clearing House in London began in the 1770s. See Campbell-Kelly and Aspray (1996), pp. 15–18.

[4]Humphrey (1995), p. 4.

[5]Evans and Schmalensee (2005), pp. 40–41.

[6]Klebaner (1974). See also Fernelius and Fettig (2006).

Visa, so it is worth describing in detail. The float on a check creates a kind of short-term, no-interest loan for the check writer; the writer has already received the goods or services, but the actual funds are not withdrawn from the writer's account until the check is cleared and settled. The value created by this time lag is often too small for a consumer making a low-value purchase to notice, but for high-value transfers between business or banks themselves, this float-value often becomes a significant motivator for resisting changes to the payment mechanism.

In 1913, The Federal Reserve System was established primarily to reform the US banking system in general, but part of their mandate was to improve the way checks were cleared as well. The creation of the Fed had two important effects on this check clearing and settlement process. First, the new Fed structure created a mechanism for funds transfer that was as easy and efficient as the correspondent model, but with a simple hierarchical organization and a national scope. All nationally-chartered banks were required to become members of the Federal Reserve System by maintaining a reserve deposit account at their local Federal Reserve District Bank.[7] These reserve accounts created a way for the Fed to not only control the money supply, but also transfer funds between member banks in the district by simply debiting one reserve account and crediting another. The District Banks then maintained reserve accounts with each other, which allowed for easy transfer of funds between banks in different districts. This system almost completely eliminated the need to move physical currency around the nation.[8]

This new funds transfer system had a subtle, though perhaps unintended effect on the nature of money: it made it more abstract. Within the Federal Reserve System, money was now less of a "thing" and more of a concept.[9] The transfer of money no longer required the movement of physical objects, only the mathematical manipulation of numbers written in an account book. For the average consumer, "money" was still physical coins, and when necessary, paper notes, but for those involved in the operation of the banking system, money was quickly becoming something more akin to socially-guaranteed information. The processing of payments using computer networks depends on just this kind of conceptual move, and as we shall see, creating a similar conceptual move within the minds of consumers was one of Visa's central missions. This is not to say that the Fed made this move with electronic payments in mind, or that we should interpret this move as being the first step on an inevitable path toward electronic value exchange. Rather, we should see it as a conceptual move that occurred for reasons specific to the time, but was nevertheless a necessary condition for future events that took place in the history of Visa and other electronic payment systems.

The second effect the Fed had on payments was the establishment of a centralized, national check clearing system in 1915 that promised to be more efficient than

---

[7] State-chartered banks were also encouraged to join, but most did not as the reserve requirements for Federal Reserve members were often higher than their state-mandated counterparts.

[8] Evans and Schmalensee (2005), pp. 38–40. See also, Humphrey (1995), p. 8.

[9] A number of authors on the history of money remark that this move toward abstraction has been a general trend. See especially Richardson (1970).

the haphazard method based on clearinghouses and correspondent relationships. In effect, the Fed offered a new type of clearinghouse, similar to those discussed earlier, but now with a national scope. It was also free of charge to Fed members, as the cost of clearing was covered by the Fed itself, which in turn was funded through taxes. Just as in the other clearinghouses, the Fed mandated that participating banks clear each other's checks at par with the hope of completely eliminating non-par check clearing. Participation in the check clearinghouse was voluntary at this point, however, and only a quarter of the member banks chose to use the system. As Fernelius and Fettig observed "contrary to the Fed's hopes, most banks did not care to join the Fed in its attempt to streamline the nation's payments system because there was too much to lose by such efficiencies."[10]

The reaction to the Fed's check clearing system provides a nice example of one of the core theories from the Social Shaping of Technology position: the choice to adopt a new, more efficient technological system is not always a given. From an engineering perspective, system efficiency is its own justification, and engineers are often perplexed when more efficient technologies are not universally adopted. When we take a historical perspective, however, we can see that increased efficiency is not always a benefit to all groups within the system. If increases in efficiency will harm a powerful group, that group will resist that change or even shape the system in such a way as to heighten the inefficiency. In the case of payment systems, float creates a powerful economic incentive for those that find themselves on the paying side of transactions more often than the receiving side. That group tends to resist changes to the payment system that would make it more efficient, reducing the time it takes to settle a transaction, thereby reducing the float. Conversely, those that would benefit from an increase in efficiency will fight for those changes, and the resulting power struggle will shape the development of the system.[11]

The member bank's reluctance to use the new par check clearing system forced the Fed to take more aggressive action, forcing its members to clear at par regardless of how the checks were presented, and pressuring the non-member banks to do the same. Litigation, legislation and industry changes caused the number of non-par banks to fluctuate over the next six decades, but by 1972 all states had finally outlawed the practice of discounting checks, enforcing a par-clearing system nationwide.[12]

While there is some disagreement as to whether the Fed's check clearing system is indeed more efficient than the traditional correspondent and clearinghouse arrangements (which are still used today, albeit to a lesser degree), the elimination of non-par check clearing created the *expectation* that the processing of these kinds of payment instruments should be free, especially to merchants. This created not only a preference on the part of merchants for payment by check as opposed to payment methods that incurred a discount (as payment cards would), but also a hostility to

---

[10] Quote from Fernelius and Fettig (2006). For historical points, see Evans and Schmalensee (2005), pp. 41–42.

[11] For another example based on the choice between water and hand milling, see Bloch (1999).

[12] Evans and Schmalensee (2005), pp. 41–42, Fernelius and Fettig (2006).

paying a fee to process anything that resembled or was marketed as a replacement for a check. As we shall see, this expectation would become a key dynamic in the history of not only the Visa in particular, but also the shift toward electronic funds transfer systems in general.

Early Charge Cards

Shortly after the Federal Reserve System was established, the first charge card systems began to appear. These systems were offered by specific large-scale merchants, or by a network of merchants within a specific industry or geographic area, and they allowed consumers to purchase goods and services on short-term credit, requiring full payment at the end of the billing cycle.

Customers generally did not pay a fee to have or use these cards, nor did they pay interest on the short-term credit extended to them, so the systems themselves tended to lack profitability. Profit, however, was not the purpose of these systems. Instead, merchants offered these systems for two other reasons. First, they believed that customers purchasing on credit tended to buy additional or higher-priced items than those who were paying with cash. Second, they believed that the cards tended to create a loyalty, or brand affinity, for those businesses that would otherwise be competing strictly on price. The cards not only carried a reminder of the merchant's name, they also lent a certain amount of prestige and recognition to the cardholder, which in turn encouraged the cardholder to shop at the merchant's store to the exclusion of others.[13]

What made these systems innovative was not the idea of buying items on credit. The idea of "buy now, pay later" was nothing new at the time. Mandell reminds us that "retailers drifted into the credit card industry simply by conducting business as usual. In the United States, a large proportion of retail sales, particularly of discretionary items, had always been made on credit."[14] Calder makes a similar point, arguing that most purchases in the nineteenth century were made on credit, not only because most consumers were farmers and thus received the bulk of their income only at harvest time, but also due to the chronic shortage of coins and the unreliability of paper currency during this period.[15] What made these systems innovative was the ability to use a card, or similar device, to identify one's account to a centralized credit system that was available at multiple locations, or multiple merchants within an industry-specific network.

---

[13] Mandell (1990), p. 18. Note that the loyalty reason actually seems a bit tenuous. If a cardholder could obtain a card from one merchant, that same cardholder could likely obtain cards from competing merchants as well, as there was no centralized credit reporting agency that would stop a consumer from obtaining multiple cards. If cardholders tended to be more loyal to a given merchant, it may be for more complex reasons.

[14] Mandell (1990), p. 17.

[15] Calder (1999).

Western Union and the Department Stores

Western Union was one of those large-scale merchants that offered credit accounts to both businesses and recurring customers. Western Union also had a centralized accounting and billing office so that customers could charge their telegrams at any one of Western Union's numerous locations, but they needed a way to identify the customer to the billing system. In 1914, Western Union issued what is believed to be the first consumer charge card—a small rectangular piece of paper, containing the account number, the name and address of the person or company responsible for paying the charges, and a signature line.[16] The card identified the billing account, and the signature could be used to authenticate the cardholder.[17]

There were actually two types of cards, those for government officials and employees, and one for "representatives of business concerns and other responsible customers." Either type could be used to charge telegrams, as well as other services, at any Western Union location in the United States or Canada. The clerk would record the card number on the message, or a separate "toll ticket," and submit that to the central accounting office for billing.[18]

Department stores soon followed with cards or other tokens of their own.[19] Typically these cards were issued only to wealthier customers, who embraced the cards not only because they simplified their payments, but also because they lent a certain amount of prestige.[20] These cards were again only charge cards, so having one meant that you could pay off an entire month's purchases at once. The loyalty these cards created, or the merchant's perception of that loyalty and its value, became an important dynamic in the history of payment card systems.[21] As we shall see, the major department store retailers in America refused to accept bank-issued credit cards for many years, for fear of loosing this loyalty. Visa recognized this very real concern, and eventually developed the idea of co-branded loyalty cards that offered customers incentives to shop at specific merchants.

The early department store cards required clerks to hand-copy the account information from the card to the sales draft. This of course introduced the possibility

---

[16] Jutilla (1973), pp. 8–10.

[17] It is perhaps not accidental that Western Union was at the forefront of payment systems innovation, as they also introduced the first electronic money transfer service in 1871.

[18] Western Union Telegraph Company tariff manual, provided through personal correspondence with Harold Smith, former operations employee and webmaster of Western Union Retirees web site, and Carlos van Orden, another former Western Union employee. Some early authors mistakenly claimed that these cards were made from embossed metal, like a military dog tag, and journalists have tended to propagate this error in their articles. These authors likely confused this card with the "charga-plates" discussed later in this section.

[19] One early department store "card" was actually a small elliptical metal fob meant to be put on one's key chain.

[20] Mandell (1990), p. 18.

[21] Again, the loyalty argument may have had more to do with how merchants *perceived* the potential loss of loyalty rather than any real consumer affinity.

Fig. 1.1 Department Store Charge Fob. (author's personal collection)

of copying the number incorrectly or illegibly. To address these problems, the Farrington Manufacturing Company of Boston developed their "charga-plate" system, which was widely adopted by department stores starting in 1928. These were reconfigured metal address plates like the kinds used in addressing machines of the time. They were small metal rectangles embossed with the account number, customer name, and address on one side. A bit of paper was affixed to the other side that identified the issuing store and contained a line for the customer's signature. These plates were then used with a new device called an *imprinter*, which would squeeze the plate against a new standardized sales draft. This draft contained an additional carbon paper layer, which automatically transferred the embossed account details on the charga-plate to the top layer of the draft.[22] This method was not only a more reliable way to transfer the customer's identity to the sales draft, but also an important precursor to making the drafts machine-readable in the future.[23]

Up until this point, retail charge cards were issued by each particular merchant, and could be used only at that merchant's locations, but in the early 1930s, a new model began to emerge—several smaller retailers, who were normally competitors, banded together to form cooperative payment card systems. In these systems, a cardholder could use the same card (often a charga-plate) at multiple merchants. In a few systems, the central organization would extend the credit and collect from the cus-

---

[22]Mandell (1990), p. 18.

[23]Mandell notes that when Standard Oil of California switched to metal embossed plates in 1952, errors in identification were cut by 94 percent and drafts returned to the stations due to the inability to establish identity were cut by 80 percent (Mandell 1990, p. 23).

Fig. 1.2 Front and back of a typical Charga-Plate from the 1930s, including carrying case. The customer's name, signature and address have been blurred for privacy (author's personal collection)

tomer via one bill, while in others the central organization would simply issue the plates and the individual merchants would bill customers separately. These networks of competing retailers were often quite extensive. For example, the Retail Service Bureau of Seattle included over a thousand retailers by 1936.[24] These organizations were similar in concept to Visa, though they were owned by the retailers and not the banks, and were limited to a specific geographic area.

---

[24] Mandell (1990), p. 18. Unfortunately, Mandell provides little detail about these cooperatives, and no other author mentions them. If they are the first instances of a set of competitors cooperating to provide a common payment system, they are of great historical importance.

The Oil Industry

In the early 1920s, charge cards began to spread to the oil industry. In 1924, General Petroleum Corporation of California began issuing what they called "courtesy cards," and other gasoline retailers quickly followed suit.[25] These were charge cards, made from paper, that were handed out by station managers to repeat customers. With this card, a customer could charge gasoline and related purchases at any of the stations in the same franchise, which could extend over a considerable geographic distance. These programs typically operated at a loss, but the oil companies persisted because their prime concern was not profit, but brand loyalty. Gasoline is a relatively undifferentiated product, and there is little that ties a customer to one gasoline station over another, especially while traveling.[26]

Any loyalty generated by oil cards helped to not only increase the franchise's sales, but also enroll new stations into the network. Oil companies could promise owners of new stations that they had a large number of loyal, card-carrying customers that would choose a station in their branded network over others. Due to the nature of automobile travel, motorists would often find themselves in unfamiliar places, and would naturally choose a gasoline station where they could use their card. Additionally, the card offered the new station manager a way to extend credit to his customers without the hassle of accounting, billing and collecting.[27]

But the ability to leverage cards when signing new stations was dependent on a large cardholder base. In order to build that base quickly, these early oil cards were given out quite liberally. Mandell notes that the mere fact that a customer owned a car was often enough evidence for a station manager that the customer was credit-worthy.[28] In 1939, Standard Oil of Indiana went one step further, bypassing the station manager and distributing 250,000 unsolicited cards directly to consumers.

This episode provides us with the first illustration of the chicken-and-egg dilemma raised by multisided platform economic theory.[29] Cardholders will not carry cards until there are enough merchants that will accept them, and merchants will not agree to accept cards until there are enough cardholders that want to use them. The oil companies' solution to this dilemma was simply to mass-issue unsolicited cards to consumers, and this pattern would be imitated by other payment card systems until it was finally outlawed in the United States in 1970. Unfortunately, the benefits of this mass-issuance also came with a corresponding cost:

---

[25] Facts about BankAmericard (October 1975). See also Mandell (1990), p. 18.

[26] Mandell (1990), pp. 18–20.

[27] Mandell (1990), pp. 18–20.

[28] Mandell (1990), p. 19. Considering the price of gasoline at the time, the amount of credit exercised by any one customer would have been quite limited, so this rationale might not have been as unreasonable as it sounds.

[29] Evans and Schmalensee (2005).

large initial losses due to fraud and defaults. One man reportedly used his card to operate a long distance taxi service, charging over $500 worth of gas and oil without making any payments until he was finally arrested for an unrelated offense.[30]

The Airline Industry

The idea of the charge card then spread to the airline industry. In 1931, Century Airlines began issuing pre-paid coupon books for air travel, and after they were acquired by American Airlines, a Detroit office manager suggested to one of his large accounts that the airline could hold their coupons for them, and simply remove them from the books in response to "authorization letters" sent by the account. This program was widely adopted and eventually the books were replaced with a simple cash deposit. In 1936, the program was expanded to include other airlines and was renamed the Universal Air Travel Plan (UATP). UATP ran their own private clearinghouse to process the transactions, and by 1968 they were processing a billion dollars in sales volume across 111,000 business accounts with 1.5 million cards in circulation.[31]

UATP is another example of a payment card system that included multiple *competing* organizations that cooperated just enough to provide a universal system.[32] The member airlines of UATP were fierce competitors, yet it was in all of their interests to make airline travel easier, especially for business people. Business trips often required traveling on multiple carriers, and thus it was attractive for businesses to have one account on which they could charge all their air travel, regardless of airline. Eventually UATP evolved into a more general-purpose travel and entertainment card, extending into other travel-related merchant categories, including trains, busses, hotels and restaurants.[33]

The Great Depression and the credit restrictions imposed as America entered World War II put a halt to nearly all these systems.[34] Nevertheless, these early programs developed a number of ideas and practices that would influence the design of future payment card systems including BankAmericard and Visa: the identification card, embossed account information transferred by imprinters, cooperative joint ventures amongst competitors to provide a universal system, and mass unsolicited issuance to build the cardholder base quickly.

---

[30] Mandell (1990), pp. 19–20.

[31] Mandell (1990), pp. 20–21. 1968 statistics are from Jutilla (1973), pp. 53–55.

[32] Although the oil cards allowed customers to charge purchases as multiple stations, those stations belonged to the same franchise and thus did not compete with one another to any great extent.

[33] Jutilla (1973), pp. 53–55.

[34] Struble (1969), Facts about BankAmericard (October 1975).

Travel and Entertainment Cards

Shortly after the conclusion of World War II, the American payments industry experienced another round of innovations. A new type of payment card system was developed starting in 1949, commonly referred to as "travel and entertainment (T&E) cards" because they initially focused on supporting business people who traveled and entertained clients. Despite this initial focus, these systems quickly grew to include many types of merchants that were only loosely connected to the activities of travel and entertainment.

These systems differed from the merchant and industry-specific payment card systems in two important ways. First, instead of receiving your card directly from the merchant or a merchant cooperative, you now received your card, and its associated credit, from a third-party organization, one that was not owned by the merchants themselves. That organization also signed up merchants from many different industries to accept the card, allowing the consumer to use one card at a wide variety of establishments. Thus these systems are often called *generalized* or *universal payment cards*. On a periodic basis, the third-party organization would then pay the merchants for any charges made on its cards, and collect from the cardholders. Thus, the merchant was no longer in the credit business, and all bookkeeping, billing and collecting was performed by the third-party organization.[35]

Second, these systems were operated specifically for profit. As noted earlier, merchant-specific payment card programs were offered primarily to increase customer loyalty, and nearly all operated at a loss because the merchants did not charge any interest on the credit they extended. The T&E systems used a different business model. They "bought" the sales drafts from merchants at a discount, much like the discount on checks discussed earlier, which was commonly six or seven percent of the total. For example, if a hotel charged a business traveler $100, the T&E organization would pay the hotel $93 but collect the full $100 from the cardholder. The $7 difference would cover their costs and hopefully return a profit. Initially the cards themselves were issued without charge to build a significant cardholder base, but the various T&E organizations quickly discovered that they also needed to charge cardholders a small yearly fee in order to remain profitable, especially as the cost of funds increased.[36]

Diners Club

In 1949, Frank MacNamara and Ralph Schneider formed the first T&E payment card system, known as Diners Club.[37] MacNamara's initial plan was to create a card

---

[35]Mandell (1990), p. 26.

[36]Mandell (1990), p. 26.

[37]Some sources put the formation at 1950. It is likely that the company was formed late in 1949 and did not actually start operations until 1950.

that would be honored at restaurants all over New York City, hence the "Diners" part of the name, but it quickly expanded to also include everything from hotels and car rental agencies to florists and charm schools.[38] It became an extremely successful system, boasting 1.3 million US cardholders at its peak.[39]

The original card itself was a rather unusual design. It was made from cardstock, shaped roughly like a typical business card, with the account name, address, and number printed on the front, along with a signature line. This "card" was actually a small booklet that opened up to list all the establishments that accepted it. Initially, this was a relatively small list so it fit on just a few pages, and as the number grew, the list was separated from the card.[40]

The origin of the Diners Club idea requires some comment, as it has been inaccurately reported for many years and in many sources.[41] The story reported by the press was that MacNamara was entertaining a business acquaintance one evening in a New York restaurant, and when the bill arrived, he discovered he had not brought enough cash. To avoid embarrassing himself in front of his guest, he telephoned his wife who then drove from Long Island to deliver more cash. While he waited, he realized that a responsible business man should have a card with which he could charge a restaurant bill anywhere in the city.[42]

This story would normally lend credibility to the theory that technologies develop due to pressing social needs, but unfortunately, *it was completely fabricated*. Matty Simmons, the first press agent for Diners Club, thought that the real story lacked sufficient glamor, and invented the near-embarrassing incident, no doubt partly to encourage business people to avoid the same mistake by applying for a Diners Club card. Simmons admits:

> My story has appeared literally thousands of times in newspapers and magazines and books all over the world. In a beautiful four-color brochure, the Diners Club still evokes the legend of MacNamara sitting in that restaurant—his dinner partner long gone—waiting for his wife and dreaming of a credit card world.
> Of course, they couldn't know until reading this that the scene never took place.[43]

In reality, MacNamara simply thought of the idea one day and eventually decided it was worth trying.[44] Although it would be an overstatement to say that Diners Club was a solution looking for a problem, business people were not directly clamoring for a universal charge card. Simmons himself doubted that it would work, and Mac-Namara left the organization after only three years because he concluded it was

---

[38] 'For everything', Time (23 March 1959).

[39] Simmons (1995), p. 106.

[40] Simmons (1995).

[41] For a recent example, see Evans and Schmalensee (2007).

[42] Evans and Schmalensee repeat this story, but note that the original *Newsweek* article describes MacNamara as being at a coffee shop and forgetting his wallet altogether. Later reports tell the story as presented here.

[43] Simmons (1995), p. 26.

[44] Simmons (1995), p. 26.

only a fad that would quickly fade. The idea was not immediately obvious—it had to be explained and sold, both to consumers and merchants. Simmons described how MacNamara pitched the original idea to him:

> "It's perfect for the businessman," he enthused. "You pay all your business entertainment with one monthly check. You don't have to carry a lot of cash with you, and, most importantly, you have receipts for reimbursement from your firm and entertainment receipts for tax deductions."
>
> I listened unimpressed. He went on. "It's all of those things," he said, "but maybe most importantly, it's prestige. It's having a good enough credit rating to own one of these cards so that restaurants will treat you like somebody who's somebody. If you're a businessman and you're entertaining clients or working on a deal, the people with you will be impressed."[45]

This quote nicely summarizes how the T&E payment cards were marketed to business people, and many of these same points would be made by the bank-issued credit cards. Marketers stressed that the card was more convenient than cash, which could run out or be stolen, and more reliable than checks, which might not be honored out of town. The card also allowed the business person to delay and consolidate their actual payments, which could easily mount when traveling. The card provided automatic bookkeeping for not only corporate reimbursement, but also income tax deductions.[46] But these business functions were minor compared to the *cultural meaning* of the card: *prestige*. At this time, cards were still issued rather selectively, so not everyone could qualify for one. To have one meant that you, and consequently your organization, were worthy of what amounted to a blank check.

Diners Club built their cardholder base in much the same way as the oil industry. They initially sent unsolicited cards to "several thousand prominent businessmen with a letter revealing its wonders."[47] Simmons then began generating publicity, getting stories in every major New York newspaper. He also began advertising in newspapers and magazines, and eventually through direct mail. After the public was educated, applications began to flow in. In just one year, membership grew to over 100,000, and a similar number had applied but been rejected as bad credit risks. Initially, there was nothing to lose by applying because the card itself was free, but by late 1950, they were forced to charge a three dollar membership fee in order to generate additional revenue. Simmons writes that although they were concerned that this fee would destroy the cardholder base, it turned out to be a blessing, as the only customers who canceled were those who were not actually using the card. Inactive users still create costs in a card system, but produce no revenue, so it is in the system's best interest to reduce their number.[48]

Attracting cardholders, however, was now only one side of the equation. The T&E card systems also needed to convince merchants to accept the card, which

---

[45]Simmons (1995), pp. 21–22.

[46]This significance of this point is often missed from our current vantage point. Restaurants at this time did not provide receipts unless asked for, which was required in order to be reimbursed or to deduct business entertainment expenses on tax returns. The T&E cards provided that proof automatically.

[47]Simmons (1995), p. 27.

[48]Simmons (1995), p. 29.

entailed giving up six or seven percent of the sale to the card organization. Diners Club sold the card to merchants using a variety of tactics that would be repeated throughout the history of bank-issued credit cards. First, they commissioned a study that claimed a Diners Club cardholder typically spent 18 percent more than a cash customer, which would more than make up for the discount.[49] Second, they used the merchant's competitive position either as a carrot or a stick: if the competition had not yet agreed to accept the card, they sold the merchant on the additional revenue they would get from the lucrative business traveler if they accepted the card; once one merchant agreed to accept the card, they could then pressure the competing merchants by warning them that they would lose sales to their competitor if they did not accept the card as well.[50] Diners Club had also started a magazine that was sent to all cardholders, and they often promised full page advertisements in order to close the deal with a merchant.[51]

Some merchants, especially those that had their own industry-specific cards, actively resisted T&E cards. For example, the US Hotel Trade Association had their own program, called the Universal Travel Card, and actually prohibited their members from accepting Diners Club and other third-party cards that carried a discount.[52] In 1957, the major oil companies (with the exception of Texaco), banded together to block all third-party cards.[53] The airlines also initially refused to accept third-party cards like Diners Club, as their own card system required a healthy $425 deposit from each of their 800,000 members, which provided them with an enormous amount of interest-free working capital.[54] Large department stores also refused to accept the card—ironically, even though Alfred Bloomingdale had taken over as president of Diners Club in 1952, he could not even sign the large department store his family started.[55]

As Diners Club built its US merchant base, it also expanded internationally through franchise agreements.[56] It is not clear if UATP or Diners Club was the first international payment card, but Diners was clearly the first in the more generally-accepted T&E category.

---

[49]Simmons (1995), p. 41.

[50]Simmons describes such an episode when trying to break into the airline industry. After signing the newly-created Northeast Airlines, he called the president of Eastern Airlines. "'I just signed Northeast Airlines to a Diners Club contract,' I told him. 'Do you want all of our one million businessmen and travelers to use only Northeast on your common routes?' A week later, I signed Eastern. The rest of the airline industry fell into place soon after." (pp. 48–49).

[51]Simmons (1995), p. 41.

[52]Mandell (1990), p. 27. Like the other industry-specific cards, The Universal Travel Card was not profitable and was eventually taken over by American Express when it issued its card in 1958.

[53]Mandell (1990), p. 27.

[54]Mandell (1990), p. 28.

[55]Mandell (1990), p. 7.

[56]There is some debate over which was the first franchise. Mandell (relying on Bloomingdale) claimed it was the UK (p. 7), while Simmons recalls that it was France in 1955 (p. 37).

American Express

Diners Club enjoyed little competition throughout most of the 1950s and its yearly charge volume grew to nearly half a billion dollars.[57] In 1958 two important competitors entered the T&E card market. The first was Carte Blanche, of which little is written primarily because they always held the minority share of the T&E card market. The second, however, was of greater significance: American Express (AmEx), a company that had been in the payments industry since it invented the travelers cheque in 1891. Compared to charge cards, travelers cheques were a virtually risk-free business which provided AmEx with revenue not only from selling the checks, but also from the float realized on their cash reserves in between the time the travelers cheques were purchased and used. Many travelers cheques were (and still are) cashed long after they are purchased, and some never at all. Still AmEx saw the amazing growth and further potential of Diners Club and initially offered to purchase the company outright. According to Simmons, a deal was reached, but AmEx's chairman Ralph Reed thought the price was too high and decided AmEx should develop its own system.[58]

AmEx designed a system that was almost identical to Diners, but their card was made of a relatively new substance: plastic.[59] These new plastic cards were more durable than those made from cardstock, yet they were still lightweight. Most importantly, they could be embossed just as the old metal charga-plates were, allowing them to be used with imprinters for a more accurate transfer of the account information.

AmEx was an enormous company compared to Diners Club, and it proved to be a formidable competitor. In October, one mailed out eight million membership applications and ran full page advertisements in 23 newspapers across America. They used their relationship with the banks that sold their travelers cheques to place application forms in front of every customer. They also had an established network of travel agency offices around the world, from which they could sign up both cardholders and merchants. Their massive cash reserves allowed them to spend more on advertising in their first year than Diners Club had spent in their entire history.[60] The furor created by the AmEx advertising, however, actually helped increase demand for Diners Club as well. By 1960, Diners Club membership was over the one million mark, but AmEx was close behind with 700,000.

As we shall see repeated throughout the history of payment cards, mad rushes to acquire cardholders are often accompanied by the lowering of credit standards, and consequently, a rise in credit losses. Diners Club had always enjoyed very low losses, partially due to their strict credit controls, but also because their cardholders were mostly business people backed by their corporations. During their membership

---

[57]Simmons (1995), p. 53.

[58]Simmons (1995), pp. 61–66.

[59]Simmons (1995), p. 82.

[60]Simmons (1995), p. 70.

battle with AmEx, Diners Club's credit losses rose from a quarter percent to almost one percent, and AmEx's losses were suspected to be much higher.[61]

American Express took a large leap ahead when it computerized its bookkeeping and billing in the early 1960s. Up until this point, both American Express and Diners Club processed sales drafts and billed customer using entirely manual processes. AmEx's head of card operations came from the Air Force, where he had been in charge of data processing during World War II, and he realized that AmEx could be more efficient, and therefore more profitable, if it converted to computers. Diners Club eventually followed suit in 1967, but Simmons recalls that it was done "in a state of confusion and ineptness of classical proportions," and actually contributed to their first year of net loss since 1951.[62] The original founders of Diners Club had both died by this point, and by 1970 AmEx surpassed Diners as the premier T&E card system.[63]

AmEx also made one other important contribution that should be discussed here: the gold card. In October 1966, they began issuing special gold-colored cards with better features to their most credit-worthy members. By the mid 1960s, the number of cardholders had grown to such an extent that the card no longer carried the prestige that MacNamara thought would be its best selling point. The creation of a new tier of card allowed AmEx to continue growing their cardholder base while still offering prestige to their most profitable customers.[64]

Bank-Issued Credit Cards

Shortly after the launch of the American Express card in 1958, the American payments industry saw another series of innovations from which we can more directly trace the origins of Visa. These new payment card systems were created and operated by an actor group that had been conspicuously absent throughout the early years of payment cards: the banks.

Beyond having a new type of issuer, these new systems differed from the T&E systems in four important ways. First, they were focused more on middle-class consumers than on business people, and thus enlisted a different and more diverse set of merchants. Second, they offered a feature that some merchant-specific systems had recently developed, which would appeal to those consumers: revolving credit.[65]

---

[61] Simmons (1995), p. 75.

[62] Simmons (1995), p. 103.

[63] Simmons (1995), p. 106.

[64] Mandell credits Carte Blanche with inventing the gold card, but he may be incorrect on this point. He claims that American Express first offered their gold card in 1975 (p. 111), but other sources such as the AmEx web site say they issued their gold card starting in 1966. There is also no mention of a Carte Blanche gold card in the 1972 index of the *American Banker*. Therefore, it may have actually been American Express that issued the first gold card and not Carte Blanche.

[65] According to Mandell, The L. Bamberger and Company department store was the first to develop a system with revolving credit in 1947 and it was quickly adopted by the major New York stores

Cardholders could choose to pay the entire bill at once, or finance any portion of their purchases, repaying them over several months with interest. Third, as opposed to the T&E issuers, the banks offered their cards without any annual fees.[66] Fourth, merchants received payment for their sales drafts, less the normal discount, immediately upon deposit, as opposed to several days later as was common in the T&E systems.

Early Bank Charge Card Systems

Interestingly, some smaller banks had actually experimented with the charge card model (i.e., no revolving credit) even before the creation of Diners Club. Flatbush National Bank of Brooklyn, New York issued their "Charg-It" card in 1947, Patterson Savings and Trust of New Jersey issued a similar card in 1950, and Franklin National Bank of Franklin Square, New York began their system in 1951.[67] The idea quickly spread, and during the next four years, over 100 banks started similar charge card systems. At the end of that period, however, only 27 of those programs were still operating, and no new programs were started for the next two years.[68]

There are two main reasons why these early programs failed. First, they were unprofitable because the banks did not charge the cardholders an annual fee, as Diners Club did, and they lacked the possibility of revenue from interest charges on a revolving credit line. The reasons for not charging a cardholder fee are not discussed in the literature, but one can surmise that the main competitors for these systems were the merchant and industry-specific card systems mentioned earlier, which did not charge a fee. These competitors were also unprofitable, but as explained earlier, loyalty rather than profit was their prime objective.

These early experiments also failed because they could not build the critical mass of adopters necessary to sustain a payment card system. These types of systems have large startup and operating fixed costs that can only be offset by a large volume that brings about an economy of scale. Additionally, multisided platforms tend to have a tipping point with respect to participation—if there are not enough participants on either side, people start to lose interest and the system collapses.[69] Due to the way

---

such as Gimbels and Bloomingdales. In 1956, J. L. Hudson's of Detroit added the idea of an interest-free period. See Mandell (1990), pp. 24–25.

[66] Struble (1969), p. 5.

[67] Mandell (1990), p. 26, Struble (1969), p. 4. Note that many sources claim that Franklin National Bank was the first "credit card," but a close reading of Struble reveals that although he used the that term, the Franklin plan did not offer revolving credit and was thus similar to the T&E cards. Struble wrote in 1969, and the terms defined above were not yet used consistently. Other sources have suggested that Franklin first offered a non-revolving card, and then later added the revolving credit feature, thereby becoming the first bank credit card.

[68] Struble (1969), p. 5.

[69] Evans and Schmalensee also remind us that this tipping point does not necessarily mean that once the point is crossed, participation is entirely self-sustaining. A small change in pricing can

banks were regulated in the United States at this time, most banks could not build this critical mass. Banks were prohibited from operating across state lines, and most states did not allow banks to open more than a few branches. Some states, called *unit banking* states, restricted banks to just one physical location. This severely limited the number of customers to which a bank could issue cards, as well as the number of merchants they could enlist to accept the cards. In fact, the "Charg-It" card was accepted only in a two-block radius around the bank itself.[70] For the car-loving consumers of the early 1950s, a two-block radius was simply not enough to sustain interest.

The BankAmericard

But there was one bank in the country that had the resources, potential scale, and the corporate culture, to make it work: The Bank of America (BofA). BofA operated in California, a state which allowed banks to operate branches statewide.[71] In the late 1950s, California was also one of the most populous and wealthiest of states, and BofA had a banking relationship with 60 percent of its residents and held more than 30 percent of its deposits. With assets of $5 billion, BofA was not only the nation's largest bank, but also one of the largest in the world.[72]

As opposed to other large banks, BofA was also *culturally* predisposed to develop a credit card for the middle-class consumer. Most large banks of the 1950s did not engage in the extension of consumer credit, much less unsecured consumer credit, which was considered to be the domain of merchants and the less-than-reputable finance companies. Mandell writes that "If a bank had a consumer loan department, it was often found in the basement where no one could see the furtive borrower."[73] One critic of these early bank credit card systems complained that they were "lowering banking's image by engaging in an activity more properly associated with pawn shops."[74] Most bankers preferred to deal with safer, larger and more lucrative commercial loans. BofA, however, had a different organizational culture. Nocera explains that "It was a bank with the mentality of a finance company and proud of it."[75] It was started by A.P. Giannini, the son of an Italian immigrant, who prided

---

easily cause consumers to leave a system, resulting in a quick collapse (e.g., Yahoo bids). See Evans and Schmalensee (2005), pp. 134–139.

[70]Mandell (1990), p. 26.

[71]Nineteen states and the District of Columbia allowed statewide branching, 16 allowed limited branching, and 15 enforced unit banking. See Goldberg (1975).

[72]Nocera (1994), pp. 18–20.

[73]Mandell (1990), p. 29.

[74]Quoted in Nocera (1994), p. 24.

[75]Nocera (1994), p. 17.

himself on serving "the little fellow."[76] Ken Larkin, the BofA executive who would become synonymous with the BankAmericard program, saw it as a natural extension of the bank's business: "We were always a leader in installment credit. Anything you could buy on time we financed ... the credit card was just a natural extension of that."[77]

But the BankAmericard, as their system was called, was a slight departure from the traditional consumer installment loan. Traditional loans were secured, meaning that the item being financed could be repossessed by the bank if the consumer defaulted on the loan. The BankAmericard credit line was unsecured, and the bank had little recourse if a consumer could not pay. Traditional loans also required the consumer to apply for the loan, which would entail a review of the consumer's credit position, and their intended use of the funds, by a bank loan officer. With the BankAmericard, cardholders could finance anything they wished without ever visiting the bank. It was a form of self-service credit that transferred the financing decision from the bank to the cardholder. In effect, it subtly blurred the line between buying and borrowing.

The designer of the BankAmericard system, Joseph Williams, had friends at Sears and Mobil Oil, and he patterned his new system directly upon theirs.[78] The card was offered to consumers without charge. Upon receiving their bill, cardholders could pay the entire amount and not incur interest, or pay less than the total and finance the rest at the rate of 18 percent per year. Merchants were charged a six percent discount fee on their transactions, but would receive funds immediately upon deposit of the sales drafts without the need to bill or collect from the cardholders. Merchants also paid $25 a month to rent a card imprinter.

The card itself was made of plastic with embossed account information, similar to the new American Express card. Just as in the case of the charga-plate, the embossed information was transferred to the sales draft using an imprinter, which reduced the potential of copy errors. Early imprinters did not have wheels for transferring the transaction date or amount, which had implications on machine processing that will be discussed in later chapters, so merchants hand-wrote these details on the sales slip, and customers added their signature to authorize the charge.[79]

The BankAmericard also had a formalized authorization process that was based upon the department store systems, but expanded to a multi-merchant environment. Each merchant was assigned a *floor limit*, over which the merchant was required to call for authorization.[80] This authorization process will be discussed in more detail

---

[76]The history and culture of BofA is chronicled in a number of sources. See especially Chutkow (2001) and Nocera (1994).

[77]Chutkow (2001), p. 61.

[78]Nocera (1994), p. 24.

[79]Merchants were also supposed to fill in details about the goods purchased, but most found this too time consuming and neglected to do so.

[80]The term *floor limit* comes from the department stores, where it literally meant the amount under which the "floor" could authorize. Any amount above require a telephone call to the finance department (Powar interview).

Fig. 1.3 A BankAmericard from the early 1970s. The customer signature and name have been blurred for privacy (author's personal collection)

in the following chapter, but it should be noted here that at this time it was entirely manual and exceedingly slow.

The accounting side however was computerized from the very beginning, albeit in rather limited way. BofA was actually the first bank in America to use a computer, an IBM 702 installed in 1955, upon which SRI developed a program to automate BofA's demand deposit accounts.[81] To support the BankAmericard, BofA adapted this computer system to maintain cardholder accounts and process sales drafts. Instead of using magnetic ink as they did with checks, the sales drafts themselves had a punch-card as the bottom layer, which would be punched with the transaction details upon deposit.[82]

"The Drop"

Nocera writes that BofA approached the rollout of their system cautiously. They chose to test it in the relatively isolated town of Fresno, California, partly because

---

[81] The system was called Electronic Recording Machine-Accounting (ERMA). That system automated the processing of checks through the use of magnetic ink printed on the back of the checks, a technique that would eventually be used in the Magnetic Ink Character Recognition (MICR) standard in 1957. According to O'Brien, the first ERMA installation was demonstrated in San Jose in early 1956, though the BofA did not fully convert all their accounts to ERMA until 1962. See O'Brien (1968), pp. 2–5, and Campbell-Kelly (2003), p. 49.

[82] Jutilla, Derman, and Russell interviews.

they had a banking relationship with 45 percent of the families there, but also because they were not entirely sure it would work. They reasoned that if the card failed there, the bank's reputation would be damaged less than if the test were conducted in San Francisco.[83]

Just as in the case of Diners Club, the BankAmericard system faced the classic chicken-and-egg dilemma. Convincing merchants to give up six percent of the transaction and rent an imprinter for $25 a month would be possible only if there were a significant number of cardholders wanting to use the card. BofA solved the dilemma in much the same way all the previous systems did. They referred to it as "The Drop." In the weeks leading up to September 18, 1958, they simply mailed 65,000 unsolicited cards to households in Fresno. They followed this up with aggressive advertising to educate those consumers about their new card.[84]

As in the other systems, merchants faced a central tension when deciding whether to participate. Accepting the card meant possibly losing the customer loyalty built by the merchant's private card system, but not accepting the card put the merchant at risk of losing customers to a competitor that did. In general, the larger merchants with established card systems, such as Sears, JC Penney and Wards, did not accept the BankAmericard, but the smaller merchants did. These smaller merchants considered the loyalty to be less valuable than the costs of maintaining, billing and collecting on credit accounts. Ken Larkin recalled one merchant he visited:

> He had three girls working on Burroughs bookkeeping machines, each handling 1,000 to 1,500 accounts. I looked at the size of the accounts: $4.58. $12.82. And he was sending out monthly bills on these accounts. Then the customers paid him maybe three or four months later. Think of what this man was spending on postage, labor, envelopes, stationery! His accounts receivables were dragging him under.[85]

A similar set of reasons was discovered by Stallwitz in his survey of Bay Area merchants in 1968. Interestingly, the reasons given were striking similar to how the cards were marketed to merchants: it would increase their sales; reduce their risks and costs of extending credit; for competitive reasons; and for customer convenience. He noticed, however, that suburban merchants also tended to accept the card more as a personal favor to their bankers, primarily because those bankers had given them their initial business loan. He continued: "The most unusual reason for joining was put forth by one merchant who had just moved into a new store (not a related type of business) and a … sticker was already on the door. Rather than scrape it off, he signed up on his next trip to his primary bank."[86]

The BofA managed to get merchants interested, but they also needed to solve one more problem to make the system truly work: how would cardholders recognize merchants that accepted the card? Diners Club had simply provided a list of establishments to cardholders, but the number of merchants accepting the BankAmericard would potentially be far greater and more diverse. Cardholders needed a simple

---

[83] Nocera (1994), p. 25.

[84] Chutkow (2001), pp. 64–66.

[85] Quoted in Nocera (1994), p. 27.

[86] Stallwitz (1968), p. 44.

way to identify merchants that accepted the card without consulting a pre-printed list. Their solution was to create a *mark* for the system, which would be printed on both the cards as well as signs that hung in the windows of participating merchants. The mark looked a bit like a flag. It consisted of three colored bands—blue, white, and gold—running across the background, with the word BankAmericard written in white within the blue band. This was a new twist on the function of identity discussed earlier. Not only would the card identify the cardholder's account to the system, the mark on the card would also identify a participating merchant to the cardholder.

The Fresno drop went smoothly, though it attracted little attention, and consumers began to use the cards. Today it seems normal for consumers to use credit cards to pay for goods and services, but one should question *why* the people of 1958 Fresno would bother. Although the Diners Club card provided an obvious benefit to the traveling business person, the general consumer shopping locally would actually have little need for such a device. Checks were commonly accepted at local shops, most merchants already extended credit to their frequent customers, and anyone who could qualify for a BankAmericard could no doubt qualify for a traditional installment loan. Considering the manual authorization process of the time, using the BankAmericard for purchases over the floor limit would have been more time consuming, awkward and embarrassing for the cardholder than writing a check. Nocera offers three possible reasons why the card was adopted. First the BankAmericard fit with the general trend in America toward impersonal self-service. Applying for a traditional installment loan meant looking a loan officer in the eye and promising to repay the loan. The BankAmericard arrived unsolicited and the decision to finance a purchase was entirely left up to the consumer. Second, the card did offer a level of convenience through consolidation. Instead of maintaining accounts and carrying cards from multiple merchants, the consumer could carry one BankAmericard and see all their charges on one bill. But his third reason is perhaps the most convincing—consumers used the card because it was a novelty in an age and culture of novelty. Nocera writes:

> The card was a novelty at first; just as Americans spent hours staring at the test pattern of their new TV, so did the citizens of Fresno gather around the checkout counter to watch someone pay with a BankAmericard. This was the 1950s, after all, a time of wonder at the miraculous march of progress. BankAmericard was part of that march.[87]

Shortly after the Fresno drop, BofA learned that their competitors were planning to launch a card system of their own in San Francisco.[88] Nocera writes that upon leaning this, all caution was put aside. BofA began sending cards to nearly all their depositors and consumer loan customers in California, and using their extensive network of branches to enlist as many merchants as possible. Larkin later remarked that this was "a calculated risk, done just the one time to get the plan off the ground,"

---

[87] Nocera (1994), p. 28.

[88] According to *Business Week*, this was the First Western Bank and Trust Company of Los Angeles. See 'The charge-it plan that really took off', Business Week (27 February 1965), p. 58.

and they did target their efforts a bit by using lists of existing charga-plate holders provided by the retail service bureaus.[89] Over the next 13 months, BofA issued 2 million BankAmericards and signed up over 20,000 merchants.[90] It is important to note that in one move, BofA created more cardholders just in California than Diners Club had ever had nationwide.

As the cards reached the urban center of Los Angeles, BofA began to experience the inevitable effects of sending out millions on unsolicited, unsecured credit cards. The problems of fraud in the BankAmericard system will be discussed in more detail in the next chapter, but the initial effects were staggering. Delinquencies were 22 percent, compared to 4 percent on traditional installment loans. Both thieves and merchants were creating numerous fraudulent transactions under the floor limits to avoid detection. Within 15 months of the Fresno drop, the BankAmericard system had officially lost $8.8 million, but Nocera estimates that the real losses were actually closer to $20 million.[91]

Despite these early losses, BofA chose to continue the system, reducing the number of outstanding cards and weeding out dishonest merchants. By May 1961, the BankAmericard system was generating a profit, though this was initially kept quiet as the publicity from the early losses was still helping to keep other banks from developing competing systems of their own.[92]

Other Bank Credit Card Systems

Although the BankAmericard was the most successful of the early bank credit card systems, it was not alone. The other system most often discussed in the literature came from Chase Manhattan, which started the Chase Manhattan Charge Plan (CMCP) in 1958. It was never profitable though, and they were eventually forced to sell it in January 1962, partially because the large New York department stores refused to accept it.[93] Ironically, it was sold to Joseph Williams, the designer of the BankAmericard system, who had resigned after its initial losses.[94] The system was renamed Uni-Card, it was soon acquired by American Express, and finally repurchased by Chase in 1969. Mandell writes that "The second time around proved no

---

[89] 'The charge-it plan that really took off', Business Week (27 February 1965), p. 58.

[90] Nocera (1994), p. 30.

[91] Nocera (1994), p. 31.

[92] 'The charge-it plan that really took off', Business Week (27 February 1965), p. 58. For the accusation that it was purposely kept quiet, see Galanoy (1980). Mandell actually questions this profitability, claiming that BofA did not include the cost of funds or advertising in the accounting of the card system, thus making it look profitable when it actually was not (Mandell 1990, p. 58).

[93] Mandell (1990), p. 30, Jutilla (1973), p. 44.

[94] 'The charge-it plan that really took off', Business Week (27 February 1965), p. 58.

more profitable than the first," and Chase shut down the Uni-Card and eventually became a member of the organization that would become Visa.[95]

In addition to Chase and BofA, 29 other banks started credit card systems of their own during 1958 and 1959, but nearly all of these programs failed or reported massive losses during their initial years. The terrible press from these programs further discouraged other banks from starting systems of their own, and from 1960 to 1966, only 10 more banks created new systems.[96]

This trend then reversed quite suddenly. Between 1966 and 1968, 440 new systems were created, more than had ever existed before. Struble offers four possible reasons for this sudden explosion of new systems. First, by 1966 the rest of the industry finally became aware that the BankAmericard was not only making profits, but also reporting substantial increases in those profits each year. Profits were increasing primarily because the large number of cardholders were financing more of their purchases, which in turn generated substantial interest income. This good news emboldened some banks to start their own systems.[97]

Second, Struble claims that the availability of new "high-speed computers" significantly reduced the costs of operating a new card system. Indeed, the "third generation" IBM 360 line had recently been developed, and large banks such as BofA began installing them in 1966.[98] Nevertheless, these machines were still prohibitively expensive for most medium or small sized banks, so although they might have contributed to the profitability of existing systems such as BankAmericard and therefore been an indirect cause, it is unlikely that they were a direct impetus for the creation of new systems.

Third, bank credit card systems afforded banks a new way to compete with one another in a time of strict regulation. In the 1960s, American banking regulations dictated the amount of interest a bank could offer consumers on savings accounts, and completely prohibited the payment of interest on demand deposit accounts. Banks had no mechanism with which to compete, forcing many to offer gifts such as toasters to those who opened new accounts. Credit cards were a relatively new phenomenon and thus were not covered by the regulations. Banks used the credit cards to lure customers, either by offering a card when their competitor did not, or offering it with a lower interest rate. Once a bank did offer a credit card, all its competitors would no doubt respond by offering cards of their own.

Finally, Struble surmises that many banks created new systems around this time because they thought credit cards were the first step on the path toward the "cashless-

---

[95] Mandell (1990), p. 40. Mandell actually claims that Visa "acquired Uni-Card," implying that Visa purchased the portfolio, but this would be out of character for that organization, which was an association of card issuers and acquirers. Visa's chief of operations at the time confirmed that NBI did not purchase anything from Chase, and that Chase merely joined Visa and offered a Visa product (Russell interview).

[96] Struble (1969), p. 5.

[97] Struble (1969), p. 5.

[98] O'Brien remarks that the 360s were so much more powerful that they easily justified the cost of porting applications. In 1966 BofA replaced their 32 GE mainframes used for the ERMA system with just two IBM 360/65s (O'Brien 1968, p. 14).

checkless society." The wide-spread adoption of computers into banking in the 1960s brought about the idea that all value transfer could be accomplished electronically, substantially reducing operating costs for the banks. Although credit cards used paper sales drafts at this time, the back-office processing of credit card transactions was typically done using computers, and the idea of a merchant terminal that would eliminate the paper altogether was already being discussed in the late 1960s. If a banker thought that the "cashless-checkless society" might come to fruition, getting into the credit card business was the first step toward remaining relevant.

Struble's final reason leaves some room for criticism. At this time, credit card departments were the poor step-child of the bank, often located in the basement or other suitably out of the way location. If bankers seriously considered credit cards to be an important step toward a desired goal, they would have made the credit card department a more integral part of the bank's operations. It is also not clear that the majority of bankers at that time thought an electronic value exchange system was such a good idea. Many of Visa's early efforts were directed at getting their member banks to support such an idea, and speeches by Visa's founder reveal a certain amount of frustration at the lack of support from his membership.

Surprisingly, Struble omits one other cause that could easily account for the sudden growth in new card payment systems: the formation of the two major national bankcard associations and their attempts to expand their network by enlisting new banks.

National Bankcard Associations

As noted earlier, by the mid 1960s the BankAmericard system had overcome its initial difficulties and was generating increasing profits, but it was still restricted to the state of California. BofA realized that both consumers and commerce were increasingly traveling across state lines, and for their card to be truly useful, it had to be accepted nationwide. American banking regulations at the time prohibited BofA from opening branches in other states, so they decided the best way to expand the system was to license the program to banks in other states. Although BofA could have legally solicited cardholders outside of California, it would have made little sense to do so. There were no centralized credit reporting agencies at this time, so BofA had no way to establish the credit worthiness of prospective cardholders in other states without the help of a local bank. Furthermore, directly signing up merchants would have been extremely difficult, as the merchant would have had to maintain an account with a BofA branch in California. BofA created a subsidiary organization known as BankAmericard Service Corporation (BASC) that was tasked with signing up licensees and administering the entire system.

Licensee banks paid BofA $25,000 for the franchise, plus a percentage of their transaction revenues as a royalty. In return, they received the accounting software developed for the BankAmericard system, as well as an invitation to a training session in San Francisco.[99] Much to the dismay of the licensee banks, however, this training session was given by the marketing department, and much of the discussion revolved around the marketing aspects of the program. Many of the licensees discovered that they could obtain more helpful and accurate information on how to run their programs by visiting the BankAmericard processing centers, directly observing and talking with their operations people.[100]

Initially BofA licensed only one bank in any particular geographic area, essentially providing it with a local monopoly. These licenses were mostly domestic, but a few were located in other countries; Barclays Bank became the first international licensee in 1966, and the sole BankAmericard issuer in the UK. These licensee banks typically had correspondent relationships with BofA, and thus were "loyal" or at least tied to BofA in some sense. Although this practice might seem a bit exclusive or restrictive, it was likely a necessary consolation in order to entice banks not only to pay the license fee and royalties, but also to give up their chance to issue a card with their own brand.[101]

The licensing system also created a new function never before seen in payment card systems: *interchange*. Because cardholders from one bank could now use their card to make purchases at merchants represented by a different bank, the two banks needed a way to clear and settle those transactions. In all previous payment card systems, the same organization both issued the cards and represented the merchants, so all settlement and clearing was done within the same organization. Check payment systems had always experienced this scenario, and as discussed earlier, the Federal Reserve had established a national clearinghouse in 1915 for just this purpose. But in a move that may have perhaps sown the seeds of its own destruction, BASC chose not to create a centralized clearinghouse for the BankAmericard system. Instead, acquiring banks were required to mail their drafts directly to the issuing bank for payment, less a discount fee, now called the *interchange reimbursement fee*. This will be discussed in more detail in the next chapter, as it became one of the central reasons for the creation of a new independent organization.

The banks that competed with the BankAmericard licensee banks quickly reacted by forming regional, non-profit cooperative associations of their own. In many cases, these regional associations were also centralized processors. The members still issued cards, signed merchants and held the receivables, but the regional association provided the more mundane operational functions such as authorization, sales draft processing, accounting, and billing. By centralizing their operations, these associations could also achieve an economy of scale, which reduced the operating costs for each of the members.

These regional associations then joined together into a national, non-profit cooperative association known as Interbank in order to allow their cards to be used across

---

[99]Nocera (1994), p. 56.

[100]This was mentioned in interviews with Don Jutilla, director of one of the first BankAmericard licensee programs. Jutilla created flowcharts from his observations that were then used to train his staff.

[101]Initially banks were not allowed to add their brands to the card. See the next chapter for more details.

the country. National merchant acceptance was hampered, however, by their lack of a common name on the card. Although all Interbank cards contained a common mark, it was only a small "i" in one corner of the card, barely noticeable compared to the regional association's name and marks, which varied from region to region. In contrast to the BankAmericard system, which used and promoted a consistent name and mark, the Interbank system did not actively promote their common mark, and thus cards were not as readily accepted outside their issuing region.

In 1969, Interbank began to address this problem by purchasing the rights to the name first developed by First National Bank of Louisville, Kentucky, and the mark popularized by the Western States Bankcard Association (WSBA).[102] The name was "Master Charge" and the mark was the overlapping yellow and orange balls, and these were eventually used on all cards issued by Interbank members. In the 1980s, they changed names again to MasterCard and in 2006 became an independent, for-profit stock corporation.[103]

Conclusion

In this chapter we reviewed the major innovations in the American payments industry, from the formation of the Federal Reserve to the National Bankcard Associations, in order to construct a historical context for Visa's formation and development. This context helps us understand when and where many of the ideas and techniques found within the Visa system originated: the identity function of the card; embossed cards and imprinters to reduce copy errors; mass-issuance of cards to prime the system; the techniques for educating consumers and enlisting merchants; revolving credit; gold cards; common marks to help cardholders identify participating merchants; and the introduction of computers for accounting and transaction processing.

This context also establishes many of the economic, social, and regulatory dynamics that shaped (and continue to shape) the history of Visa and its system: the tradition of discounts in the clearing process; the elimination of those discounts in the Federal Reserve's check clearing system and the expectation of free processing for anything like a check; the loyalties (real or perceived) created by merchant and industry-specific card programs that are threatened by third-party universal cards; and the American banking regulations that required cooperative joint ventures for a nationwide system.

With this context established, we now turn to the formation of the Visa organization itself.

---

[102] Some sources mistakenly report that the name was created by WSBA. WSBA merely licensed the name from First National of Louisville, but WSBA did develop the mark, and made both widely recognized in the West (Honey interview).

[103] Strangely, there seems to be even less written specifically about Interbank and MasterCard than there is about Visa. Some history appears in Kutler (1994); as well as Evans and Schmalensee (2005) and Mandell (1990).

Chapter 2
Associating: Dee Hock and the Creation of the Organization

By 1968, the BankAmericard licensing program appeared on the surface as if it was a resounding success. In just two years, the number of licensee banks issuing card had grown from the initial 8 to 254, and each bank had further sub-licensed other agent banks in their territories to acquire BankAmericard transactions from local merchants. There were now 6 million cardholders, each of which could use their card at 155,000 merchants in 17 different states, as well as a few foreign countries. The system was processing $458.9 million in sales volume, and growing each year.[1] And then in October of 1968, it very nearly disintegrated.

Unfortunately, these statistics were masking several serious problems in the BankAmericard system that were threatening to unravel it from the inside out. By October of 1968, these problems had become severe enough to cause a crisis amongst the licensees, and it was this crisis that instigated the creation of the organization that would soon be known as Visa. The purpose of this chapter is to analyze what was wrong with the BankAmericard licensing system, and explain how the new organization formed to take its place was fundamentally shaped by the particular philosophy of the organization's founder.

Problems in the Licensing Program

In many ways, it should not be surprising that the BankAmericard system faced a number of critical problems at this time. When any technological system rapidly grows in scope and volume, flaws in the initial design quickly manifest themselves, causing friction and instability. In many cases, these problems can be fixed easily enough without a major rupture in the organization: more techniques and artifacts can be employed to obtain more efficient operations; policies and procedures can put in place to handle the growing complexity; new departments or committees can be added to track existing and identify new problems. If this is so, why did the

---

[1] Burroughs Clearing House (1968).

D.L. Stearns, *Electronic Value Exchange*, History of Computing,
DOI 10.1007/978-1-84996-139-4_2, © Springer-Verlag London Limited 2011

BankAmericard licensees come to the conclusion that nothing short of a new organizational structure was necessary?

I will argue in this chapter that the licensees came to this conclusion primarily because the problems facing the system were both operational *and* organizational. Several key flaws in the organizational design led to a situation where the BofA could no longer control the licensee banks, and the licensees no longer trusted the BofA in return. Computer and telecommunication technology could certainly address the operational problems, but no technical device could overcome the breakdown in the organization.

A Typical Transaction in 1968

To understand the various operational and organizational problems, we must first understand what it was like to initiate, authorize, clear, and settle transactions in the BankAmericard system of 1968. This is best done by walking through the process of a typical domestic purchase. Note that in this example, we will discuss only the details that will help us understand the specific operational and organizational problems faced by the BankAmericard system; other interesting but less relevant details will be examined in later chapters. This example is also the ideal case; the unfortunate realities of the process will be noted in the following section.[2]

Imagine yourself in 1968, holding a shiny new BankAmericard. As discussed in the previous chapter, all cards had the same blue, white, and gold bands across the face of the card so that merchants could easily identify your card as acceptable, regardless of which bank actually issued it. Merchants also hung signs with the same marks in their windows, so that you could easily identify those that accepted the card, regardless of which bank represented the merchant in the system.[3] You spy a merchant that you need to visit, select your items and present your BankAmericard for payment.

If your purchase amount is below the merchant's floor limit the merchant can complete the transaction immediately without authorization.[4] The floor limit varied by merchant type and by card type: some cards had a star on the front, while others did not.[5] The floor limit for a general merchant was typically $50 for a non-starred and $100 for a starred card, but airlines, hotels and other services were often granted higher floor limits.

---

[2]Unless otherwise noted, the information in this section comes primarily from interviews with Jutilla, Russell, Honey, and Derman, as well as Fisher et al. (1980) and Hock (2005).

[3]The merchant signs differed from the card in one strange way—the BankAmericard name was in the white band instead of the blue. This would be rectified later when the name of the system changed to Visa and the cards were redesigned.

[4]For a definition of the term *floor limit*, see p. 20 in the previous chapter.

[5]This star created a kind of early segmentation. Jutilla remarked that his friends quickly noticed the difference and would often ask him how they could get a star on their card.

If your purchase is above the merchant's floor limit, the merchant is required to call for authorization. The merchant dials the acquirer's authorization center and verbally conveys the transaction details to the authorization operator. The authorizer first determines if the card was issued by the same bank or another by looking at the first four digits of your account number. If it is the same bank, the transaction is known as *local* or *on-us*, otherwise it is known as an *interchange transaction*.

If this is an on-us transaction, the authorizer then consults a series of printed reports to determine if the transaction should be authorized. At this time, there were no interactive computer systems with CRT terminals installed at the BankAmericard authorization centers. When your bank became a BankAmericard licensee, it did receive some "computer software" from the Bank of America, but this was just a simple punch card-based accounting system. This system produced two reports to help the authorizers: a list of known *hot cards*, which were either stolen or on hold for some other reason; and a summary of each cardholder's account, listing their current balance, credit limit, purchase and payment history. The authorizer first searches through the hot card list to ensure your account number does not appear there. Then the authorizer manually wades through the massive binder of account sheets to find yours, reviews your details, and consults the hand-written list of authorizations already given since the report was last printed. If all is in order, the authorizer gives the merchant an authorization code, consisting of a few letters and digits, and the merchant writes that on to the sales draft.

If this is an interchange case, however, the merchant's authorizer does not have access to your records and is thus required to call or telex your bank's authorization center. The authorizer puts the merchant on hold, dials your bank's center and relays the transaction details. Your bank's authorizer then consults the same type of reports already discussed, and supplies an authorization code. The original authorizer then relays this code to the merchant.[6]

After authorization, the merchant then completes the sales draft. The draft is a multi-layer document: the top two layers are like tissue-paper, one for you and one for the merchant. The bottom layer is an IBM 80-column punch card, complete with the corner notch. The merchant puts your card and the sales draft into an imprinter, informally known as a "zip-zap machine," which squeezes the embossed characters on your card against the sales draft, thereby transferring your card number, expiration date and name onto each layer via carbon paper. The imprinter also holds another embossed plate containing the merchant's details. The merchant manually adds the transaction date and purchase amount to the draft, and you sign it to complete the purchase. The merchant is then required

---

[6]At this time, interchange was rare on the average, but there were localized exceptions to this. For example, the National Bank of Commerce in Seattle and Puget Sound National Bank in Tacoma experienced a high level of interchange due to the large amount of business that takes place between those two cities, which are roughly 30 miles apart. The authorization centers at these two banks simply called each other in the morning and kept a line open, allowing them to authorize interchange transactions quickly over a speakerphone (Jutilla interview).

to check the signature on the card against your signature on the draft to ensure that you are the proper cardholder, but few do. The merchant tears off the customer copy and hands it to you, putting the other two layers in the cash register.

On a regular basis, the merchant deposits the punch card layer just like a check. Unlike a check, however, the merchant receives an instant credit, less the discount, the amount of which is negotiated when the merchant signs the contract with the bank (merchant discounts at this time ranged anywhere from 0 to 8 percent, averaging 3.5 percent).[7] From the merchant's perspective, the transaction is now complete, but the clearing and settlement process has in fact only just begun.

Although the drafts are computer punch cards, they are not yet machine-readable. Banks with very low volume may just manually sort and total the drafts, but others send them to the proofing and data-entry departments to be manually key punched and proofed.[8] The drafts are then sorted by card number. On-us transactions are fed into the computer to update the cardholder accounts, and are then added by collation to the drafts already processed for each cardholder since the last billing cycle. At this time, most banks are still performing *country-club billing*, where the physical drafts are included with each statement.

All interchange drafts are then grouped and totaled by issuing bank. The merchant's bank completes a special *clearing draft* against the issuing bank for the total of all the sales drafts. The clearing draft looks very much like a cashier's check, complete with the magnetic ink routing characters, and can be submitted through the normal checkclearing system for payment. The physical sales drafts on the other hand are mailed directly to the issuing bank through the US postal system. The clearing draft is often processed before the individual sales drafts arrive at the issuer, so the issuer is forced to transfer funds, but must wait until the sales drafts arrive to reconcile and add the charges to the relevant cardholders' accounts. Once they arrive, the issuer reconciles the sales drafts against the settlement payments, and then performs the same actions the original bank did for the on-us case.[9]

Operational Problems

Within this simple transaction scenario, we can begin to see a number of operational problems that were greatly exacerbated by the system's increasing scope and sales volume.

---

[7] Jutilla (1973), pp. 49, 179.

[8] *Proofing* involves verifying that the drafts total to the same amount claimed by the depositor. This was often done by encoding the human-readable elements of a draft into machine-readable form, so that the drafts can be machine-totaled.

[9] In addition to merchant purchases, cardholders could also obtain cash advances directly from any BankAmericard bank. Although these transactions levied different fees and had no free period, they were processed in the same manner, with the bank providing the cash advance acting as the "merchant."

Authorization, Floor Limits, and Fraud

The first notable operational problem was the interaction of authorization, floor limits, and fraud. Payment card transactions differ from those in other payment systems in one important way: they are *guaranteed*. If the merchant follows the rules of the program, the merchant is guaranteed payment, even if the transaction was fraudulent. In the case of a personal check, the issuer simply returns the bad check and the merchant must absorb the loss; in a payment card transaction, the *issuer* must absorb the loss. This introduces a certain amount of risk to the issuing bank, and in an ideal world, the issuing bank would like to eliminate that risk by authorizing every transaction. This was not a realistic option in 1968, however, as the labor and telecommunication costs would easily outweigh the revenue gained from a low-value transaction. Additionally, authorizing every transaction would delay an already slow process, risking the use of cash or a check instead of the card.

The floor limit concept is essentially a cost/risk tradeoff made by the banks. Not all transactions are equally risky, and the easiest way to distinguish the higher-risk ones is by the combination of purchase amount and merchant type: a high-value purchase from a jewelry store is more risky than a low-value purchase from a shoe store. What most banks did not anticipate, however, was that criminals would quickly discover the various floor limits and make numerous under-limit charges, resulting in significant losses. A new card stolen from a mailbox could be used for a week or more before the issuing bank even saw the first sales draft, and over a month before the cardholder received the first statement for a card the customer did not even know was issued.[10] Once detected, banks would notify other authorization centers and mail a postcard to merchants that might likely see the card.[11]

But relying on the merchants to catch the cards was problematic. The main incentive for merchants to use the authorization system is the *guarantee of payment*, not the reward for catching a stolen card. The authorization process is more than just a technical function—it also formally transfers the responsibility for fraud from the merchant to the issuer. A merchant was (and still is) allowed to take a transaction above the floor limit without authorization, but the merchant then assumes the risk of fraud. If an issuer can prove that the merchant did not authorize the transaction, or that the bank warned the merchant about the card number prior to the transaction, the issuer can submit a *chargeback* into the system, which will eventually debit the merchant's account. Proving a chargeback required a manual audit, however, and most bankcard processing centers were already struggling to keep up with the sharply-increased sales volume.

---

[10]Often the cards were actually stolen by the postal sorters and carriers. The practice of mailing unsolicited cards to consumers was eventually banned by the US Congress in 1970, and most other countries have since passed similar laws.

[11]Jutilla (1973), pp. 221–223. Eventually the Visa system produced a weekly booklet of hot card numbers, but this was ultimately replaced by online authorization via inexpensive point of sale dial terminals (see Chap. 7).

Merchants were also not inclined to call for authorizations due to the delay it would cause at the point of sale—sources from the time estimated that the average authorization took anywhere from five to twenty minutes, depending on how quickly the merchant could get through to the authorization center, and how quickly the merchant's bank could call or telex the issuing bank in an interchange case.[12] Stallwitz found that nearly all merchants in his study complained about the speed of authorization, and some admitted that they encouraged the use of cash or a check-when the purchase was above their floor limit.[13] Others would rely on their own assessment of the customer (often based on appearance) and take the card without authorization, or simply reuse an authorization code from a prior transaction as it was unlikely that the issuing bank would detect this under the manual system of the time.[14] Stallwitz also found that suburban merchants in particular would avoid consulting the hot card lists and calling for authorization as it might offend their customers and risk the loss of the sale. Lastly, some merchants were themselves creating or participating in fraudulent transactions. Restaurant cashiers would make additional sales drafts with a customer's card, or less reputable merchants would submit under-limit drafts using a stolen card and split the proceeds with the thief.[15]

The actual amount of fraud occurring at this time is difficult to estimate as banks were not required to disclose such information, nor were they particularly eager to do so. Those that did were either inconsistent in the way they calculated and reported losses, or as Spencer Nilson claims "doctored the records so that it would come out to a ratio acceptable to their peers."[16] Nevertheless, Nilson and others attempted to estimate how much the banks were losing on their card programs. Unfortunately, the estimates are difficult to compare as they are for different time periods, different sets of card programs (e.g., bankcards only, bank and T&E and retail, etc.), and different loss categories (total losses as opposed to losses specifically attributable to fraud). Nilson estimated that *fraud-specific* losses on bankcards increased from a mere $140,000 in 1967 to $2.2 million by 1969.[17] Various Federal Reserve studies reported that *total* losses for bankcards rose from $12 million in 1967 to $115.5 million in 1970.[18] Nocera claimed that throughout the late 1960s, the Chicago banks alone lost over $25 million, and the New York banks over $250 million.[19]

---

[12] "It took about 15 to 20 minutes to make a $35 purchase, which didn't make you very popular at the point of sale" (Russell interview). See also Stallwitz (1968), pp. 44–45.

[13] Stallwitz (1968), p. 45.

[14] Reusing authorization codes became much easier to detect after NBI computerized both authorization and clearing and settlement, the story of which will be told in the next two chapters.

[15] Jutilla (1973), pp. 219–229, Nocera (1994), p. 30, Galanoy (1980), p. 149.

[16] Nilson (11 April 1977), Report No 161. The general accuracy of the Nilson Report was contested by many of my interview sources, so some of his claims and statistics should be approached with caution.

[17] Nilson (11 April 1977), Report No 161. Dollar amounts are in USD.

[18] 1967 data from (Federal Reserve System July 1968); 1970 data reported in Brooke (18 May 1971).

[19] Nocera (1994), p. 61.

The growing amount of fraud was clearly a concern for those banks participating in the BankAmericard licensing program. Beyond the actual monetary losses, the shocking headlines were creating a *perception* that fraud was rampant and bankers were doing nothing to protect their cardholders.[20] This perception could not only erode the confidence of cardholders and merchants, but also attract the unwanted attention of lawmakers and regulators. Indeed the US Congress held hearings on the practice of mailing unsolicited cards in 1967 and was drafting legislation to not only prohibit it, but also protect consumers from the cost of fraudulent charges.[21] As is typical, these hearings became a thinly-veiled public trial of the entire bank credit card industry, accusing the banks of fueling inflation and tempting innocent consumers to abandon the traditional values of thrift in favor of reckless debt spending.[22]

Clearing and Settlement of Interchange Transactions

The second major operational problem area was the clearing and settlement of interchange transactions. Like a check, a payment card sales draft is a claim on funds that must be cleared and settled with the issuing bank. If a different bank would acquire that transaction, there would have to be a mechanism by which the draft can be routed to the issuer, and payment made to the acquirer.

As noted in the previous chapter, most banks at this time cleared and settled their checks through the national clearinghouse operated by the Federal Reserve. It would seem that using this same system to clear and settle credit card sales drafts, which were small in number compared to checks at this time, would be a sensible thing to do. The bankcard associations approached the Fed about processing credit card drafts, but the Fed refused to handle them.[23] Technically, it would have required

---

[20]For example, see Galanoy (1980). Formerly the Director of Communications for NBI, Galanoy accused bankers of being blinded by their desire to build an all-encompassing electronic funds transfer system, ignoring the costs of fraud to consumers. For an example of this concern voiced in the popular press, see O'Neil (1970).

[21]These laws were passed in 1970 as an amendment to the Truth in Lending Act (Brandel and Terraciano 1980; Fisher et al. 1980, p. 257). The 1967 hearings are documented in 19th Congress, First Session (8 and 9 November 1967).

[22]Dee Hock provided perhaps the best rebuttal to this in a 1979 interview: "Sure, consumer debt is high, but if you want the consumer to stay out of debt, business and government have to set the example. If we expect consumers to reduce debt and increase savings, then we must create an environment without inflation and with tax laws that favor saving and not debt. After all, interest paid on debt is tax deductible and interest earned on savings is taxed. How can that encourage thrift? We should not criticize the consumer who is learning to play the government invented game of buying now through debt and paying later with inflated dollars." Streeter (1979), p. 75.

[23]Russell interview. Hock also commented on this in a 1974 speech: "Had the Federal Reserve agreed when asked (and they were) to clear bank card activity, would the service have evolved as it subsequently has? ... It is clear there would be no BASE II and no INAS today had the Federal Reserve said yes, and clear that present bank card service would be radically different" (Hock 1974, p. 21).

some modifications to the automated systems: the sales drafts were 80 column IBM punch cards, larger in size than most checks of the day; and they encoded information as punched holes instead of magnetic characters printed along the bottom edge. But the technical reasons were secondary to the more ideological belief that debt instruments, especially those involving a discount, simply did not belong in the Federal Reserve's clearing system.[24] Recall that one of the Fed's goals was to eliminate discounts on cleared checks, so it is not surprising that they would refuse to process BankAmericard transactions.

With the Fed's refusal to handle credit card drafts, the BankAmericard Service Corporation (BASC) was faced with a problem: how should the licensee banks clear and settle their interchange transactions? One logical option would have been for the BASC to create their own centralized clearinghouse for BankAmericard transactions, but the BASC chose not to do this, partly because the amount of interchange was still very low in the late 1960s.[25] Instead, the BASC stipulated that acquiring banks must mail interchange drafts directly to the issuing bank, similar to the way they handled out-of-town checks in the nineteenth century. The issuing bank would then reimburse the acquiring bank, less a discount fee, called the *interchange reimbursement fee*.[26]

This solved only the clearing half of the problem—the licensee banks still needed a way to settle those transactions (i.e., transfer "good and final funds" from the issuer to the acquirer). Recall that the Federal Reserve System eliminated the need to transfer physical currency between banks when settling payment transactions, and the BASC decided to leverage this system by creating a special *clearing draft*, which looked like a bit like a cashier's check. To receive payment for a set of interchange drafts, acquirers completed one of these clearing drafts against the issuer for the total amount of the sales drafts, less interchange fees, and submitted it along with their other inter-bank funds transfer requests.

This separation of the clearing draft from the sales drafts allowed banks to use their existing funds transfer mechanisms, but it also created a timing problem that jeopardized the functioning of the entire system. When the issuing bank received payment notice of the clearing draft, it would enter that amount into a suspense ledger and wait for the individual sales drafts to arrive in order to reconcile and bill the cardholder. Unfortunately, this often took quite a long time. This is how Visa's founder described it:

> Meanwhile, the merchant bank, having already been paid and under immense pressure to handle its own cardholder transactions, had no incentive to process [interchange] transactions and get them to the issuing bank for billing to the cardholder. Since each bank was

[24] Russell interview.

[25] Sources estimated that it was between one and five percent of transactions at the most. There were of course localized exceptions to this. In regions where banks were not allowed to operate branches across an entire metropolitan area, the interchange level would naturally be higher.

[26] Note that the laws governing checkclearing discussed in the previous chapter did not apply to credit card sales drafts. Any similarity in their clearing method was coincidental and not required by law. The legal basis for credit card sales drafts came from the contracts signed by licensee banks, cardholders, and merchants (Katz interview).

both a merchant-signing bank and a card-issuing bank, they began to play tit-for-tat, while back rooms filled with unprocessed transactions, customers went unbilled, and suspense ledgers swelled like a hammered thumb. It became an accounting nightmare.[27]

This immense backlog in the system also compounded the fraud problems discussed earlier. Issuing banks would have no way of knowing if sub-floor-limit fraud was occurring on a card until the actual sales drafts arrived and were processed. By the time they arrived, thousands of dollars worth of fraud could have taken place.

Even when the sales drafts did arrive, it was often the case that their total did not match the clearing draft amount. Many smaller merchant banks would simply run an adding machine tape over the drafts instead of key punching them, and would inevitably make mistakes. Chuck Russell, who succeeded Hock as CEO, recalled that "Banks couldn't balance from day to day because they couldn't get their drafts drawn on other banks settled. It was a disaster."[28] To provide a sense of the scale of the problem, he relayed this story:

> I was shown a room that was warehoused-sized, full of IBM 80-column tab cards (which were the drafts) that they couldn't settle. We're talking millions and millions of dollars ... they had never got the debit or the credit side of the transaction through clearing because they couldn't find them![29]

Finally, it should be noted that not all banks experienced problems to the degree described here. But the lack of a centralized clearinghouse, compounded with the timing problems introduced by the clearing drafts, created operational problems that were most definitely threatening the overall system's stability and impeding its future growth.[30]

Organizational Problems

Although the operational problems just described may have had potential solutions within a health franchising organization, the organization had problems of its own that further compounded the operational difficulties. It was these organizational problems, even more than the operational ones, that convinced the licensees that a new organizational structure was necessary.

The BankAmericard licensing system, like any cooperative payment system, faced a central organizational tension—balancing competition and cooperation.[31]

---

[27] Hock (2005), p. 77.

[28] Russell interview.

[29] Russell interview. The "stacks of unprocessed drafts" story was also relayed by others in various forms.

[30] Jutilla indicated that his bank was typically able to reconcile, but the delays in receiving the interchange drafts were especially dangerous due to fraud. He concluded that the system could not have survived the way it was as the transaction volume increased.

[31] Evans and Schmalensee (2005).

The licensing system created a new meta-organization comprised of *competing* financial institutions that needed to *cooperate*, at least to some degree, in order to provide a universal payment system that none could have realistically provided alone. Competing organizations in a marketplace normally seek their own self-interests in an assumed zero-sum game for market share. A cooperative organization, on the other hand, offers a different possibility—if all members cooperate, they can provide a larger, universal system that allows them all to benefit even more than if they chose not to cooperate. In other words, each participant's slice of the cooperatively baked pie would likely be larger than any pie the participant could have baked alone. To accomplish this, however, they need mechanisms that would create trust within the organization, mechanisms that balance out their power and interests and dictate how inter-organizational work will be accomplished. In other words, they need something akin to a constitution, as well as *operating regulations*, to which all member organizations agree. As we shall see, the licensing program's key organizational problems lay precisely in these balancing mechanisms and operating regulations.

Under the BankAmericard licensing system, BofA retained not only the ownership of the BankAmericard name and marks, but also all the power, and this led to a fundamental distrust between BofA and the licensees. The licensees knew that BofA would have opened branches in their territories if the banking regulations had allowed it, and if those regulations ever changed, BofA could easily revoke their license and become the sole BankAmericard issuer.[32] The licensees also doubted if BofA had the desire and even the ability to solve the operational problems discussed earlier.[33] The licensees believed that any solutions developed by BofA would naturally be in BofA's best interest and not those of the licensee banks.

Although BofA retained nearly all the power in the system, their power to enforce and modify the operating regulations was neutered by two critical flaws in the license contracts. First, the contracts lacked mechanisms for financially punishing banks that skirted or bent the operating regulations, nor did they contain a method for resolving grievances between the licensee banks. The only recourse BofA had was to revoke a bank's license, but since most of these banks held large correspondent deposits with the BofA, and were dominant in their geographic area, this was not likely to happen. Second, the contracts also lacked a clause allowing BofA to change the operating regulations in response to new developments. If BofA needed to modify or add a rule, they had to re-negotiate a new contract. Again, BofA had no recourse if banks simply refused to sign the new license, which they often did if the rules were not in their best interests.[34]

The fundamental distrust and the flaws in the contracts created a number of organizational instabilities. The most significant and pernicious was the tension over the

---

[32] Hock (2005), p. 85. Of course, these regulations were abolished in the 1980s, but by then it was too late, as the Visa system had already been established.

[33] Russell interview. The BofA paid very low salaries at the time, and the most talented operational people tended to go to their main local competitor, Wells Fargo, which was a member of the Interbank system.

[34] Katz interview. See also Hock (2005), pp. 83–87.

interchange reimbursement fee. As noted earlier, this fee was paid by the acquirer to the issuer during the settlement of an interchange transaction.[35] At this time, the intent of the fee was to compensate the issuer for the cost and risk of extending the cardholder credit for the transaction. The rule established under the licensing system for interchange fees was essentially unenforceable. This is how Bennett Katz, Visa's long-time general counsel, described it:

> When I came on board, the rule was... if a customer of your bank goes into a merchant belonging to another bank, outside of that territory, then the bank that signed the merchant has a choice as to what it sends to the issuer. It could send the amount of the discount that it received from the merchant less a processing fee (for processing the transaction), or if it didn't want to calculate each and every one... it could send the average discount it was getting from all of its merchants less a processing fee. Well they would say 'my average is two percent.' How are you going to audit that? And if the merchant put up a big deposit, their merchant discount might be close to zero, and the issuer would get almost nothing!
> So the issuer has all the costs because he's extending the credit and eating defaults, but he was getting almost nothing when the customer traveled. The losses were horrendous. It was literally chaos in the BankAmericard system.[36]

Tensions Come to a Head

In October of 1968, the BASC called a special meeting of the licensees to discuss the operational and organizational problems facing the BankAmericard system. Card program managers from each of the licensee banks descended on Columbus, Ohio, but the BASC neglected to send their most senior officers. The licensees were incensed that the BASC apparently did not recognize the seriousness of the situation, and began to make accusations that the BASC was either unwilling or incapable of solving the system's problems. By the middle of the second day, the meeting had devolved into "acrimonious argument."[37] Unsure of how to rescue the situation, the BASC representatives attempted to create a committee of licensees that would look into the most critical problems. One of those selected to be on the committee, however, had a different idea of what it would take to solve the system's problems, and after lunch the rest of the licensees were greeted by the card-center manager from the Seattle National Bank of Commerce: Dee Ward Hock.

Dee Hock

To tell a complete history of Visa's origins, one must give significant time and credit to Dee Hock. Historians of technology are usually quite reticent to spend too much

---

[35]The acquirer paid this out of the discount fee collected from the merchant in return for immediate and guaranteed payment. In the case of a cash advance, however, the flow is reversed: the issuer pays the acquirer, because the acquirer assumes all the costs.

[36]Katz interview.

[37]Hock (2005), p. 84.

time focusing on any single individual, fearing that they will fall foul of the dreaded "inventor-hero" myth. This sort of history, all too common in the popular press, simplifies technological history by focusing on one particular person (typically a man), often portraying that person as a forward-thinking genius heroically fighting against the stodgy and uninventive status quo. Through a flash of inspiration and sheer tenacity (as the story typically goes), the inventor-hero brings about a completely novel technique or device that forever changes a reluctant industry.

The trouble with this kind of heroic saga is that it typically falls apart when one starts to dig deeper into the case. As argued in the previous chapter, most technological systems are based upon, or at least shaped by, other innovations that came before. Most are the product of many different minds and hands, working and negotiating with each other over many years. Most require a legion of individual workers not only to build the initial system, but also to keep it in good repair and working over time. That is to say, despite our tendency to associate innovations with a single heroic figure, a more nuanced understanding of the case often reveals key contributions from many different people over longer periods of time.

In our effort to avoid the inventor-hero style of history, however, we have sometimes neglected to give proper credit where that credit is due. In the case of Visa, a deep study of the case does expose several other individuals who played key roles in bringing the system to life and keeping it running on a daily basis, but one still cannot escape the critical, and perhaps most important role played by Hock. He, more than anyone else, established the principles by which the organization was designed and intended to function, and set the agenda for that organization's actions during its formative and most prolific years. Thus, it is appropriate to spend some time understanding not only who Dee Hock is, but also how his ideas on money and organizations shaped his vision for what Visa could become.

Hock's Personality

All that said, it is still a difficult task to describe Dee Hock, as his character is frustratingly complex. Those that worked at Visa during Hock's reign would invariably start telling "Dee stories" during our interviews, and since no single story could entirely capture his character, they just kept telling more of them. Tom Cleveland, who eventually became Visa's Chief Financial Officer, wrote a series of sixteen stories totaling fifty pages in an attempt to capture what he called "the Dee Hock experience."[38] Sources used a wide variety of adjectives, but none of them seemed to be sufficient: inspirational; intimidating; clairvoyant; clever; shrewd; aggravating; fair; brutal; demanding; and brilliantly eccentric. Many said he was the most decent human being they had ever met, and most said he was nearly impossible to describe fully.

---

[38]Cleveland (1999), p. 1.

Interestingly, all of the stories combined to describe Hock as simultaneously having one character trait and its opposite. He was the most inspirational of leaders, but could also be the most denigrating. One employee said that he was like an "emotional roller-coaster"—he could completely demoralize you in one breath and then boost your ego to new heights in the next. Another employee remarked that he sometimes could be demanding to the point of being insensitive, but immediately came to her tangible assistance when personal tragedy struck. Hock advocated decentralized autonomy for his employees and gave them enormous leeway at times, but would ultimately micromanage every detail he could. Every piece of correspondence that left the Visa offices during the first few years was personally reviewed by Hock, and he reportedly obsessed about the design of each new office or data center space, even down to the location of the electrical sockets. In short, his personality is complicated and often paradoxical.

One way in which we might untangle his personality a bit is to examine the way Hock tells his own life story.[39] Hock's autobiography is revealing, not only as a chronicle of his times at Visa, but also as a window into the way he views himself and thus a clue to his deeper, more unconscious motivations.[40] He opens his autobiography with his birth in 1929, at the start of the Great Depression. He describes his upbringing as part of a poor family in rural Utah, living in a cramped one-room cottage with no plumbing and a wood stove that doubled as a cooker and heater. He characterizes himself as a curious child, a voracious reader, and a keen study of nature. He notes that his penchant for books and long walks in the country began to estrange him from his family and friends and make him feel misunderstood, leading him into an interior world in which he dreamt of greater things. He recounts how in his youth he worked a number of harsh, manual-labor jobs, which as he reminds the reader, "proud men did, without whining. 'Root, hog, or die' was the homily of the day." He describes how he learned to argue persuasively on his high school's debate team, and how he was the first person in his family to attend college, at which he obtained an associates degree and an interest in the classics of Western thought. He ends the segment on his early life by marrying his childhood sweetheart, and taking an entry-level job in a small local consumer finance office to provide for his new family.[41]

Hock's own portrayal of his early life, almost the stereotype of the pioneering self-made American man, makes several claims that I think are key to understanding not only his general character, but also the motivations behind a number of his actions that I will discuss in later chapters. First, he strongly emphasizes his *humble origins* in order to establish that he did not come from privilege. Second, he portrays himself largely as *self-taught*; his schooling was limited and when teachers enter the story, they merely expose or introduce him to sources that he alone then reads, interprets, and understands. Third, he highlights the hard-working nature of his community as well as his own experience with manual labor in order to

---

[39] Hock (2005).

[40] For issues surrounding the reading of autobiographies, see Smith and Watson (1996, 2001).

[41] Hock (2005), pp. 15–29.

self-identify as belonging to the working-class. Fourth, he hints at *feeling like an outsider*, misunderstood by those with more limited imaginations.

All of these claims combine to create one important yet unspoken overtone that runs throughout his entire autobiography: he wants to make it absolutely clear to the reader that he was *not a typical banker*. Hock was not born into an important or wealthy family, nor was he the son of a banker. He did not grow up in a suburb of New York, San Francisco, or any other banking capital. He did not attend the right schools, nor did he earn an MBA from a prestigious graduate school. Most telling of all, his first job was at a consumer finance company, not at a large commercial bank.

Although Hock would eventually become the CEO of a significant international banking organization, earn a commensurate salary, and commune with some of the most powerful bankers in the world, he continued to think of himself as that self-made, pioneering man from humble origins who would always remain somewhat of an "outsider" to the typical world of banking. In some ways, Hock enjoyed his outsider status: it allowed him to ignore conventions, take risks, and break down conceptual barriers that typical bankers considered immovable. In other ways, however, that outsider status sometimes drove Hock to seek acceptance amongst his banker-peers: as we shall see, his attempts to seem equal or even more important than his powerful member bankers created frictions that contributed to his eventual dismissal from Visa.

Views on Organizations

Hock's first professional job was with a consumer finance company in Los Angeles starting in 1951, and it was here that he not only learned the business of lending, but also began to develop his concepts about organizations. During this time, Hock became increasingly suspicious and critical of what he called "mechanistic, command-and-control organizations."[42] These types of organizations are typified by the centralization of power, the creation of bureaucratic hierarchies, and the use of technology and highly-rationalized rules to control an increasingly specialized and deskilled set of workers.[43] For Hock, this concept of organizational design was bred from "industrial age thinking" and the "machine metaphor," where an organization is viewed as a sort of machine with humans as the cogs and wheels.[44] Hock sees these organizations as fundamentally flawed—in these kinds of organizations, "purpose slowly erodes into process," "procedure takes precedence over product,"

---

[42] Hock (2005), p. 36.

[43] Hock purposely does not cite his sources, but this is of course reminiscent of Burns and Stalker's 'mechanistic' and 'organic' organizational spectrum. See Burns and Stalker (1961). One can also detect resonances with General System theory, Chaos theory, and what is now beginning to be called "ecological thinking."

[44] Hock (2005), pp. 37–38.

and "the doing of the doing" causes nothing of substance to get done.[45] Furthermore, Hock argues that command-and-control organizations are actually incapable of dealing with their increasingly complex and dynamic challenges, and because this is still the dominant organizational form, we are in "the midst of a global epidemic of institutional failure."[46]

Hock would eventually develop a different concept for organizations based on his observations of natural systems.[47] He created the neologism "chaordic" to describe his new concept and defined it as "The behavior of any self-organizing and self-governing organism, organization, or system that harmoniously blends characteristics of chaos and order."[48] In contrast to the command and control organizations, chaordic organizations are decentralized, self-organizing, self-governing, exhibiting emergent properties. The obvious implication is that they are also more flexible and adaptive.[49] But this concept was still rather nascent in Hock's mind at this time, and we shall see how he continued to develop it through the creation of the Visa organization, which he considered to be the first, albeit flawed, implementation of this new concept.[50]

Hock began to implement some of these new organizational ideas while working for the consumer finance company in Los Angeles. Unfortunately for Hock, that organization did not share his vision, and they eventually parted ways. It was at this point that Hock learned his most important lessons about consumer lending. While he was still employed, he had gotten into "considerable debt" through the use of credit cards, and had no savings to live upon. Hock took multiple jobs to pay it off, and he and his wife vowed never to carry so much debt again. He wrote, "It is amusing now to remember how we shredded every credit card in our possession, swearing never to have another."[51] Although this makes an amusing anecdote, it also reveals Hock's motivations for creating Visa's first debit card soon after the organization was formed.[52]

Hock moved to Seattle and interviewed for a job at the National Bank of Commerce in 1965.[53] He played several menial roles within the bank before being picked in 1966 to help start their newly-licensed BankAmericard program. He and his boss were given a ridiculously short time in which to start the program—90 days—and

---

[45] Hock (2005), p. 36.

[46] Hock (2005), p. 11.

[47] Hock (2005), pp. 248–249.

[48] Hock (2005), p. 13.

[49] Burns and Stalker argue that this organic style of organization is more effective for firms in highly-dynamic markets, while the mechanistic style is best for stable markets. Hock, however, would question if any organization exists in a stable context, and point out that mechanistic organizations will ultimately fail due to their inherent flaws.

[50] Hock (2005), pp. 248–249.

[51] Hock (2005), p. 40.

[52] See Chap. 8.

[53] Dougherty (1981), p. 13.

by the end of their training session in San Francisco, they realized that they were in "deep trouble."[54] Hock discovered that there was "bad blood" between the BASC and BofA's own card operations center, and that the card center "had no capacity to comply with rules prescribed in the licensing agreements."[55] The training, provided by the marketing department, amounted to encouragements to mass-issue the cards, with no practical advice on how to handle the aftermath. Hock and his boss spent the next week visiting every card center they could in order to learn the realities of credit card operations. Hock summarized: "Within a single week, our original belief that the BankAmericard franchise would provide a well-marked, expeditious road to the future had been shattered by what we had learned."[56]

The highly dynamic, unpredictable nature of the endeavor provided Hock with another chance to try out some of his new organizational concepts. He suggested that they "abandon tradition, throw detailed planning to the winds, rely on a clear sense of direction, a few simple principles, common sense, trust in the ingenuity of the people, and let the answers emerge."[57] Despite numerous setbacks, his new organizational style proved effective, and with great effort they issued 100,000 cards and signed up enough merchants, all within 90 days. Throughout the process, Hock had become a believer in the future of payment cards, but not because of their financing capabilities. Hock wrote that while he was organizing the new program, he was also reading about the possibilities of a more complete integration of computers and banking. "Giving people another way to borrow money interests me not at all," Hock recalled, "What credit cards might become is something else again."[58]

Views on the Nature of Money

Hock had been slowly coming to the realization that "money" had become nothing more than "guaranteed alphanumeric data" and that a bank is nothing more than an "institution for the custody, loan, and exchange" of this data. Furthermore, that data was increasingly being stored and manipulated by computers, and would eventually "move around the world at the speed of light at minuscule cost by infinitely diverse paths."[59] He then came to one of his most important conclusions:

> Any institution that could move, manipulate, and guarantee alphanumeric data in the form of arranged energy in a manner that individuals customarily used and relied upon as a measure of equivalent value and medium of exchange was a bank. It went even beyond that. Inherent in all this might be the genesis of a new form of global currency.[60]

---

[54] Hock (2005), p. 61.

[55] Hock (2005), p. 61.

[56] Hock (2005), p. 61.

[57] Hock (2005), p. 62.

[58] Hock (2005), p. 69. Although these quotes come from a retrospective biography, his speeches from the 1970s contain similar sentiments.

[59] Hock (2005), pp. 95–96.

[60] Hock (2005), p. 96.

Hock realized that if this was actually the case, the implications were enormous:

> If electronic technology continued to advance, and that seemed certain, two-hundred year old banking oligopolies controlling the custody, loan, and exchange of money would be irrecoverably shattered. Nation-state monopolies on the issue and control of currency would erode.... The vast preponderance of the system would fall to those who were most adept at handling and guaranteeing alphanumeric value data in the form of arranged particles of energy.[61]

Lastly, Hock realized that he, and most of his fellow bankcard managers, had misunderstood what business they were in:

> It seems ordinary and obvious now. It was a revelation then. We were not in the credit card business. "Credit card" was a misnomer based on banking jargon. The card was no more than a device bearing symbols for the exchange of monetary value. That it took the form of a piece of plastic was nothing but an accident of time and circumstance. *We were really in the business of the exchange of monetary value.*[62]

Creation of National BankAmericard Inc.

At the licensees meeting in 1968, Hock convinced the BASC representatives that merely investigating a few of the most serious operational problems would do nothing to save the system. Instead he proposed a "cohesive, coherent, self-organizing effort involving all licensees to examine all problems plaguing the system."[63] The BASC representatives were naturally reluctant to agree, but they had little reason to object—Hock's proposal did not require them to commit to any policy recommendations made by the licensees, nor could the BASC prohibit the licensees from meeting on their own and making plans that might exclude the BofA.

Hock created a matrix of committees to investigate the problems of the system. He divided the United States into eight regions and each region formed separate committees to focus on four functional areas: operations, marketing, credit, and computer systems. After performing some initial research, the committees began to report:

> The complex of committees had but one redeeming quality: It allowed organized information about problems to emerge. It took only two cycles of meetings to realize that the problems were enormously greater than anyone imagined—far beyond any possibility of correction by the existing committees or the licensing structure—and growing at an astonishing rate. Losses were not in the tens of millions, as everyone had thought, but in the hundreds of millions and accelerating.[64]

It quickly became obvious to Hock that the licensing system could not survive as it was structured. The problem was not a lack of technology—it was a *fundamental*

---

[61] Hock (2005), p. 97.

[62] Hock (2005), p. 98. Emphasis in original.

[63] Hock (2005), p. 87.

[64] Hock (2005), p. 91.

flaw in the organizational design. If the licensing organization could barely function in the United States and a few other countries, it had no chance of expanding into the ubiquitous worldwide system that Hock envisioned. His new organizational ideas had been successful in the highly dynamic and chaotic context of starting a new card program at a particular bank, but could they also work to organize a system that involved hundreds, and eventually tens of thousands, of independent organizations spread across different countries, subject to different regulations? If so, there was an enormous opportunity:

> Any organization that could guarantee, transport, and settle transactions in the form of arranged electronic particles twenty-four hours a day, seven days a week, around the globe, would have a market—every exchange of value in the world—that beggared the imagination. The necessary technology had been discovered and would be available in geometrically increasing abundance at geometrically diminishing cost. But there was a problem. No bank could do it. No hierarchical, stock corporation could do it. No nation-state could do it. In fact, no existing form of organization we could think of could do it. On a hunch I made an estimate of the financial resources of all the banks in the world. It dwarfed the resources of most nations. Jointly they could do it, but how? It would require a transcendental organization linking together in wholly new ways an unimaginable complex of diverse institutions and individuals.[65]

Organizational Dreams

Hock selected three members of the national executive licensee committee, which had overseen the work performed by the regional committees, to help him think through a design for a new organization. They checked into the Alta Mira hotel in Sausalito, California for a week of discussion. The location was perhaps fitting—it is perched upon a hill across the bay from San Francisco's financial district, home of the BofA. It was here that Hock and his colleges, "the founding fathers," planned what amounted to a revolution against the BofA's licensing system.

Hock recounts that on the fourth night he began to realize that if the methods of biological evolution could produce such complex organizations as brains and immune systems, not to mention larger and more diverse systems such as rain forests, marine and weather systems, the same sort of principles employed by humans might be able to create the kind of complex, self-organizing system he wanted to achieve. He concluded, "What if we quit arguing about the structure of a new institution and tried to think of it as having some sort of genetic code?"[66] He continued, "If institutions have no reality save in the mind, might their genetic code have something to do with beliefs—with purpose and principles?"[67] What if they came to agreement on the purpose and principles of the new organization, and then let it self-organize according to those?

---

[65] Hock (2005), pp. 98–99.

[66] Hock (2005), p. 108.

[67] Hock (2005), p. 109.

Hock presented his ideas the next morning and the group formed the following principles, which would in turn become the basis for the new organization's constitution:

> *What if ownership was in the form of irrevocable rights of participation*, rather than stock: rights could not be raided, traded or sold, but only acquired by application and acceptance of membership?
> *What if it were self-organizing*, with participants having the right to self-organize at any time, for any reason, at any scale with irrevocable rights of participation in governance at any greater scale?
> *What if power and function were distributive*, with no power vested in or function performed by any part that could reasonably be exercised by any more peripheral part?
> *What if governance was distributive*, with no individual institution or combination of either or both, particularly management, able to dominate deliberations or control decisions at any scale?
> *What if it could seamlessly blend cooperation and competition*, with all parts free to compete in unique, independent ways, yet able to yield self-interest and cooperate when necessary to the good of the whole?
> *What if it were infinitely malleable, yet extremely durable*, with all parts capable of constant, self-generated, modification of form or function without sacrificing its essential purpose, nature, or embodied principle, thus releasing human ingenuity and spirit?[68]

Hock persuaded the other licensees to agree to these principles, but as he admits, this may have had more to do with their beliefs that the entire project was likely doomed to failure anyway. Hock recalled:

> In the beginning, none of the licensees thought that the Bank of America would surrender ownership of a trademark and licensing system that assured them a quarter percent or more of the revenues of every participant in perpetuity. No one thought that banks would voluntarily surrender a portion of their autonomy to an external entity in order to act together for a common purpose. No one believed that such a horizontal grouping of competitors could exist within the spirit and constraints of antitrust laws. And no one dreamed the emerging ideas would bring together in common ownership and enterprise people and institutions of every race, language, custom, and culture—every economic, legal, philosophical, and religious persuasion in the world.[69]

Hock then presented the principles and a rough idea of the new organization to Ken Larkin, BofA's Senior Vice President in charge of the BankAmericard program. Larkin's response was less than encouraging and the BofA initially resisted any attempts to curtail their power or control over the system. The BofA, however, actually had little choice but to capitulate and allow Hock to pursue the new structure. The system was clearly falling apart, and there was a very real danger that the licensees could organize a new competing system on their own and exclude the BofA, or simply join the rival Interbank network. Hock used his talents of persuasion to argue that it was actually in BofA's best interest to support the new organization, as it had the potential of generating far more revenue for them in the long run, and eventually they agreed to do so.

---

[68] Hock (2005), pp. 109–110. Emphasis in original. Although Hock wanted to balance malleability and durability, the former seems to have won out over the latter. Visa restructured into a public stock-issuing corporation in 2008, essentially abandoning these principles.

[69] Hock (2005), p. 112.

Hock began crafting the organization's structure, bylaws, and operating regulations. It would be a membership cooperative where the members would also be the joint-owners. In essence, the customers and owners would be the same, so there would be no divided loyalty. It would be non-stock, and membership would be non-transferrable, so that ownership and participation would forever be linked. Membership qualifications would be set by the Board, but then any organization meeting those criteria must be allowed membership. Both membership fees and voting rights were determined by the amount of volume a member generated, linking taxation and representation. Operating regulations dictated not only how inter-member work was to be accomplished, but also how members would be penalized when they violated them. But most importantly, members would agree to abide by a common set of bylaws and operating regulations "as they now exist or are hereafter modified."[70] Thus Hock ensured not only that the new organization could enforce the rules, but also that they could modify and extend them as needed without renegotiating contracts.

Interestingly, Hock claims that he always wanted to include participating merchants as full owners and members in the new organization, but the idea was always strongly resisted by the licensee banks.[71] At the time, the licensee banks were concerned that giving merchants voting rights would endanger the merchant discount, which was a key source of revenue for acquirers. Hock also claims he wanted to include all the cardholders as owner/members, but that would have added a layer of complexity and chaos comparable to a democratic nation-state, and perhaps would have been unrealistic.

The bylaws acted like a kind of constitution for the new organization. They enshrined Hock's principles, and although they could be amended by the Board of Directors, doing so required an 80 percent majority vote. This ensured that the organization could adapt if the principles no longer made sense, but they also could not abandon them without an overwhelming consensus.

The Board of Directors for the new organization was also designed to balance the interests and power of all the members, regardless of size and location, and to provide the larger banks with "blocking power" on key issues such as budgets and fees.[72] Each Board member would come from a different bank, so that no one bank could dominate policy regardless of volume. Each of the eight regions would be allocated one Director in order to ensure that all regions were equally represented. Five "at large" Directors would be elected by the general membership. One Director would be elected by the smallest banks in the system. Any bank that generated more than 15 percent of the sales volume would be able to appoint their own Director.[73] The president of the new organization (which would be Hock) would also have a seat on the Board, but could not serve as chairperson.

---

[70] Hock (2005), p. 124.

[71] Hock (2005), p. 161.

[72] Honey interview.

[73] This was eventually reduced to five percent (Honey interview).

The functional committees would also remain in the new organization, though they would be split into two levels. Hock felt that it was important to keep the Board members occupied with the large and important policy decisions, while sub-committees handled the matters of minutia.[74] Thus he created a lower layer of "advisor groups," which were comprised of card-center managers. These groups reviewed policy proposals made by the central organization's staff, and occasionally drafted some of their own. The advisor groups then made recommendations to the Board-level committees, which were comprised of Directors, plus a member of the central organization's staff. The Board-level committees then voted whether to bring the policy before the entire Board. Certain committees, however, such as the one for operations, were eventually given the power to approve changes to the operating regulations on their own without a full Board vote, as these changes were numerous.

In practice, the committees and advisor groups also provided the staff of the new organization with a testing ground for innovative ideas, enabling them "take the temperature" of the membership on important issues.[75] The staff could thus determine which issues would become politically contentious, which required some alteration, and which could be proposed with confidence at the full Board meetings. The relationship was symbiotic, as the committee and group members often became the champions of certain issues, enabling NBI's staff to appear as neutral advocates for the needs of the system as a whole.

Organizational Realities

The complex structure of the Board and committees was certainly a political masterpiece, and in principle, it ensured that while groups had blocking power, no one bank or person could dominate the organization. In practice, however, the design did allow one person in particular to exert enormous influence: Dee Hock. By stipulating that the president of the new organization could not chair the Board, Hock had limited his own power to that of persuasion, but as Nocera remarked, "this was Hock at his most coy. It was precisely his ability to persuade that made him powerful."[76] Chuck Russell, who would succeed Hock as CEO in 1984, noted that Hock also used the structure of the Board and committees to his advantage:

> ...[Hock] structured the Board in such a way that *he* ran the company and there was no question about it. What he did, he very cleverly split up the power of the big banks into different groups. And if you get a Board that is widely split, *management* runs the company. Dee understood that; he understood it very well, and he taught it to me very well, because when I took over, man I kept that thing split into smithereens. You want a Board of at least 25 guys, because they'll never accomplish anything. Then you want to form lots of

---

[74] Honey interview.

[75] Honey interview.

[76] Nocera (1994), p. 92.

committees to supposedly do something, but you very strategically put fighting banks on each committee.[77]

A number of sources remarked that during the first decade of the Visa organization, it was in essence a dictatorship, and the only true power-broker was Hock. This was in part due to Hock's early successes in automating the core system processes, which will be discussed in detail in the upcoming chapters. In the minds of the member banks, Hock literally *saved the system* as well as their card programs, turning them from a source of major losses into a profit-making department. This gave Hock a large amount of influence with the Board, and its structure further ensured that he could shape the system toward his own vision: "the world's premier system for the exchange of value."[78]

Convincing the two hundred fully-licensed banks, and their thousands of sub-licensees, to join the new organization was no easy task, but Hock was persuasive and persistent. In 1970, only 90 days after Hock began the formation process, all the licensees had agreed to join, and the new organization was legally formed as a Delaware membership corporation named National BankAmericard Incorporated (NBI). The BofA became just another member, though they retained five special seats on the Board for the first few years to recognize their unique contribution in forming the original system.[79]

The exact legal description of the organization is a "for-profit, non-stock membership corporation."[80] This rather unusual classification is actually quite important. Banks at this time were not allowed to own stock in anything but a Bank Service Corporation (BSC), but BSCs were also subject to stringent regulation. By creating NBI as a non-stock membership corporation, Hock cleverly enabled the banks to "own" it through membership while at the same time avoided unwelcome government regulation.

Although NBI was legally formed as a for-profit enterprise, its owners were its customers, so it effectively operated as a non-profit entity. Because it did not issue any stock, and therefore had no market capitalization nor paid any dividends, any "accumulated net revenue" from member fees was used to finance the ongoing work of the organization. The Visa organization continued this structure and method of operation until its recent reorganization into a publicly-traded stock corporation. Although the member banks still own the majority of the corporation, non-member organizations and personal investors may now purchase shares in Visa, and consequently, will expect healthy returns on their investments. Only time will tell if this need to meet investor's return expectations will fundamentally alter Visa's motivations and priorities.

---

[77] Russell interview.

[78] According to Nocera, Hock actually convinced the Board to adopt a resolution with that exact wording, even though most of the members had no idea what he meant by that.

[79] Nocera (1994), p. 92. These seats were reduced by one each year until Ken Larkin was the only remaining director from the BofA.

[80] Katz interview.

An New Kind of Organization?

Although Hock's methods for arriving at the NBI organizational structure may have been novel, the resulting structure itself was not terribly unique. Most joint ventures in the banking industry, both before NBI and since, have taken similar approaches to ownership and governance, though NBI's complex representational design may have allowed more of a diversity of voices, at least in principle. The airlines had also created a similar organization for their Universal Air Travel Plan discussed in Chap. 1. This kind of structure can also be found in other industries besides banking and payments: for example, regional multiple listing services in the American real estate industry are typically owned by multiple competing brokerage firms, each of which owns and has representational governance over a central organization that provides informational services for the network.

But NBI was only the start of what would soon become the larger, multi-layered, worldwide organization eventually known as Visa. Starting in 1972, Hock began to implement the same sort of organizational design at the international level, resulting in a new kind of organization that has few if any parallels. For Hock, it was this worldwide version of the organization that was the first, albeit flawed, example of a "chaordic" organization, one that seamlessly blended elements of chaos and order. This worldwide organization went beyond the typical international joint-venture to encompass tens of thousands of financial institutions in hundreds of countries, dealing with a wide variety of currencies and banking systems. The members of this international organization were often themselves national systems like NBI, each of which was subject to the international rules, but could also enforce additional local rules that made sense for the specific country. I will describe the creation and structure of this worldwide organization in Chaps. 6 and 9.

Conclusion

In this chapter we examined what was wrong with the BankAmericard licensing system, noting that, while the operational problems may have had technical solutions within the existing organizational structure, that structure had severe problems of its own that made the existing structure untenable. This ultimately led Hock and his fellow licensees to revolt against the Bank of America and form a new, jointly-owned organization known as National BankAmericard Incorporated (NBI) in 1970.

In the next chapter we will turn our attention to NBI's first steps, especially how Hock and his new staff solved several of the most pressing organizational problems. At the heart of these solutions were the operating regulations, a series of rules that governed everything from the physical design of the card, to the fees each party must pay to process transactions, to the rights and responsibilities each party has during a transaction dispute. As we shall see, these rules, along with NBI's role as a kind of judiciary, helped restore not only order to the inter-organizational workflow, but also a minimal level of trust between the members that was necessary for the system to survive, function, and grow.

Chapter 3
Crafting the Social Dynamics: Staffing, Operating Regulations, and Advertising

Now that the independent organization was formed and functional, Hock and his new staff turned their attentions toward solving the remaining operational and organizational problems noted in the previous chapter. Foremost amongst these was the need to establish a common set of rules that would dictate how inter-organizational work was to be done, how disputes between member banks were to be settled, and how fees would be assessed. The rules needed to be clear and apply consistently to all members, but they also needed to be flexible so they could adapt to the rapidly changing technological, financial, and cultural landscape of the early 1970s.

NBI took the approach of codifying these rules into a set of "operating regulations," or "op-regs" in Visa-speak, and including a clause in the member contracts that bound each member institution to abide by these regulations "as they now exist or are hereafter modified."[1] This allowed the operating regulations to become the rulebook by which the game was played, specifying everything, from the appearance of the physical card to the fees that must be paid to process transactions, to the rights and responsibilities each party has during a transaction dispute.

The purpose of this chapter is to explain how these rules were formed and enforced, while analyzing the role they play within the NBI/Visa organization. I will argue that these regulations are a key part of what makes the Visa system "work" at the inter-organizational level. The computer systems and telecommunications described over the next four chapters are most certainly what makes the system work at the technical level, but these technical systems alone cannot explain or account for how the overall payment system was able to function and grow during its first few decades. Visa's technical infrastructure was, and still is, very adept at moving transactional information between system participants, but it was the operating regulations that allowed those participants to coordinate their work in response to that information.

The operating regulations establish the "rules of the game," and as such, created a common set of expectations and incentives amongst member banks, merchants, and cardholders. These expectations and incentives helped not only to coordinate

---

[1] Hock (2005), p. 124.

D.L. Stearns, *Electronic Value Exchange*, History of Computing,
DOI 10.1007/978-1-84996-139-4_3, © Springer-Verlag London Limited 2011

inter-organizational work, but also to balance out the conflicting interests of these various participants, many of whom are competitors of one another. In this way, the operating regulations, and Visa's role in adjudicating and enforcing them, created the conditions by which system participants could ultimately trust each other, just enough, in order to enable the system to function and grow.

Building a Staff

Before a new set of operating regulations could be crafted, Hock had a much more pressing task before him: building a staff that could help him achieve his vision of a worldwide system for electronic value exchange. The formation of the NBI organization had largely been driven by Hock alone, but developing that organization into a smoothly functioning system required talented and dedicated employees that could thrive in a high-pressure, low-specification work environment. In many ways, NBI was similar to the high-technology Internet startups of the 1990s, where work hours were long and operational plans shifted as quickly as the tides in the San Francisco Bay. More importantly, it was very unlike the typical banking work environment where the core processes had already been worked out to a large extent and systematized into predictable routines.

To his credit, Hock surrounded himself with people who had *complementary* and *not identical* skills, personalities, and ways of thinking. Hock was an idealistic visionary who could see clearly the direction he wanted to go, but lacked many of the practical skills that were necessary to build such a system and keep it running day-to-day. He needed committed people who not only shared his vision, but also knew how to break that vision down into achievable steps and do what was necessary to bring it to fruition. It was during these first few years of the organization that most of its key employees, those who will be mentioned often throughout the remaining chapters, were hired, and most of them stayed with the organization for their entire careers.

These key employees, however, did not comprise NBI's first staff. To get the new organization started, the BofA provided Hock with a small staff of executives, many of whom came from the now less-relevant BankAmericard Service Corporation (BASC). Since Hock had just personally led a revolt against the Bank of America (BofA) and the BASC, and since his views on organizations and money were quite different from most bankers, it should not be surprising to learn that most of this initial staff were rather unimpressed with the young, opinionated upstart in charge of the organization. Not long after this staff was assembled, these initial executives went so far as to plan a "palace revolt" to get rid of Hock. Unfortunately for them, Hock learned of the plan and summarily fired every last one of them, sending a clear message to the BofA that he was now in charge, and was there to stay.[2]

---

[2]Cleveland (1999). Confirmed in Russell interview.

Hock's own recruiting efforts were more favorable, and one of the first people he brought on board would soon become his most trusted ally: a bank operations expert named Chuck Russell. Russell had quite a bit of experience with bank credit cards: he started Pittsburgh National Bank's proprietary card program in 1965, was a founding member of Interbank, serving on their operations committee, and later established Wachovia's Interbank card program in 1968. Russell complimented Hock's abilities and personality in a few important ways. First, Russell was a practical bank operations person who could put Hock's creative vision into action. Second, although Hock had spent some time at a bank, his roots were much more in finance companies and consumer lending, and Russell's more extensive banking background allowed him to temper Hock's enthusiasm with the realities of a more traditional banker's perspective. Lastly, while Hock could easily be abrasive and stubborn, the member bankers found Russell much more approachable and helpful. Ken Larkin, who led the BankAmericard licensing program, summarized their complimentary differences well: "When I want vision, I go to Dee. When I want something done, I go to Chuck."[3]

Russell and Hock created a powerful team, and both of them were necessary to build and manage NBI during its early years. Russell noted:

> We covered each others' blind sides beautifully.... If I was Marshal and I was trying to figure out how to invade Europe, Dee would be my guy. If I wanted someone to lead the charge, it sure as hell wouldn't be Dee! He'd be thinking three moves down the board and get killed in the process.[4]

Russell would later succeed Hock as CEO in 1984, retiring from Visa in 1994. A number of sources remarked that the Hock/Russell team was crucial to Visa's success, and it is likely that this collaboration between a visionary, charismatic leader, and a practical operational engineer is a necessary component of what makes technical systems successful in general.

In addition to Russell, several other key figures were also hired during the first two years of the organization, and each played an important role in crafting the organization and its operational systems. Bob Miller, one of Hock's colleagues at the National Bank of Commerce, joined the effort shortly after NBI was formed. Bennett Katz, Visa's long-time chief counsel became the eighteenth employee in 1970. Ron Schmidt, the financial architect behind the new interchange fee, quarterly profit analysis and functional cost study (discussed in detail in the next sections), joined at the beginning of 1971. Aram Tootelian, Dave Huemer and David Goldsmith were hired in 1972 to lead the development of NBI's computerized authorization system, which I will discuss in detail in Chaps. 4 and 5. Finally, Bob Sanders was hired to develop NBI's adversing and marketing campaigns, described briefly at the end of this chapter.

---

[3]Russell agreed with this quote and responded: "I think I played a great buffer role." (Russell interview).

[4]Russell interview.

The Operating Regulations

One of the first challenges Hock and his new staff faced was establishing a new common set of rules that would govern the functioning of the system. When creating NBI, he encoded many of his basic principles into the bylaws of the organization, which could be altered only by a supermajority board vote, but these were more akin to ideals than day-to-day operational rules. NBI had its Constitution, but it now needed a series of laws that would describe how the inter-organizational work was actually to be done, who would pay whom for what services, and how rule violations, transaction disputes, and fraud were to be handled.

Recall that under the BankAmericard licensing system, each bank negotiated and signed a separate agreement with the BofA, and all changes to those agreements required re-negotiations. When banks violated the rules in these agreements, the BofA had little recourse beyond expelling the bank from the system, a consequence that was unlikely considering that many of the licensees maintained significant correspondent reserves with the BofA. This made it difficult for the BofA to enforce the rules and alter them as circumstances changed, resulting in an inflexible and ultimately brittle structure.

The rival Interbank system had adopted a different approach. They established a common set of regulations by which all the members agreed to abide, and formed a committee of representatives from the member banks to maintain those rules. Not surprisingly, NBI adopted a similar approach to Interbank, and NBI's first set of operating regulations were almost a verbatim copy of Interbank's with the branding details altered to fit the BankAmericard.[5] To become a member of NBI, banks had to contractually agree to abide by the operating regulations "as they now exist or are hereafter modified," allowing NBI to adjust and craft them in response to a rapidly changing technical and social context.[6]

Changes to those rules were then discussed and approved by the advisor groups, which were made up of representatives from various member banks. The advisor groups proved to be particularly useful for two reasons. First, they allowed NBI's staff to "take the temperature" of the membership on potentially controversial issues without causing widespread or intractable debate. Second, if the advisor groups liked the ideas, they would then act as advocates for them, making it seem that the ideas came from the general membership and not NBI's staff. Regulation changes were then voted upon by the Board of Directors (or one of their sub-committees), which was carefully structured by Hock to provide adequate representation for all types of member banks within the system (those within a given geographic area, those smaller than a certain size, etc.).

The full set of operating regulations covered numerous topics and got quite detailed, but there were three broad areas that are important to review here. First, the regulations clearly specified all the physical attributes of the card itself as well as the various advertising marks and their allowed usages. Second, they stipulated rules by

---

[5]Russell interview.

[6]Hock (2005), p. 124.

which inter-organizational work was to be accomplished, and who would pay for what services. Third, they established a process for handling and resolving disputed transactions, putting NBI in the role of judiciary. Each of these areas contained rules that were intended to craft the social dynamics of the system so that the participants could trust each other, just enough, to balance the system and allow it to function and grow. Let us look at each of these in turn.

The Card and Marks

One important distinction between the early Interbank and the BankAmericard systems was their approach to the physical design of the card and usage of the advertising marks. Because the Interbank system was comprised of many pre-existing regional systems with different established names and marks, Interbank required only a small "i" logo to be placed in one corner of the card's face, while the rest of the card used the local name and marks. This made it difficult for cardholders to realize that their cards were accepted at merchants outside their local areas, and for merchants to recognize acceptable cards from different regions, as the primary marks on the cards and merchant windows would be completely different. The common "i" logo was simply too small and insignificant to be recognized intuitively by merchants and cardholders as the common mark.

The early BankAmericard system, on the other hand, was built by licensing the BankAmericard name and its blue-white-and-gold (BWG) bands design to other banks, so the domestic card designs and merchant signage were almost entirely uniform. A BankAmericard issued by BofA in California looked almost identical to a BankAmericard issued by banks in New York or any other state, the only difference being that the local bank was allowed to include their own name in addition to "BankAmericard," but only in smaller, less-prominent type. Many of the international licensees were allowed to use more culturally-appropriate names, but they were still required to use the BWG design across the entire face of the card, making it fairly obvious that they were at least related if not the same.

The NBI operating regulations continued this approach, and as I will describe in Chap. 6, the international and domestic cards were eventually brought under a common name and graphic design philosophy. This made it easier for cardholders traveling abroad to quickly and reliably identify merchants that accepted the card, even if the cardholder and merchant did not speak a common language. It was not until the late 1980s that the BWG band design was reduced to a smaller logo on the card face; by then, the recognition of, and expectations about, the marks were established firmly enough that there was less risk in giving the member banks more of the card face for graphical differentiation.[7]

The graphical consistency of the cards and merchant signage also allowed NBI to conduct national advertising on behalf of the member banks, the details of which I

---

[7]Chutkow (2001), p. 215.

will describe later in this chapter. Although this could be seen as simply an efficient centralization of a common task, we shall see that NBI's intentions for these early advertising campaigns were actually far deeper, and the effects were much more powerful.

Inter-Organizational Work and Fees

The second relevant area of the operating regulations covered how the inter-organizational work was to be accomplished, what fees would be charged for the various interchange services, and which party would be responsible for fraudulent or disputed transactions. Although the operating regulations did stipulate some of the rules by which acquirers interacted with merchants (e.g., merchant screening, inspection and auditing) and issuers with cardholders (e.g., common requirements for cardholder agreements), most of these regulations pertained to the inter-organizational work conducted between member banks and NBI; how the banks interacted with their merchants and cardholders was largely left up to the individual banks, subject of course to the relevant Federal and State banking regulations.

The most important inter-organizational work conducted in the NBI system was the authorization, clearing, and settlement of interchange transactions, and the operating regulations contained numerous, explicit rules dictating exactly how each step should be accomplished. Having a clear and comprehensive set of rules was quite crucial; by the time NBI formed there were already thousands of banks participating in the system in some form or another, and both the number of participants and the transaction volumes were growing by about thirty percent per year. In order to keep up, especially once interchange authorization and clearing became electronic (see the next two chapters), each bank needed clear directions as to how it should submit and receive transactional information sent through the system, how to handle abnormal cases, and how to rectify errors.

One particularly important aspect of these rules was ascription of liability for fraud. As opposed to other forms of payment, NBI transactions were (and still are) guaranteed from the merchant's perspective provided the merchant follows the relevant rules stipulated in the operating regulations. In the early 1970s, the rules dictated when the merchant was required to call for authorization, what transactional details must be captured on the sales draft, and how the merchant was to submit the drafts to the acquiring bank. The following of these rules transferred not only *funds* from the cardholder to the merchant, but also the *liability* for fraud from merchant to issuer. Cardholders and their issuers could still dispute the transactions (the process for which is described in detail in the next section), but unless they could show that the merchant or acquirer did not follow the rules, the issuer was responsible for the loss.

In addition to the rules stipulating how inter-organization work was to be accomplished, this section also contained a series of rules regarding the fees assessed by the system for various services. These fees constituted the basic economic dynamics of the system, most of which are still at play today.

When crafting these basic economic dynamics, the NBI staff had to answer a set of questions that are essential to any payment system: who pays, who benefits, and who gets to decide?[8] Although it might seem a bit self-referential, payment systems cost money to operate; every exchange of money requires a bit of that money to facilitate the exchange itself. All payment systems have fixed costs, and most also have per-transaction costs that must be paid by someone if the system is to continue operating. The question is, who should cover these costs? The party on the buying end, the party on the selling end, or some combination of the two?

Cost reimbursement is certainly required, but fledgling cooperative payment systems like NBI also had to concern themselves with another, perhaps more important economic dynamic: balancing incentives in order to attract banks, merchants and consumers to participate in the system in the first place.[9] Payment systems are useful only when buyers, sellers, and their financial agents (i.e., banks) all decide to participate in sufficient numbers, and one of the factors that determines their decisions are the fees they have to pay in order to participate. In the early 1970s, NBI was still the minor player in the credit card industry compared to Interbank, and credit cards accounted for only a small percentage of overall consumer payments, so NBI's new prices had to be high enough to attract new card-issuing banks, but low enough to allow acquiring banks to offer competitive discount rates to new merchants. From a system competition perspective, the question was also: who is *willing* to pay and *how much* can we charge yet still attract new participants?

There are no "natural" or perfect answers to these questions, and in most cases, the answers depend heavily on the systems's historical context. They may also change over time as participants negotiate with each other. In the United States, the costs of cash and the national check clearing systems have traditionally been funded by taxpayers and administered by the Federal Reserve, but NBI and other private payment networks typically do not have access to public funds, and thus must raise their own funding by charging some set of their participants for their services.

In the case of NBI, they inherited the model whereby the merchant pays for the service through a transaction discount while the cardholder pays nothing. The BofA adopted this model because it had been well-established by the various travel and entertainment cards of the 1950s and 1960s, and the merchant-specific cards before them. By the 1970s, consumers had become accustomed to the idea that credit cards were free if balances were paid each cycle, and would likely resist additional usage fees, though several banks did attempt such charges as the cost of credit rose. Merchants were willing to pay the discount on credit cards primarily because they were used for a small percentage of their overall transactions, and the card systems provided studies showing that consumers purchased more on average when they were allowed to use a credit card instead of cash or check. As we shall

---

[8]For a discussion of this in the context of the UK's planned point-of-sale electronic funds transfer system, see Howells and Hine (1993). For an excellent analysis of the way different value systems can influence answers to these questions, as well as design priorities, see Kling (1978).

[9]For an expression of this in the language of multisided platform economics, see Evans and Schmalensee (2005).

see, when the percentage of credit transactions rose, and when debit cards with discount fees were introduced to replace checks, the merchants attempted a revolt, challenging the fees in court.

Although the basic "merchant-pays" model was inherited and not likely to change, NBI still had to determine *how much* merchants should pay, and how much of that should flow back to the card-issuing banks. This was ultimately determined by the interchange reimbursement fee (IRF), first discussed in Chap. 2, which was the percentage acquirers paid to issuers during the settlement of interchange transactions. This fee would effectively set a minimum amount for the merchant discount, as acquirers had to charge merchants something higher than the IRF in order to make a profit. Too high of a fee would discourage new merchants from accepting the card, but too low of a fee would discourage banks from issuing the cards.

The interchange reimbursement fee has always been a source of controversy in the NBI/Visa system. At the core of the issue is a basic question: is it a form of anti-competitive price-fixing, or a necessary aspect of a cooperative payment system? Because this fee is agreed upon by a group of competitors for their own benefit, and because it effectively establishes a minimum for the merchant discount fee, many merchants have argued that this is indeed anti-competitive, and on occasion the US Department of Justice has agreed.[10] Visa has typically responded that all cooperative payment systems require these kinds of fees, not only to help cover the participants' operating costs, but also to provide the correct economic incentives for both issuers and acquirers. From Visa's perspective, the fee is a method of obtaining an *economic balance*, providing both acquirers and issuers with sufficient profit while remaining competitive with other payment card systems.[11] This shift in language from "cost reimbursement" to "economic balance" is of course not accidental; as automation reduced transaction costs as well as fraud, and as the cost of credit reduced in the 1980s and 90s, the rate could no longer be justified purely as a cost reimbursement.

Over the years, this fee has also created controversy between the member banks, as each has tried to tip that balance in their own favor. On average, this fee constitutes ten percent of an issuer's revenue, so banks that specialize in issuing often want to increase this fee.[12] Not surprisingly, those that specialize in acquiring fight to reduce it. When NBI formed, most member banks performed both roles, but as the business matured, banks began to specialize in one role or another, creating a certain partisanship regarding the direction, and eventual segmentation, of the interchange fee.

The primary issue with the interchange fee under the licensing system was that it was vague and unrealistic to audit, so NBI's staff realized that they needed to establish a fixed interchange fee that was consistent and unambiguous. But they were faced with a difficult problem—how should they calculate the rate? Setting a proper rate depended on knowing not only the true costs of interchange transactions,

---

[10]For a review of Visa's antitrust battles, see Mann (2006) and Evans and Schmalensee (2005).

[11]For a very detailed theoretical model of four-party payment systems and the need for an interchange fee, see Baxter (1983).

[12]Schmidt interview.

but also the entire economics of the system, neither of which were well understood in 1971. The industry was still very young, and most bankcard programs did not delineate their costs by function, much less by transaction type. Many of the small rural banks barely had accounting systems at all.[13]

It was clear that more information was needed to understand the economics of the business. To begin gathering it, NBI established a requirement in late 1970 that all member banks must submit a "certificate of sales" each quarter, which reported their basic operational information such as number of accounts, sales volume, delinquencies, charge-offs, and the like. This information not only helped NBI calculate member fees, but also provided them with the data they needed to build a basic economic model of the business. This information was eventually compiled and summarized by Ron Schmidt into a quarterly "profit analysis report" that was then made available to all the membership starting in third quarter of 1971.[14] Thus, for the first time each member could now see how their program compared to others in the system, as well as how the system was performing as a whole.[15] Furthermore, Hock could use these reports at the Board meetings to prod directors of under-performing banks to improve their programs. As with any network industry, improvements in one element of the system often brings about a benefit to all.

The quarterly reports also served another important function at the time. Throughout 1970 and 1971, industry papers such as the *American Banker* were publishing articles about the huge losses incurred by bankcard programs, questioning whether this endeavor could ever be profitable.[16] According to these articles, many banks were considering giving up on the card business altogether. The quarterly reports provided a concrete rebuttal, showing the member banks that some of them were indeed beginning to turn a profit.[17] Furthermore, each bank could now see how their programs compared to others, creating an incentive for improvement. But most importantly, the reports encouraged the member banks to ask NBI to take an *active* role in helping the individual programs achieve profitability; if a bank was struggling, they could call NBI and a team would visit them to study their procedures and costs, and to share best-practices learned from other banks in the system. NBI was thus helping banks *learn from one another* for the benefit of the entire system.

---

[13] Schmidt interview.

[14] Schmidt interview. See also Brooke (6 August 1971), p. 1.

[15] These reports were actually quite detailed. Banks were grouped by the sizes of their portfolios, whether they did acquiring, issuing or both, and whether they used a third-party processor or not.

[16] For example, see the series of articles that begins with Brooke (18 May 1971), p. 1. In the 14 June edition (p. 5), there are a few letters to the editor in response to this series. In one, a bankcard manager wrote "My very candid opinion is that, after having operated a credit card operation, I can see nothing in store for the future of this operation but disappointment. Evidently, many banks are reluctant to admit their mistakes and prefer to continue to lose money for their institutions rather than admit they were wrong."

[17] According to the American Banker, one third of the member banks were profitable by 1971. See McKenna (19 June 1971), p. 3.

The quarterly reporting data helped NBI understand the general economics of the system, but they still did not contain enough detail about costs to determine an optimal interchange fee rate. Thus, NBI began a detailed research project that would eventually produce what was known as the "Functional Cost Study," first published in the fourth quarter of 1971. While, the quarterly profit analysis reports provided a high-level overview, the functional cost study was a very detailed examination of the functions performed, and costs incurred, by a typical program. Most banks had never examined their programs this closely, so a team comprised of NBI staff and Arthur Andersen consultants visited the bank, observed their operations, and studied their accounting records.[18] This process required about two weeks of research in each bank, plus two or three weeks of additional analysis, but the results provided the bank and NBI with detailed information about costs and problem areas. The bank then knew where to target their efforts, and NBI could construct a more accurate economic model of the system.

All of this information would eventually help NBI set an optimal rate for the IRF, but unfortunately NBI could not wait for all the studies to be compiled. The rules governing the IRF under the licensing system needed to be fixed, and that meant specifying a new fixed rate in the operating regulations, but Schmidt was still in the field researching the member banks. He was asked to estimate a new rate based on his work so far, and the model he and his Arthur Andersen consultants were building calculated a rate around 2.6 percent, but this seemed too high to Hock. At this time acquirers were sending issuers about 2 percent on the average, and according to Schmidt, Hock felt that the new rate could not be any higher than that, so he proposed a rate of 1.95 percent instead. Interestingly, Schmidt remarked that in his opinion, 1.95 percent was suggested instead of an even 2 because it would appear as if it had been arrived at through sophisticated calculation, and not simply decided upon through instinct.[19]

Dispute Resolution

The last major area of the operating regulations to discuss concerned how disputes over interchange transactions were to be resolved within the system. Dispute resolution is a critical feature of any cooperative network of competitors; without it, the competitive members would have no way to resolve disagreements that invariably arise, especially when money is involved. From the beginning, Visa defined a chargeback and arbitration process that would provide a reasonably fair and equitable method for resolving these disputes.[20]

---

[18]These were called "Profit Improvement Teams (PITs)" (Honey interview).

[19]Schmidt interview. Of course, NBI continued to adjust the fee based on the results of the studies once they were available.

[20]Information about dispute resolution comes from interviews with Tindal, Baum, and Kollmann, all of whom managed the process and served as arbitrators.

The process has remained essentially the same throughout the years, though it has been modified slightly based on experience. The process typically begins when a cardholder complains about a particular transaction. This complaint can be raised for a number of reasons: the cardholder did not conduct the transaction (or does not wish to admit to it[21]); the transaction was keyed incorrectly or was processed multiple times; the merchandise was "not as advertised"; the merchandise was never received; was defective or damaged in shipment; etc.[22] If the issuer thinks the complaint is valid, the issuer then submits a chargeback transaction through interchange. Because the original transaction had already been cleared and settled, the issuer essentially puts through a compensating transaction, "charging back" the acquirer for the original amount plus a penalty fee. The acquirer then has a certain number of days to research the transaction on their side, after which they can either close the case or "represent" the transaction through interchange. Originally, the operating regulations allowed the transaction to bounce back and forth a few times, but today, the issuer and acquirer must resolve the dispute after one cycle, or submit it to Visa for arbitration.

Initially, the group that handled chargeback disputes within NBI was the same group responsible for maintaining the operating regulations. In the early 1970s, interchange volumes were still rather low, and disputes were less common, so the arbitration process was simply a side job of those maintaining the regulations. As interchange volumes increased, so did the disputes, and Visa reacted by developing a more complex, formalized arbitration process, and staffing positions within the operating regulations area to manage it.[23]

This group's primary responsibility is to shepherd cases through NBI's formal arbitration process. When two members cannot resolve a chargeback dispute amongst themselves, they submit it to this group, along with all the supporting documentation, and a fee to discourage frivolous cases. In the early years, the cases were reviewed and decided by an ad-hoc committee composed of mid-to-upper-level managers, but today the dispute resolution group itself acts as the "court." In most cases, the applicable rules are fairly clear and unambiguous, but the cardholder/issuer and merchant/acquirer testimonies conflict. The court then does their best to review all the available evidence and decide which party is correct.

In some cases, however, the dispute is based on differences of *interpretation*; that is, the evidence might be clear, but the two parties have different opinions as to

---

[21] Several interviewees indicated that male cardholders would occasionally conduct morally questionable transactions that they later regretted, and instead of admitting to them, would claim their card had been lost or stolen. Unfortunately for these cardholders, their signatures on the original sales drafts would be retrieved, making the transactions more difficult to deny.

[22] Consumer protection laws in the United States allow cardholders to refuse payment for goods that are "not as advertised" or defective if they are purchased within a certain, limited geographic range from the cardholder's residence. In other countries this may not be a legitimate complaint.

[23] Unfortunately, statistics on the number of disputes raised for arbitration are not available to the public, but interview sources indicated that they were relatively few, perhaps a dozen per week, less than a tenth of a percent of all chargebacks. The dispute resolution staff actually spends more time educating and fielding general questions from the membership.

whether their actions adhered to the rules. For example, the rules require merchants to compare the signature on the sales draft with the signature on the card, but what constitutes a match? Two signatures that might seem similar-enough to a merchant might seem completely different to an issuer or cardholder. Initially, the rules did not clarify what it meant for two signatures to "match," and the members of the arbitration committee were forced to make their own judgments on a case-by-case basis. As the number and dollar value of these kinds of disputes increased, this quickly became untenable, and the rules were eventually modified to require only that the *content* of the signatures matched, and not the hand in which they were written.[24]

Although they may be rare, these differences in interpretation are always a possibility in rule-based systems. As Wittgenstein argued, a rule in itself cannot fully specify what it means to follow or not follow the rule.[25] The interpretation of a rule is necessarily bound up with participants' attempts to follow it, disputes over those attempts, and judgments made by a commonly-recognized authority as to whether those attempts were correct or not. In this case, Visa acts as the commonly-recognized authority, establishing a canonical interpretation of the rules through their arbitration decisions.

As discussed in the signature example, NBI/Visa also has the luxury of modifying rules that are seen as too vague or problematic. Visa's ultimate goal is to minimize disputes and arbitration cases, so if particular rules cause too many interpretation disputes, Visa suggests changes to clarify them. Although the operations committee must approve those changes, they have little incentive to resist, as disputes reduce the overall efficiency of the system, and in turn, the profitability of the member's card programs.

Additionally, the dispute resolution group takes an *active* role in educating the membership about the chargeback and arbitration rules. The operating regulations are actually quite detailed, and currently fill multiple printed volumes, so it is not uncommon for a member to be unfamiliar with certain sections. The resolution group helps to educate the members on the entire process, including their rights and obligations. They also send out regular communications, informing the members of new rules and their implications, or recent arbitration decisions that might help clarify how the rules should be interpreted.

The decisions handed down by Visa's "court" are typically final, but under certain circumstances, such as high-value transactions, the loser is allowed to appeal the decision. There are currently several layers through which the case can be appealed, with the Board of Directors acting as the final, supreme arbiter. Interestingly, Visa's arbitration process is not entirely binding; the members still retain the right to bring suit against one other in their country's legal system if they do not like the result of the arbitration.

---

[24]Honey interview. Note that this rule typically applies to fraudulent transactions involving a lost or stolen card that has since been recovered. If the contents of the signatures on the sales drafts do not match the card, the merchant or acquirer must absorb the chargebacks. If the contents do match, even if they are in a completely different hand, the issuer must absorb the loss.

[25]Wittgenstein (1958), §201–202.

It should be noted here that although Visa's chargeback and arbitration process is well designed, it is by no means perfect. Powerful members can and do abuse the mechanism for their own gain. Smaller banks have been known to pay questionable chargebacks from intimidating issuers without a fight, primarily because they lacked the resources to investigate the matter and collect the necessary documentation. Those reviewing the cases are humans, and as such, can never be completely impartial. Lastly, members have occasionally felt that the arbitration process did not produce the correct result, and have chosen to continue fighting in the civil court system.

The Significance of the Operating Regulations

Although the operating regulations are perhaps not quite as exciting to historians of technology as the computer systems discussed over the next four chapters, they are nevertheless a critical aspect of what made the NBI system "work" at the inter-organizational level. Most authors have ignored the regulations, or merely mentioned them in passing, but in order to truly understand how the early NBI system managed to stabilize, grow and ultimately become the largest payment network in the world, we must examine them more closely to see their significant effects on the system's social dynamics.

First, at a very practical level the operating regulations provided a central co-ordination mechanism for inter-organizational work. In Gerson's terms, they acted as a sort of *bracket*, a mechanism that connects multiple organizations together in a mutual interdependence, while at the same time maintaining their distinctions.[26] As several organizational scholars have noted, inter-organizational work does not simply happen on its own—cooperative systems like NBI must create mechanisms involving artifacts, techniques, and rules that guide and facilitate exchanges between participating organizations, resulting in coordinated work at the overall system level. NBI was expanding at a fairly aggressive rate, and without this coordination mechanism, it would have been exceedingly difficult for the member banks to keep up with the transactional volume, much less handle the anomalies, crises, and errors that invariably occur when the operations of several thousand independent organizations interact. Clear and comprehensive operational rules allowed the system to increase outward in scale by expanding the number of participants, while still enabling them to coordinate the work they needed to accomplish together.

Second, the fees established by the operating regulations, especially the interchange reimbursement fee, not only helped the system to stabilize, but also created the economic model that would propel it forward. Although its very name indicates that it was initially thought of as a cost recovery fee, NBI eventually began to see the interchange reimbursement fee as a mechanism for balancing out the various economic interests of the system's participants. Initially the fee was set higher in order to encourage more banks to issue the cards, but was eventually lowered and split

---

[26]Gerson (2008).

into different levels for different merchant classes and transaction types in order to attract and retrain merchants (see Chaps. 7 and 8).

Third, the operating regulations, and especially Visa's interpretation and enforcement of them, helped the various participants trust each other, just enough, to allow the system to function, grow, and expand. The member banks, many of which were direct competitors of each other, naturally had troubles trusting each other when it came to fees, fraud liability, and disputed transactions. The consistent fees, clear rules, and especially the adjudicated dispute resolution process all helped to create a framework for trusted cooperation between the member banks.

But the member banks were not the only participants in the system that needed to trust one another; the operating regulations, especially those that governed the use of the marks and the handling of disputed transactions, also helped cardholders and merchants develop just enough trust to conduct transactions when more interpersonal sources of trust were absent. When a BankAmericard holder presents a card to a merchant displaying a sign bearing the same marks, the cardholder knows that the merchant is trusted by the system, and merchant knows the same about the cardholder. The merchant also knows that if the relevant rules are followed, the transaction is guaranteed and the merchant will be paid even if the card proves to be fraudulent. The cardholder also knows that if the merchant enters the transaction incorrectly or fraudulently, the cardholder can dispute the transaction and ultimately have it arbitrated if necessary. The cardholder and merchant need not trust one another directly; instead, their trust is in the marks and the rules of the system represented by them. I will return to this and expand this idea more fully in the concluding chapter.

National Advertising

In addition to crafting the social dynamics of his staff and his new organization, Hock also set about crafting the social relations between the new NBI organization and its cardholding public. In April of 1971, NBI began running print and television advertisements with their now iconic tag line "think of it as money." From the outside, this may have seemed like any other series of BankAmericard ads, but for Hock, this campaign was his chance to communicate his ideas about the nature of money directly to the cardholders, and he took it very seriously. As Tom Cleveland noted, "There was never a doubt about what was priority one in Dee's mind regarding the relative importance of issues at Visa—how Visa appeared in the market place, from media ads to brochures to corporate business cards, nothing went anywhere without Dee's expressed approval."[27] NBI reportedly spent $2 million of its own money, plus "substantial additional funds" from NBI member banks to promote the message across a variety of media.[28] Luckily for NBI, it also received

---

[27]Cleveland (1999), p. 26.

[28]'BankAmericard starting ad campaign urging public to think of card as money', American Banker (10 March 1971), p. 1.

some extra free advertising when Hank Aaron hit his 755th home run directly over the BankAmericard "think of it as money" billboard, a scene that was often repeated on television for several weeks afterward.

The message of the campaign was twofold. First, it proclaimed to consumers that the BankAmericard is a "modern sensible medium of exchange." The phrase "medium of exchange" is important here—for Hock, the BankAmericard was not just a credit card, it was a *medium of exchange*, and thus a *new kind of money*. This was graphically reinforced by showing a BankAmericard held by a money clip, decorated with a coin. Already we can see Hock pushing the card away from the limited notion of credit, toward the broader concept of value exchange. This campaign, as well as those that followed it, began to *redefine* the card in consumers' minds, transforming it from a vehicle solely for consumer credit to a general-purpose payment device suitable for all kinds of routine purchases.

The second message was to encourage "responsible use of the card" with the followup tag line, "If we didn't think you could handle it, we wouldn't have given it to you." This was not only an effort to educate consumers about how to use the card, it was also an attempt at a rebuttal against the various accusations the press and legislators were hurling at the banks throughout the late 1960s. As noted earlier, a Congressional investigation in 1967 summoned several prominent bankers to a hearing in which they were publicly criticized for sending unsolicited credit cards to consumers who did not understand the nature of compounding interest and consequently found themselves quickly in a financial distress they would have otherwise avoided. Life magazine also ran a scathing cover story against credit cards in 1970, claiming that "In a rush to 'get their plastic on the air,' banks randomly fired off credit cards." It continued:

> They did so, in many cases, with a kind of eager innocence which none of them would have countenanced for a moment in firms with which they did business; a few of them, caught up in the excitement of the unfamiliar chase, seem to have become as blithely careless of consequences as a drunken sailor shooting craps in a Mexican whorehouse on New Year's Eve.[29]

The article went on to quote from a study of 84 card-issuing banks conducted in 1969 for the Charge Account Bankers Association, in which they found "only a fifth of the banks investigated checked the credit background of those to whom cards were mailed," and "a fifth of the banks [in the study] did not even bother to find out if [an applicant] had a job."

Articles like these were naturally shaking consumer confidence in the cards, as well as the banks that issued them, and NBI's advertisements sought to reassure cardholders that the banks were taking the criticism seriously. Those involved in the credit card rush of the late 1960s readily acknowledged in interviews that procedures were lax or bypassed altogether at many banks in an effort to get cards issued quickly, so NBI had quite a bit of ground to reclaim in the battle of public perception. By reclassifying the card as a new form of money, as opposed to an instrument

---

[29]O'Neil (1970).

of uncontrolled credit, NBI hoped to regain the public's trust in this new payment instrument.

It should be noted, however, that these advertisements were also an excellent expression of one of Hock's most basic beliefs: the cards offer a valuable service, and consumers are entirely capable of using them responsibly. Hock's political beliefs would commonly be classified as libertarian; he believed that the majority of Americans would be far better off without the government telling them what they can and cannot do. In a 1979 interview, he stated these beliefs quite clearly:

> Why do people always think of consumers as a mass of ignorant people needing help? If you talk to them as individuals, you will have trouble finding helpless, confused, ignorant people. The average man on the street is not stupid. He is the soundest, most prudent, solvent and dependable part of the economy. Each individual is a far better judge of his needs, desires, and financial affairs than many give him credit for.[30]

Whether or not Hock was overly optimistic about the financial capabilities of the average American, quotes like these help us to see that his motivations were to provide consumers with an array of payment services, letting each decide when and where to utilize their various pools of funds, be they lines of credit or deposits.

The "think of it as money" campaign was only the first of many national and eventually international advertising efforts conducted by NBI, the details of which have been documented quite extensively in the organization's own corporate biography.[31] Each of these campaigns explicitly sought to redefine the card as being a new type of global currency, one that was accepted "everywhere you want to be." Each strived to change the way consumers thought about the card, moving it away from its historical association with consumer credit and toward an association with money and payments in general. The card was no longer simply something you used to finance purchases more easily; it was now something you used in lieu of cash and checks, something that could become the only payment device you would ever need.[32]

Conclusion

In this chapter we reviewed how Hock and his early staff set out to craft a few key social dynamics at three levels of the system: the central organization's staff; the overall NBI association; and the cardholding public. We saw how Hock rebuffed an attempt to oust him, and how he surrounded himself with employees who shared his vision, but also had complementary skills to his own. We also saw how the operating regulations, which governed the use of the marks, the processing of interchange

---

[30]Streeter (1979), p. 75.

[31]Chutkow (2001).

[32]This is similar to Mackay and Gillespie's observation that firms attempt to construct ideologies for consumers via marketing during the adoption of a new technology. See Mackay and Gillespie (1992).

transactions, the critical interchange reimbursement fee, and the dispute resolution process, helped not only to coordinate work between the member banks, but also to build just enough trust amongst the system participants to allow the system to stabilize, function, and grow. Lastly, we saw how NBI used national advertising to communicate Hock's conception of what the card really was, and attempt to repair the BankAmericard's image in the wake of the late 1960s credit card rush.

This crafting of the system's social dynamics was a key and necessary step in the system's development. The computer and telecommunication systems described over the next four chapters were certainly necessary components as well, but they were not in themselves sufficient to account for the system's growth and ultimate success. Without these first steps, the NBI system might have become very adept at moving transactional information between system participants, but its organizational problems would have made it difficult for the system to survive.

Chapter 4
Automating Authorization: BASE

With the new organization formed and its operating regulations established, the key organizational issues that we discussed in Chap. 2 were for the most part addressed. The various competing member banks now had an organizational structure and a set of rules they could use to cooperate and coordinate their work. But the organizational issues were only half of the problem—the operational issues surrounding the authorization, clearing and settlement of interchange transactions were still waiting to be solved.

In this chapter, we will focus on how NBI and others addressed what was considered to be the most critical of these operational problems: authorization. By 1970, the slow and cumbersome manual authorization process was holding back further expansion of the various payment card systems, and several industry leaders began developing what they considered to be appropriate solutions. NBI's staff kept a close watch on these experiments, eventually developing their own national electronic authorization system, BankAmericard Authorization System Experimental (BASE), which was first put into production in April of 1973.

The Need for Automated Authorization

Of the many operational problems facing the bankcard systems in general, and the BankAmericard system in particular, authorization was seen as the most important. This was for two reasons: first, the delay and hassle involved in obtaining an authorization was beginning to affect consumers' desires to use the card, and merchants' willingness to accept it; second, the floor limits, which were intended to ease the former concerns, were simultaneously making it difficult to control the increasing levels of fraud, which was in turn further eroding consumer confidence. Without the continued participation of both cardholders and merchants, all the bankcard systems would quickly collapse. This is how one of the industry leaders described the situation:

> Vital—critical—all important. These words you have heard to describe the urgency that surrounds our troubles with authorization. And I suppose what frustrates so many of us is

D.L. Stearns, *Electronic Value Exchange*, History of Computing, 71
DOI 10.1007/978-1-84996-139-4_4, © Springer-Verlag London Limited 2011

the conviction that this one trouble can be resolved. If authorization is so vital, so critical, if it can generate more business for the card, if it can lead to a reduction in fraud and credit losses and effect greater economies in our operation—then why, as the little boy says, can't I have one of those things, Daddy?[1]

In Hughes's terms, the authorization process had become a "reverse salient," that is, an element holding back, or even thwarting, the development and growth of the overall system.[2] Hughes argued that when confronted with a reverse salient, actors seek to correct it by constructing one or more "critical problems," the articulation of which often guides them toward, or even directly implies, certain solutions.[3] In the case of bankcard authorization, the industry leaders constructed two critical problems. First, the local *authorization decision* was too slow, and often not available, because it required *human intervention*. Second, *interchange authorizations* were too slow because they required manual "two-legged" calls or telexes between the acquiring and issuing centers. The solution implied by the first problem was replacing the human authorizers with automated, computerized logic. The solution implied by the second problem was enabling electronic communication between the centers, either computer-to-computer, or computer-to-terminal. Building an effective nationwide card system, and its accompanying authorization system, ultimately required solving both problems, but local authorizations were automated first, primarily because they did not require cooperation and coordination between independent, competing organizations.[4] Therefore, we will begin by charting the various ways in which organizations automated their local authorization decisions.

Automating Local Authorizations

National Data Corporation (NDC) of Atlanta seems to be the first processor to offer some sort of computerized authorization to its subscribers.[5] NDC began operations in 1968 as the primary processor for the Chicago-area Interbank members, but eventually expanded to handle processing for a number of merchant-specific card

---

[1]Brooke (11 August 1971), p. 6.

[2]Hughes (1983), p. 79.

[3]MacKenzie further points out that historians should never treat reverse salients or critical problems as "given, independent of the actors involved." In the midst of events, actors may not agree on what goal should be obtained, what is hampering progress toward it, and how it might be solved. Causation may also run the other way—actors may formulate critical problems based on what they can accomplish, and then argue for a corresponding reverse salient. See MacKenzie (1987), pp. 197–199. In the case of authorization, there seems to have been rather widespread agreement that it was a significant problem area, though I will note the few minor disagreements regarding how it should be solved.

[4]Recall that in a local authorization, the acquirer and issuer are the same organization, or are served by the same processor, so political issues are largely removed.

[5]National Authorization Joint Feasibility Study Final Report (29 January 1971), p. 8.

systems, oil industry cards, and two NBI member banks. NDC also provided "after-hours" authorization services for banks that wanted to operate their own center during the normal working hours; after the bank's center closed, they would switch their phone network so that calls would go to NDC instead. Because NDC was a processor for many issuers and acquirers, they took the approach of centralizing all cardholder data onto one computer system from which they could make automated authorization decisions. Merchants called one of NDC's four regional authorization centers, where less-skilled, clerical operators keyed the transaction information into terminals, which in turn communicated over 2400 baud modems with NDC's central computer (a UNIVAC 494) in Atlanta. The key aspect of this system was that the authorization decision was entirely automated; subscribers could define the rules used to make the decision, but the rules were then executed without human intervention. Most subscribers opted for *negative authorization*, meaning that card numbers were simply checked against a "derog" file, which contained accounts on which purchases should not be authorized. Some, however, took advantage of NDC's scheme for *positive authorization*, which maintained an "open to buy" amount for the particular account, as well as a history of transactions over the previous seven days. The automated decision significantly sped up the authorization process, resulting in an average local authorization time of just twenty-two seconds. NDC's system, however, could authorize transactions only for cards issued by one of their subscribers—interchange authorizations required an additional, "two-legged" call to the issuer's center.[6]

Credit Systems Incorporated (CSI), the regional processor for Interbank members in Missouri, Kansas, Illinois, and Kentucky, also began offering computerized authorization to its subscribers in early 1971.[7] Their system was similar in concept to NDC's, but was augmented to offer a completely automated interface for the merchant. Merchants could use a touch-tone telephone, a relatively new device at the time, to enter the transactions details, guided by voice prompts. The computer system (an IBM 360 with a tone frequency decoder) translated the tones into an authorization request on their local cardholder data and used the response to select the appropriate pre-recorded message that was played back to the merchant. Interestingly, the system itself never responded with a pre-recorded denial; if the automated rules could not authorize the transaction, the call was switched to a human authorizer who reviewed the transaction and account details on a terminal and made a final determination.[8] Similar to NDC, CSI's system could authorize transactions only for cards issued by one of their subscribers, but in the case of an interchange authorization, the merchant phone call was automatically switched to the issuer's center, and the merchant spoke directly with the issuing authorizer.

---

[6]National Authorization Joint Feasibility Study Final Report (29 January 1971), pp. 8–9.

[7]'Fast credit card authorization is offered to banks and merchants by CSI', American Banker (6 January 1971), p. 8.

[8]Unfortunately, the article did not mention a reason for this design choice, but there are two possibilities: first, because a denial embarrasses and erodes the confidence of a legitimate cardholder, such a decision should be verified by a human; second, it may have been culturally inappropriate for a denial to come from an automated, impersonal recording.

In June of 1971, Omniswitch began what seems to be the first test of merchant point-of-sale (POS) terminals with a bankcard program.[9] Like the charga-plate system mentioned in Chap. 1, these counter-top electronic devices helped to reduce data entry errors by directly reading and transmitting the card information.[10] The ABA had publicly endorsed the magnetic stripe (often abbreviated "magstripe") in early 1971 as the preferred method for making the cards machine-readable and defined a format for encoding the account information upon it.[11] As a result, a number of manufacturers began producing terminals in 1971 designed to read the ABA format and transmit the card data across standard telephone lines.[12] But these early terminals were quite bulky and expensive, ranging from $500 to $1,000 each, so they were appropriate only for larger merchants who generated numerous card transactions. Omniswitch's system will be discussed in more detail in the next section, but it should be noted here that the POS terminals further decreased the average authorization time to just fifteen seconds. Interestingly, Omniswitch found that this response time was almost too fast for merchants, and built in a "delay factor... to facilitate human reaction time."[13]

NDC also added POS terminals to their authorization system in the summer of 1971, but instead of reading a magstripe on the back of the card, their terminals optically scanned the embossed characters on the front. These terminals, manufactured by Data Source Corporation, were adopted mostly by the oil companies, who felt little need to follow the ABA magstripe standard. With these terminals, NDC's average authorization time was reduced to just seven seconds.[14] In October of 1971, City National Bank and Trust (CNBT) of Columbus, Ohio began what they called an "electronic funds transfer pilot test."[15] This test used similar technology to those already mentioned, but as the name suggests, it had a much more ambitious objective.

---

[9]Wiegold (18 June 1971), p. 1. See also, 'Omniswitch tests merchant-to-bank authorization system', Payment Systems Newsletter (July 1971), p. 4. Whether Omniswitch was actually the first to test POS terminals is somewhat unclear. The news articles imply this but are also vague enough to create doubt. I have not yet found an earlier report about POS terminals in the banking news sources. Tom Schramm, Omniswitch's VP of operations, noted that he thought they were at least one of the first to test them, if not the first (Schramm interview).

[10]Note that these terminals performed authorization only. Merchants were still required to use a standard imprinter to complete a paper sales draft for clearing and settlement.

[11]'Magnetic stripe for credit cards urged by ABA unit', American Banker (16 February 1971), p. 1. See also 'ABA adds to guides for magnetic card coding', American Banker (18 March 1971), p. 1. Interestingly, the airlines favored putting the stripe on the front of the card, but the ABA decided that this "would seriously deface the logo of the bank plans," and chose instead to put it on the back. The Japanese banks, however, put the stripe on the front of their cards for many years (Conway interview).

[12]Manufacturers included IBM, Data Source, Addressograph, and Transaction Technology Incorporated, a subsidiary of First National City Corporation (now known as CitiCorp).

[13]See Omniswitch Tests Merchant-to-Bank Authorization System, p. 5.

[14]'NDC credit authorization pilot underway', Payment Systems Newsletter (July 1971), p. 7.

[15]'Electronic funds transfer test announced by City NB&T', Payment Systems Newsletter (July 1971), p. 5. See also Brooke (14 July 1971), p. 1. CNBT is now known as BancOne. They remained at the forefront of technological innovation, providing the bank processing side of the

It was not merely a test of computerized authorization equipment; it was a test of the very idea of full electronic funds transfer (EFT). A spokesman described their intent:

> What we really hope to do is to peek into the future and learn the sequence of social and technological developments that will bring about a society where most sales involve the electronic transfer of data and funds, instead of cash and checks.[16]

CNBT was an NBI member bank, and one of the few at that time that shared Hock's vision for an electronic value-exchange system, but it was not entirely clear in 1971 if the public would accept such an arrangement. In fact, the Federal Reserve Bank in Atlanta commissioned a study on the public reaction to electronic payments earlier that year, and the final report stated that the public was overwhelmingly against any kind of electronic payments system.[17] Undeterred, the head of the research group surmised that this had more to do with a lack of understanding as to how such a system would actually work. The lesson was that any system developed would require extensive consumer education in order to gain acceptance. A key element of CNBT's test was to determine if a particular set of consumers would accept the idea of electronic payments and use them to the exclusion of cash and checks.

The test was fairly small, and was conducted in the favorable location of Upper Arlington, a wealthy suburb of Columbus. CNBT issued two different cards to 20,000 residents and installed 58 IBM POS terminals at 29 merchant locations. The first card was a modified form of their standard BankAmericard, featuring a magstripe on the back. With it, cardholders could make credit purchases at participating merchants, where all purchases were electronically authorized using automated logic regardless of amount (a condition known as a *zero floor limit environment*). Although merchants still completed a paper sales draft, it was reported that the authorization request actually caused an immediate debit to the cardholder's credit line, and a corresponding credit to the merchant's account.[18] Thus the paper sales draft functioned mostly as a receipt for the customer, and not a claim on funds, as the transaction was already cleared and settled electronically.[19]

The second card was specially designed for use in the new Docutel "Automated Total Teller," which could accept deposits/payments and transfer funds between accounts, in addition to dispensing cash. With the combination of both cards, consumers could significantly reduce their use of checks, limit the amount of cash carried at any one time, and perform nearly all their banking tasks without ever visiting a physical branch.

After four months, the bank declared the test to be a success, both technically and culturally, but the degree of its success is debatable. A spokesman reported that the "bank is finding not only that the new technology involved works, but also that the

---

Merrill Lynch Cash Management Account (CMA), the first investment account that could be accessed using checks or a payment card. See Nocera (1994), pp. 159–199.

[16]Jelliffe (July 1971), p. 6.

[17]Brooke (9 July 1971), p. 1.

[18]Jelliffe (July 1971), p. 5. See also Brooke (28 January 1972), p. 1.

[19]Whether merchants were still required to deposit the paper drafts is not mentioned.

public will *adapt to change*."[20] The language here was no doubt chosen carefully—the public may be willing to "adapt" to change, but very few were actually demanding it. Although the merchants were enthusiastic, the cardholder reaction was decidedly lukewarm—only 20,000 transactions were processed within the first 100 days, just one for each card issued. It was clear that consumers were still using cash and checksfor most purchases.

Despite CNBT's inability to convince their customers of the benefits of full EFT, these early systems did convince issuers of the feasibility and benefits of replacing human authorizers with computerized logic. Many organizations continued the trend by automating their local transactions in a similar manner throughout the rest of the 1970s. Interchange authorizations, however, still required a manual, two-legged call or telex, resulting in multiple-minute authorization times for those traveling outside of their area, and limited non-local fraud detection for the issuers. One system that promised an innovative solution to this problem was Omniswitch.

Automating Interchange Authorizations

The Omniswitch organization was originally formed in 1969 to provide New York merchants a single, centralized authorization service for all Master Charge cards. The New York metropolitan area was one of those where banking regulations and competition made it relatively common for the merchant and cardholder to be represented by different banks. Most of the Interbank members in that region belonged to the Eastern States Bankcard Association (ESBA), who also performed their processing, but the First National City Bank (FNCB, later Citibank) did not, as they had converted to Master Charge from their proprietary "Everything Card" and thus already had their own processing center. Omniswitch eliminated the need for merchants to determine which center to call, providing them with one point of contact for all Master Charge authorizations, regardless of issuer. Omniswitch began offering this service in June of 1970.[21]

Because FNCB was uninterested in transferring their cardholder data to ESBA's computer, Omniswitch developed the innovative approach of "switching" the authorization request messages to the appropriate computer system, similar to how a networking switch routes packets to the appropriate node on a computer network.[22] Merchants called Omniswitch's data center in Lake Success, NY, where operators keyed the requests into an interactive computer terminal. The Omniswitch computer

---

[20]Brooke (28 January 1972), p. 1. Emphasis added.

[21]Information on Omniswitch was collected through interviews with Tom Schramm, former VP of Operations. Schramm also provided reports, presentations, and news clippings from the time, allowing me to verify his comments with the written record. The most detailed news story on Omniswitch is Brooke (11 August 1971). Schramm came to NBI in 1974.

[22]To be clear, Omniswitch's innovation was the switching of *authorization* request messages, not the switching of digital messages in general. For the development of packet switching, see Abbate (1999).

(an IBM 360/40) then used the first few digits of the card number to determine the appropriate destination: the ESBA computer, which was literally across the room; or the FNCB authorization computer, which was about 9 miles away.[23] The Omniswitch computer transmitted the messages to the issuer's computer system, where they were processed without human intervention. One of three replies could be returned: an approval with a corresponding code; a denial; or a "referral," meaning that the operator should connect the merchant to the issuer's center to obtain further details. As noted earlier, Omniswitch began testing POS terminals in 1971, and also offered a voice-prompted touch-tone interface.

This switching technique had two important advantages over the consolidation approach taken by organizations such as NDC. First, it made it politically easier to expand the geographic reach of the system, as banks and processors could maintain control over their cardholder data and local authorization decisions, but utilize Omniswitch to process interchange authorizations at nearly the same speed. The decentralization of cardholder data also pleased a US Senate sub-committee that was concerned about potential loss of privacy due to data consolidation.[24] Second, it also made it technically easier to expand the system, as supporting a new processor required only the development of a relatively simple bridging program, what we would today call a "driver" or "provider." Processors could and did use a wide variety of computer hardware and software for their local processing, but they could still communicate through Omniswitch to other issuers, as Omniswitch provided all the necessary protocol conversion.

Although Omniswitch began with only two nodes, it quickly expanded to five by the end of 1971. Because most of these nodes were themselves multi-bank processors, the Omniswitch network effectively provided interchange authorization services for 286 banks and 100,000 merchants spread across 11 states. Throughout 1971, Omniswitch routed 4.5 million transactions, and handled a peak of 2,500 merchant calls per hour at their Lake Success authorization center.[25]

Omniswitch was able to have this multiplicative effect because of the specific history of Interbank's formation and growth, which was quite different from that of the BankAmericard system. The Interbank system began as an alliance between regional processors, each of which served many organizations, while the BankAmericard system began by licensing individual banks. From an organizational perspective, Interbank was a network of networks, while BankAmericard was a simpler star network of individual nodes.[26] Thus, Omniswitch could provide interchange authorization for numerous banks by connecting only a few processors. From a technical perspective, this reduced their complexity, as well as their transaction load. Most

[23] Schramm interview.

[24] Omniswtich (1971), p. 20.

[25] Omniswtich (1971), pp. 7–8. See also Quigley (1 December 1971), p. 8A.

[26] Although a few NBI members used third-party processors (such as NDC) in the early 1970s, the vast majority did not.

of the authorizations could be handled within the local processor, and only a small percentage of those required interchange.[27]

Omniswitch continued to expand, and in January of 1972 they agreed to add a new node that dramatically increased their scope: NDC, the large processor mentioned earlier.[28] With the NDC connection, Omniswitch now provided interchange authorization for 2,800 banks, which comprised 72 percent of the entire Interbank system. Although Omniswitch and NDC formed a new organization called Nataswitch to govern the connection, it was technologically just another node on the Omniswitch network.

Omniswitch was actually designed from the beginning to be a dependable nationwide authorization system, and thus developed many of the features that would later appear in the systems built by NBI and Interbank. For example, although issuers typically performed positive authorization, Omniswitch also maintained a file on its computer that could be used for negative authorization if the communication lines failed, or if the issuer's system was unavailable or unresponsive. Any authorizations made under these conditions were logged and sent to the issuer electronically when their system became available again. Omniswitch also maintained a redundant IBM 360 as a hot backup and could switch to it almost instantaneously if the primary system failed.[29]

The Joint National Authorization System

Omniswitch established a model for how to build a decentralized national authorization system by networking together the existing local centers and switching authorization requests between them. This was something NBI, Interbank and American Express all wanted to provide, and during Omniswitch's first year of operation, their representatives met to discuss the possibility of developing one joint computerized system that could provide authorizations anywhere, at any time, for any card program.[30] From a systems engineering perspective, it seemed wasteful to develop separate authorization systems for each card network, as they would all need to do essentially the same task. It seemed far more "logical" to combine efforts and build one shared system.

---

[27] There were of course localized exceptions to this, as in the New York area. Also, a few acquirers contracted Omniswitch to handle their merchant calls directly via inbound Wide Area Telephone Service (WATS) lines.

[28] Brooke (4 January 1972).

[29] Schramm interview. Confirmed in Brooke (11 August 1971).

[30] This was actually not the first or last time a joint system was proposed. As NBI was forming, Bank of America and American Express proposed developing a joint system to which they would then sell access, but found few takers. The ABA Monetary and Payments System (MAPS) planning committee also proposed a centralized system run by the large commercial banks, but also failed to generate any action. See Hock (2005), pp. 164–165 and Brooke (3 May 1971), p. 1.

The participants formed an advisory team, which investigated the technical feasibility of such a system and compiled their final report in January of 1971.[31] In it they concluded that such a system was indeed feasible, and recommended using the message-switching technique developed by Omniswitch. They estimated that a single switching center could be operational in eighteen to twenty-four months, and two more could be added by 1976, to handle the expected increase in volume.

A shared system may have been technically feasible, but was it politically so? Hock was vehemently opposed to it because he thought that a single, shared system was antithetical to his vision:

> From my perspective, neither the institutional nor technical thinking made sense. It was just another attempt to centralize power and control. ... Creating a single, monopolistic, electronic payment system seemed ... [to be] an attempt to wrap the substance of the future in order to perpetuate past forms. It was contrary to all my beliefs about the nature of organizations and the possibilities inherent in electronic communications. Exchanging authorization information and monetary value in the form of electronic particles ought to be a highly decentralized, competitive business. Trying to design and impose a single, monolithic system on such an essential flow of information seemed absurd.[32]

Hock may have also been opposed to the system because NBI would be only one of many organizations controlling its destiny. Hock's more ambitious goals required a large-scale computer network similar to what the joint feasibility study was proposing. If he did not control it, he would lack the ability to dictate the development of the system to ensure that his goals could be achieved. Once a shared system was in place, it would also become difficult to convince banks to fund a second, private network to deliver the services Hock ultimately wanted to provide.

At the time, NBI's Jack Dillon also claimed that the US Department of Justice was starting to object to the idea of the banks and the T& E companies cooperating to build a joint system.[33] This is not mentioned in Hock's autobiography, nor Visa's corporate history, but it is entirely possible that the DOJ would object to such a system. Because acquirers (and ultimately merchants) pay to authorize transactions, such a jointly-owned system would result in a fee set by a number of competitors. The DOJ tends to interpret these activities as price-fixing and thus a breach of antitrust regulations. Because those who lose an antitrust lawsuit are required to pay treble damages, many organizations will choose to abandon efforts that the DOJ even hints might become questionable.

At the June 1971 Charge Account Bankers Association conference in the Bahamas, Hock announced that NBI would abandon the joint effort, take a "unilateral approach" to national authorization, and develop its own private system.[34] Interbank followed suit, and the joint effort effectively dissolved.[35]

---

[31] National Authorization Joint Feasibility Study Final Report (29 January 1971).

[32] Hock (2005), p. 165.

[33] Brooke (4 November 1971), p. 1.

[34] 'Card groups take own authorization paths', American Banker (29 June 1971), p. 1.

[35] Unfortunately for Omniswitch, CSI was given the contract to build the Interbank National Authorization System (INAS). According to Schramm, the reasons were "entirely political." FNCB, who

NBI's BASE

Having decided to develop their own system, NBI did what most firms at that time did: hire a consultant and put out a Request For Proposals (RFP). Of the sixty vendors interested, NBI invited twenty-one to attend a meeting on 8 October 1971, where NBI presented their needs. At this time, NBI was primarily interested in buying an existing system in order to offer a national authorization service in the shortest amount of time possible. In fact, the RFP required that any proposed system must be operational within twelve months.[36]

Although the requested system, which was given the tentative name of "Bank-Americard Authorization System Experimental (BASE)," was primarily intended to provide authorization services, the RFP revealed that Hock already had much larger plans. National authorization was merely "the first phase of a more comprehensive nationwide bank information processing system."[37] Building BASE would create a computer network connecting the seventy-six existing BankAmericard centers and processors spread across the nation, and once that network existed, authorization was only one of the many possible services NBI could offer. From the beginning, Hock was intending NBI to be the electronic hub through which all electronic value-exchange transactions flowed.

Thirteen vendors submitted proposals in November 1971, and at the time NBI was confident it could offer a nationwide authorization service by the second quarter of 1972.[38] But in late February 1972, NBI announced that it had rejected all thirteen proposals as none "satisfied enough of [their] functional needs."[39] This very careful statement attempted to gloss over a much worse reality as Hock later admitted: even the best bid was several times more than their allocated budget, twice as long as their desired schedule, and "no vendor was willing to warrant the performance of the system."[40] Hock was told that this was customary in the computer industry and that he should just go back to the NBI Board and ask for more money and time. But that would have been antithetical to Hock's personality, not to mention damaging to his reputation, and quoting Emerson's "Trust thyself," he declared that NBI would design and build their own system within the budget and timeframe already approved by the Board.[41]

---

was part-owner of Omniswitch, had also designed their own competing system that they wholly-owned. FNCB represented both Omniswitch and their own system in the selection process, and their conflict of interest caused them to downplay Omniswitch in favor of their system, which was not even operational at the time. CSI eventually won the contract because their system was functioning, and their leader was also leading the overall selection process. Omniswitch was eventually abandoned once INAS became operational.

[36]Brooke (4 November 1971), p. 1.

[37]Brooke, NBI Plans.

[38]Brooke, NBI Plans.

[39]Brooke (21 August 1972), p. 1.

[40]Hock (2005), p. 171.

[41]Hock (2005), p. 171. Although it was risky, Russell agreed with Hock, provided they hired the right people to build and operate it (Russell interview).

Acquiring the Talent

NBI needed help, however, as they did not have the necessary staff in 1972 to design and build a large-scale computer system. In fact, NBI's complete staff totaled less than 20 employees. They contracted with TRW, one of the thirteen vendors who had submitted a proposal, to design and coordinate development of the system. NBI also hired Aram Tootelian away from TRW, where he had been the General Manager of the Information Systems Division, to lead NBI's new Systems and Technology Division. Tootelian had an almost serendipitous background: while working for IBM, he had learned about the Sabre online reservation system built for the airlines, designed and built several bank information systems involving long-distance terminals, and had worked on the TRW Credit Data account, which provided online credit information to banks. While at TRW, he also learned the high-reliability and fail-safe techniques they had developed for top-secret aerospace projects, and even built a computerized simulation of the US payments system for the Federal Reserve. Tootelian remarked that he was the "only person" who could have built BASE, because his background had provided all the required skills and techniques.[42]

Tootelian then hired two others that would become key players in the design and construction of BASE. Dave Huemer, who had been at California Computing after receiving a doctorate in mathematics from Cal Poly Pomona, came as the Director of Systems Operations, responsible for the data center and all its associated hardware. David Goldsmith, who was conducting sales and executive education for IBM after earning his MBA, joined as the Director of Development, responsible for software development and member bank training.

Hock assigned Tootelian's team a formidable task: establish a nationwide computer telecommunications network; install terminals in each of the BankAmericard centers around the country and train each center's staff on how to use them; obtain all the necessary computer and networking hardware; build a data center to house that hardware; install four regional concentrator minicomputers; write, test and debug software that could provide online switching of authorization messages twenty-four hours a day, seven days a week; and staff a call center that could take merchant calls after the local card centers closed for the night. And all of this had to be done by 1 April 1973, just nine months away.

Despite the usual association with that day of the year, Hock was not joking. Throughout his time at NBI/Visa, Hock never allowed a technology project to extend over twelve months. He maintained that if you give computer people more time, they will just consume it, so he always insisted on shorter projects with uncompromising deadlines. As the overall payment system grew, deadlines became even more important, as changes to the central computer system necessitated parallel changes to the members' computer systems as well. Many sources from the systems area indicated that they felt this adherence to short project cycles was a key element of their success.[43]

---

[42]Tootelian interview. A biographic sketch may also be found in Brooke (21 August 1972), p. 1.

[43]For a treatise on scheduling techniques for software projects, see Brooks (1995). Although Brooks encouraged developers to be more aggressive about defending how long it takes to write

Design of the System

At the heart of BASE was a Digital Equipment Corporation (DEC) PDP-11/45 mini-computer, housed in NBI's newly constructed data center in San Mateo, California, just down the peninsula from their San Francisco headquarters.[44] This central computer acted as a real-time switch for authorization requests, which could either come from acquiring authorization centers, or directly from the electronic cash register systems of large national merchants.[45] Acquiring centers entered their request into a Harris-Sanders model 804 terminal (often shortened to "Sanders terminal"), which could queue up to ten messages in its internal memory. Periodically a regional concentrator, which was a DEC PDP-11/20, polled the terminals in its area, collected all pending requests and sent them on to the central switching computer. The switch would determine the issuer from the first few digits of the card number, and forward the request to the appropriate destination. The network was supplied by AT&T and operated at a "blazing" 2400 bits per second.

The issuers also had a Sanders terminal in their authorization center, on which new requests would appear. But because many issuers experienced such low volumes at this time, it was common that nobody would be sitting in front of the Sanders terminal to see the incoming authorization request. To remedy this situation, NBI asked Sanders to add a small bell to the terminal, the clapper of which could be triggered electronically when a new request arrived. Convincing Sanders to add the bell proved to be one of NBI's more difficult tasks in building BASE, but Sanders eventually relented, and issuing authorizers learned to jump to their terminals when they heard the bell ring. After making the authorization decision (either by using their own computer system or printed reports), the issuing authorizer typed the response into the terminal, which was then routed back to the acquirer's terminal through NBI's central switch.

Although most NBI member banks had not yet automated their local authorizations, a few of the more technically-advanced banks had done so, and these banks wanted a direct CPU interface to BASE.[46] But connecting a bank's computer system to BASE was problematic at two levels. At the networking level, the DEC PDP-11 used a different communications protocol than the IBM mainframes used by most banks. To enable the systems to communicate, NBI developed a program called the Bisynchronous Communications Module (BCM), which translated the DEC protocol into something the bank's computer could understand. This allowed the computer systems to talk, but what they talked *about* was still an issue. At the

---

a program properly, he also acknowledged that shorter schedules with clearly defined milestones greatly increased the chances of staying on schedule and delivering something genuinely useful.

[44] Derman and Tootelian interviews. See also Brooke (21 August 1972), p. 1. Hock had originally requested that the computer be installed in a closet near his office in the BofA building, but was eventually convinced that this would be impractical (Totten interview).

[45] Brooke (21 August 1972), p. 1.

[46] Only four banks had direct interfaces when BASE began operating. See Brooke (29 August 1973), p. 1.

application level, the format used by BASE for authorization request and response messages was typically different from those the banks used in their systems. Thus, banks were required to develop a second program that translated BASE's messages into those used by their internal systems. This allowed BASE to treat all end-points on the network in a uniform manner.[47] Over the next few years, NBI helped all the member banks and processors develop such CPU interfaces, as they greatly reduced the overall authorization time.

On the merchant side, a few of the large, national retailers also had direct connections into BASE.[48] From a business perspective, these merchants were still represented by an acquiring bank, to whom they also paid merchant discounts. But from a data processing perspective, their electronic cash register (ECR) systems were connected directly to BASE, and thus they were effectively their own processor. As we shall see, this dichotomy eventually caused merchants to question why they were paying a fee to a bank that seemingly did little work for them. This climaxed when NBI (by then renamed to Visa USA, Inc.) signed up JC Penney, then the third largest department store chain in the US, in exchange for a direct business and data processing relationship with Visa, bypassing the merchant acquiring bank altogether.[49]

BASE was also built from the beginning to offer a constant, reliable service. Nearly every piece of the system had a redundant backup, including standard dial-up telecommunication lines that could be used if the leased lines failed. Nevertheless, even if the central computers and telecommunications were functioning, there was no guarantee that the issuer would respond to the request in an acceptable amount of time. To ensure a reliable service, BASE also had the capability to "stand-in" and approve transactions when the issuer did not respond in a timely manner. The central computer could use a negative file, as well as a file containing recent account activity, to approve or deny requests according to rules established by the issuer. The issuer was then notified of all activity when its system came back online. Interestingly, there was also a "VIP file" containing numbers that should automatically be approved without consulting the issuer. Both the negative and VIP files were maintained through the Sanders terminals, or via tapes mailed to NBI's data center.[50]

Additionally, NBI also had the ability to stand-in for acquirers after-hours, or during especially busy periods. When an acquirer's center closed for the night, they could switch their phone network so that authorization calls went directly to NBI's data center in San Mateo. NBI's own authorization operators handled the calls, entering the requests into their own Sanders terminals. Some smaller centers found this

---

[47] Fojtik and Derman interviews. Eventually, these message formats were changed and standardized through ANSI and ISO. See Chap. 7.

[48] Brooke (21 August 1972), p. 1. The article makes no mention of who was connected in this way, just that some were. It should be noted, however, that these were not the major department stores, as they did not accept bankcards at this time.

[49] Streeter (1979). The details of the JC Penney deal will be discussed in Chap. 9.

[50] Tootelian and Derman interviews. See also, Brooke (21 August 1972), p. 1.

so convenient that they simply contracted with NBI to handle all their authorization calls.[51]

It is also interesting to note how the distribution of work in BASE reflected Hock's organizational philosophy. The local card centers maintained their autonomy, and NBI provided only those services that local centers could not accomplish on their own. Each BankAmericard center or processor was responsible for interacting with their merchants, and maintaining their cardholder accounts. All local authorizations could still be handled by the center itself, but interchange authorizations could be switched through BASE. This design was not only politically attractive, it was also very efficient—the transaction load was distributed amongst the centers, and only the interchange traffic came through BASE, which was still a small percentage of transactions at this time.

NBI's decision to use the DEC PDP-11 instead of an IBM mainframe was somewhat surprising and deserves some comment. Most of the banking industry had standardized on IBM hardware, but Hock was in the middle of a personal feud with "Big Blue." Sources differ as to the exact cause, but all agree that IBM promised something to the fledgling NBI but later reneged, which infuriated Hock.[52] At the time NBI was a relatively small, unimportant account for IBM, but in Hock's mind, he was the future of banking and global value exchange. Although Hock vowed that he would never do business with IBM again, as we shall see, he changed his mind a few years later when the transaction volume proved too much for even the most powerful of the PDP-11 series.[53]

One cannot help but notice the similarities between the functional design of BASE and that of Omniswitch, but it does seem that this was a case of independent, parallel invention, rather than one of direct influence.[54] Although Tootelian was aware of Omniswitch, and although NBI's management would have certainly learned the essential details of Omniswitch from the Joint Authorization System Feasibility Study, Tootelian maintains that the design of BASE came entirely from his past projects and what he considered to be "common sense."[55] In many ways the

---

[51] Not surprisingly, this created some tension between NBI and the various third-party processors. Organizations such as NDC already offered after-hour services to card centers, and they considered NBI to be encroaching on their business. NBI eventually discontinued this service when processors like NDC and First Data Resources offered to handle calls for both Master Charge and BankAmericard authorizations, something NBI could not do.

[52] For Hock's recollection see, Hock (2005), pp. 172–173.

[53] See Chap. 6. Tootelian also remarked that DEC could deliver the hardware when they needed it, while IBM could not, and that the DEC was a simpler, yet perfectly adequate computer at the time. Derman added that DEC was also adept at real-time data transmission, which is primarily what they needed.

[54] Hughes actually predicted that when a reverse salient occurs, historians will often find cases of multiple independent inventions. See Hughes (1983), p. 80.

[55] Tootelian interview. Other sources involved in the BASE design had never even heard of Omniswitch, or considered it inconsequential. Keep in mind that BASE was developed in a very different world: Omniswitch served members of the Interbank system, and mostly those on the East Coast.

similarities are not surprising—switching authorization requests would have been the only politically acceptable solution for the BankAmericard system, and the ability to stand-in for issuers is a feature that naturally follows from the desire to maintain a constant, reliable service. Although it may have been technically feasible to centralize cardholder data into one computer system, as NDC had done, NBI member banks would have never agreed to that loss of control.[56]

It should also be noted that there was a significant difference in network scale between BASE and Omniswitch. As discussed earlier, Omniswitch could provide interchange authorization switching for the majority of the Interbank members by connecting only a few large processors. BASE on the other hand, initially needed to connect seventy-six individual bankcard centers and processors, and be able to accommodate more as the membership continued to increase. More members also meant a higher percentage of interchange transactions, and the overall system volume was growing at an alarming rate. During the construction of BASE, the sales volume generated in the US BankAmericard system grew by thirty-two percent, and the first quarter of 1973 set a record with a staggering forty-one percent growth from the same quarter the previous year.[57] This quickly inflating scale posed unique challenges that required different approaches, such as the regional concentrators, special queueing logic, and an automatic retry in the event of a load spike.

The Development Process

The process of putting together BASE requires some explanation, as it has been somewhat misrepresented in the two existing sources on Visa.[58] Here is how Hock recalled it in his autobiography:

> Swiftly, self-organization emerged.... Leaders spontaneously emerged and reemerged, none in control, but all in order.... Position became meaningless. Power over others became meaningless. Time became meaningless. Excitement about doing the impossible increased, and a community based on purpose, principle, and people arose.... A few who could not adjust to the diversity, complexity, and uncertainty wandered away. Dozens volunteered to take their place. No one articulated what was happening. No one recorded it. No one measured it. But everyone felt it, understood it, and loved it.[59]

Although Hock's account of the process sounds almost like the ideal working environment, it unfortunately fails to correlate with the recollections of others who

---

[56]Whether this was actually technically feasible is debatable. NDC was a processor for many issuers, but not for an entire system. The computer technology of the time may not have been capable of handling all data related to the BankAmericard program, and even if it could, it would have limited the system's ability to grow, causing yet another reverse salient.

[57]'BankAmericard sales', American Banker (1 February 1973), p. 2 and 'Word bankamericard volume sets record', American Banker (2 May 1973), p. 3.

[58]Hock (2005) and Chutkow (2001). Chutkow based his version largely on Hock's autobiography with some added detail from interviews.

[59]Hock (2005), pp. 173–174.

were directly involved in the development of BASE. To be clear, I am not trying to argue that Hock is deliberately misleading the reader or deliberately fabricating his account; instead, I am arguing that his retrospective interpretation of those events is highly influenced by his own philosophical project (explained below), and has tended to misrepresent a few important historical aspects of the process. In cases like these, it is the historian's job to collect and compare as many relevant recollections as possible in order to triangulate the most probable account, and in this particular case, Hock's recollections simply do not seem to correspond with the testimony of others, as well as the contextual situation.

To be fair, there are many sentiments in this quote that are supported by the testimony of others. First, those building BASE were genuinely excited by what they were doing, and many commented that they felt like they were changing the world. Second, the physical environment was also quite informal—they used hospital curtains to divide the unused space in the data center into work areas, rearranging them as needs changed.[60] Lastly, because the project had such a tight schedule and small staff, the process was a bit more chaotic than a typical TRW or IBM systems development effort.

But Hock's account is somewhat misleading in a two important ways. First, the process was far more organized and controlled than he implies. TRW, the primary contractor, as well as the previous employer of Tootelian, made their name by applying to the civil sector the same rigorous project management techniques they developed while working on aerospace projects for the US military.[61] Those involved in the BASE project characterized it as highly-organized, though somewhat less formal due to the relatively small size of the team. Goldsmith stressed, "I've never had the privilege of being involved in such a well-organized project... For each specialty, there was basically one cook stirring the broth. Not half a dozen. There was no committee approach to anything."

In fact, the BASE project would have never succeeded without this degree of organization, because much of the actual construction work was sub-contracted to other, off-site firms. AT&T supplied the network, DEC installed the regional concentrators, and perhaps the most critical piece, the software, was built by a vendor named Compata. The delivery schedules for all these elements had to be tightly-coordinated in order to guarantee that the system could be assembled, tested, and put into operation within the abbreviated schedule.

The primary management and coordination technique used on the BASE project was what they referred to as the "war board." A former project manager explained how it worked:

> ...in the data center..., they rented more room than they needed and they had this open area, and [George Glaser of McKinsey Consulting] put on this big flat wall all the tasks that needed to be done. It was basically a big PERT chart, but it was really more like a line of balance chart. It listed all the tasks that had to be done, and it moved left to right with time. The way he would track progress was that he had a holder for those disposable coffee cups,

---

[60]Totten, Derman, Goldsmith interviews.

[61]Dryer (1998, 2000).

and he tied a string to it and used that to mark the line of balance. And he would just move the cup down the way, and as it progressed, people would report where they were in their activities. It was a very effective thing.[62]

The Program Evaluation and Review Technique (PERT), and its associated graphical representations, were originally developed for the US Navy's Polaris missile project, and it was exactly the opposite of undirected self-organization.[63] PERT was developed precisely because existing management techniques were failing to control the increasingly large and complex technical projects developed by the military after World War II. As a product of the highly-rationalized discipline of Operations Research, the PERT method promised to help beleaguered managers regain top-down control over technical projects, identify critical paths, and better predict when milestones would be completed.

The second misleading aspect of Hock's account was his use of such passive language. He seems to imply that the organizational power structure somehow dissolved and that disgruntled employees simply "wandered away" on their own accord. In reality, Hock's management style, as well as the styles of those that ran the BASE project, were much closer to a typical, authoritative director. John Totten, who compiled the requirements for BASE as a TRW contractor, and later returned to NBI as an employee, commented on Hock's account:

> ... some of the self-organization happened because people were responsible for a given task and had to fill in their progress on it. But Dee, in my judgement, never let anything just truly "float." He would say that he had all these freedoms and such, but I can remember one of his classic lines was "titles aren't important around here, as long as I'm CEO." He sometimes professed a more open management style than he really practiced.[64]

Tom Honey, who would soon join NBI and create its first debit card, echoed this:

> From my experience with Dee as a new product/service developer and from observing his style with others, one was given latitude and support to do what had to be done often with unrealistic deadlines, but he made sure (and nobody questioned) who was really in charge. Rule No. 1 was that Hock was in charge and you were accountable to meet the deadline. Rule No. 2 was that if Hock was unreasonable by placing more demands on you (whether valid or invalid) that could keep you from meeting the deadline with what he wanted, you had better refer to Rule No. 1.[65]

Win Derman, who would soon be hired to manage the BASE II project, further commented that Hock had a kind of "love/hate" relationship with the technologists: "He knew he needed us, but he didn't trust us to save his life."[66] Hock had literally wagered his career by becoming the general contractor for BASE, and he certainly would not trust the outcome to an undirected, self-organized process.

---

[62]Totten interview. Note that this horizontal bar expression of a PERT model is often referred to as a Gantt chart.

[63]Fazar (1962). There is some dispute as to how seriously PERT was actually used on the Polaris project, and how much it contributed to the project's ultimate success. See Sapolsky (1972).

[64]Totten interview.

[65]Personal correspondence with Tom Honey, 9 December 2006.

[66]Derman interview.

The purpose of Hock's idealistic portrayal becomes more clear when this account is read within the context of his entire book. Throughout the book, Hock is trying to argue that self-organizing systems (which he terms "chaordic") are actually more effective than traditional "command-and-control" organizations. A key element of his proof for this claim is the success of Visa, and therefore, it is critical that he portrays both the internal and external Visa organization as being self-organizing.[67] The development of BASE provides a tempting example, as the individual employees and contractors were given quite a large amount of autonomy in order to complete the project in such a short time, but it is misleading to imply that the leaders were not in control of the overall project, or that the process was not highly organized.

Despite a few minor problems (such as the terminal key caps having square pegs while the Sanders keyboards had round holes), the system was completed within the $3 million budget and on time.[68] On 4 April 1973, the system was put into limited production, and by 1 May it was used twenty-four hours a day, seven days a week. After it ran successfully for a few months, NBI held a formal press conference to announce the system, which was then renamed to the more assured "BankAmericard Service Exchange."[69] NBI employees and member bankers, however, would continue to refer to it by its acronym: BASE.

Effects of the New System

Once BASE began operation, it generated some immediate, noticeable effects. An interchange authorization that previously took four to five minutes could now be obtained in just fifty-six seconds, and merchants could now authorize transactions twenty-four hours a day, seven days a week.[70] Although fifty-six seconds seems like an eternity from our current perspective, in 1973 this made the system *fast-enough* to be a viable competitor to cash and checks, removing one of the critical barriers to adoption.[71]

Thresholds such as "fast-enough" or "good-enough" are an important but often overlooked dynamic in the history of technological systems. From an engineering perspective, claims are often made that one system should be chosen over another because it is faster, more reliable, etc. Human consumers of technological systems, however, often make their adoption choices based upon *thresholds of indifference*— once a user's experience of the system is that it is fast enough, it becomes an acceptable and viable choice, and it makes little difference if another system is claimed

---

[67]By *internal*, I mean the NBI staff, and by *external*, I mean the association of members.

[68]Brooke (11 May 1973), p. 1. See also O'Neil (1973, 116ff). Key caps story from BankAmericard World (June 1973), p. 2.

[69]'BASE unveiled in S.F.', BankAmericard World (June 1973), p. 1.

[70]Brooke (11 May 1973), p. 1. Note that for transactions involving issuers that did not have a direct CPU interface to BASE, the average authorization time was closer to a minute and a half.

[71]Nocera makes a similar point when he says "... it was the difference between deciding to use a credit card and deciding that it was easier to use cash" (Nocera 1994, p. 103).

to be faster.[72] From the consumer's perspective, all systems that are faster than the threshold are equally suitable, and the customer's ultimate choice will then depend upon other factors. Of course, these thresholds will vary from group to group and will tend to "ratchet up" over time.[73] They can also be influenced by rivals who actively seek to persuade groups that their current expectations should be higher.[74]

Although there were some immediate effects, it should be noted that most of BASE's benefits were realized over a much longer period of time. After it was put into production, BASE did nothing to increase the speed of purely local authorizations—those were dependent on the acquirer/issuer's own authorization process and were never even routed to BASE. Merchants were also still operating with floor limits, so low-value transactions required no authorization at all.[75]

The one key demographic that did notice BASE's immediate effects were business travelers. Because banking regulations prohibited banks from operating across state lines, and because many states further restricted banks to operating within a local region, business travelers would typically require interchange authorizations when paying for large-value transactions such as hotels, airline or train tickets, or rental cars. Before the creation of BASE, it was not uncommon for business travelers to drop off their BankAmericards at the front desk before heading to breakfast, as the hotel might require an hour or more to authorize payments for all those leaving the hotel. Now these transactions could realistically be completed as the cardholder waited, greatly improving the utility of the card.

BASE also provided a *platform* upon which the system could expand and improve. Specifically, BASE enabled NBI to accomplish four things over the next few years. First, NBI could now expand the system by recruiting additional member banks without compounding the problems surrounding manual interchange authorization. Although only a small percentage of transactions required interchange authorization in 1973, that small percentage would continue to grow in absolute terms as more members joined the association. Second, NBI could also now encourage consumers to travel with their card, using it in non-local settings, which would naturally increase the percentage of those transactions requiring interchange authorization. This was attractive to NBI not only because it made the card more useful,

---

[72]I first used this term in 1995 when designing a software library for accessing databases. When we needed to determine our success criteria for performance, I realized that most of our consumers would have a threshold of indifference—any library that met that threshold would be sufficient, as the library would then have little effect on the overall performance of the consumer's application. Once we reached that threshold, our development time would be better spent on other tasks.

[73]Rochlin makes a similar observation regarding consumer expectations of reliability. See Rochlin (1993), p. 17.

[74]Perception of speed is also as important as any sort of objective measurement of performance. Today, many grocery POS terminals will encourage the cardholder to swipe their card while the checker is still adding items to the total. By doing so, the POS terminal can capture the card information, prepare an authorization message in memory, and open a connection to the acquirer, all while the clerk finishes dragging your items over the scanner. By overlapping these tasks, the consumer perceives the overall authorization time to be shorter.

[75]The merchant was required to check the number against the warning postcards, but as noted in earlier chapters, this was commonly ignored.

but also because an increase in interchange authorizations would result in an increase in fees paid by the members. This meant more operating revenue for NBI, which would enable them to automate more functions and expand their processing capability. Third, as more member banks automated their local authorizations, NBI could begin to reduce floor limits, which would help reduce fraud and bad credit charge-offs.[76] Lastly, and most importantly, BASE created an online computer network connecting all the member processing centers, and this network made it easier to automate other interchange-related functions.

Conclusion

In this chapter, we saw how the authorization process had become the critical operational issue for all the bankcard systems, and NBI in particular. Various industry leaders formulated two critical problems: the local authorization decision was too slow because it required human intervention; and interchange authorizations were too slow because they required manual "two-legged" calls or telexes. The solution implied by the first problem was the replacement of human authorizers with automated, computerized logic, and we reviewed the various ways in which organizations accomplished this in the early 1970s. The solution implied by the second problem was the development of high-speed electronic communication between the card centers, and we discussed how both Omniswitch and NBI developed similar but independent switching networks.

In the next chapter we will turn our focus to NBI's solution to the second operational problem discussed in the previous chapter: clearing and settlement of interchange transactions.

---

[76]Floor limits were not entirely removed until after the development and mass-adoption of inexpensive dial-up POS terminals, which I will discuss in Chap. 7.

Chapter 5
Automating Clearing and Settlement: BASE II and III

With interchange authorizations automated via BASE, NBI turned their attention to the other half of their operational problems: clearing and settlement. In this chapter, I will discuss NBI's next major computer system development projects, known as BASE II and III. BASE II replaced the cumbersome mailing of paper drafts between members with a centralized, batch-oriented, electronic clearinghouse. BASE III was intended to replace the old BofA punched-card accounting system given to new members with a modern, sophisticated mainframe computer program capable of seamless integration with BASE I and II. Although BASE II was highly successful, building generic software for the member banks' processing centers was not only a significant departure from NBI's core purpose, but also an activity they did not entirely understand. As a result, the BASE III system failed to meet its objectives, and was eventually canceled. As we shall see, however, Hock ultimately managed to turn this first serious defeat into a personal victory that helped to ensure the financial success of the organization.

Truncating the Paper: BASE II

In Chap. 2, I described the manual, tedious, and error-prone process for clearing and settling interchange transactions in 1968. Although the BankAmericard organization had been restructured in 1970, and the switching of interchange authorizations had been automated in 1973, there was still no centralized clearinghouse. Acquiring banks continued to sort and mail the physical sales drafts to each issuing bank, where they were reconciled against clearing drafts that had already been received and paid separately.

The member banks were able to cope with this process while the volumes remained low, but as more banks joined NBI, and the sales volume increased by 30 to 40 percent each year, so did the number of interchange transactions. During 1972, the NBI member banks exchanged 95 million drafts, and they projected that this would rise to 225 million by the end of 1975.[1] It was clear that without an automated, centralized clearinghouse, the BankAmericard system would grind to a halt.

As noted in the previous chapter, automating interchange authorizations was just the first phase of Hock's overall plan to build an electronic value exchange system. Once BASE was put into operation in 1973, Hock quickly began the second phase, which was aptly named BASE II.[2] In this phase, he intended to automate the clearing and settlement of interchange transactions, but instead of using high-speed Magnetic Ink Character Recognition (MICR) readers and sorters as the Fed had done with checks, he wanted to *truncate* the paper, transforming the sales drafts into electronic records, and clearing them through a centralized computer system.[3] Using this approach, interchange transactions could be cleared and settled as early as the night after they were deposited.

But building an electronic clearing system would require engineering more than just computers and telecommunications. It also required the "engineering" of a more cultural dynamic: the consumer preference for country-club billing.[4]

Country-Club, Descriptive, and Facsimile Billing

In 1973, most NBI member banks performed *country-club billing*, which is the practice of returning the punch-card layer of each sales draft to the cardholder, along with a summarized bill. The term originates from the traditional practice of country clubs in the US, nearly all of which would bill their members by returning the "chits" signed when charging purchases at the club.[5] For most cardholders, however, this billing method was not as reminiscent of the genteel country club as much as it was of their monthly checking account statements. At this time, most banks returned canceled checks to account holders, providing them with not only a visual memory of the transaction, but also a legal proof of payment. Thus, it seemed "natural" to return bankcard sales drafts as well.

Interview sources noted several reasons why many cardholders preferred country-club billing. First, the drafts provided them with instant visual memories of each transaction, as merchants occasionally wrote a short description of the purchased merchandise in the detail area. Second, cardholders could also quickly verify their

---

[1] 'NBI planning paperless card drafts', American Banker (18 December 1973), p. 1.

[2] The original working name for BASE II was actually "Shared Paperless Activity Network" or the "SPAN between the banks" (Derman interview). "Paperless" commonly appeared in the names of electronic clearing systems at this time, highlighting that the primary goal was to eliminate the flow of paper.

[3] Note that with the passage of the "Check 21" Act in October 2003, checks in the US may now be truncated and cleared electronically. See Wade (28 October 2003), p. 23. In fact, some merchants now simply pass checksthrough a scanner and hand the physical paper back to the customer.

[4] My language here draws upon John Law's idea of "heterogenous engineering." See Law (1987).

[5] Jutilla (1973), p. 181.

signatures on each draft to ensure that each was a legitimate charge. Third, those who kept the customer receipt layers from the time of sale could easily compare those against the punch-card layers returned by the issuer, ensuring that amounts had not been altered, and noting which transactions were still pending. Fourth, for those who did not wish to keep the customer receipts, the punch-cards returned by the issuer could be used as an evidence of payment for expense reports and income tax returns. Technically, bankcard sales drafts were not legal proofs of payment like canceled checks, but they were effectively treated as such by cardholders, their employers, and most importantly, the US Internal Revenue Service.[6]

Country-club billing was also advantageous for smaller issuers. Because the drafts were punch-cards, they could be sorted, tabulated and collated by rather simple mechanical devices, instead of expensive mainframe computers.[7] Summary bills could be generated using the old BofA software that was still given to new members when they joined NBI. Additionally, because the drafts were returned to the cardholder, the issuer did not need to capture the merchant names and locations in electronic form, as they were printed directly onto the drafts.

An alternative to country-club billing, called *descriptive billing*, began to appear in the late 1960s, but was not widely used in the BankAmericard system until after BASE II was completed.[8] In this method, the issuer captured the information from the sales drafts in electronic form, stored it in a computer file, and sent cardholders only a simple list of their transactions. For each transaction, the statement listed the purchase or posting date, the merchant name and location, and the amount. Because the transaction information was reproduced in descriptive form, the physical drafts were not returned to the cardholder.[9] The issuer stored the drafts for a short period of time, and then maintained a microfilm copy in case the cardholder disputed the charge.

The descriptive billing method was preferred by issuers with larger volumes because it required handling the paper only once, which greatly reduced their labor and postage costs. It was also preferred by NBI, because it did not require the movement of paper from acquirers to issuers. Ultimately, NBI wanted to truncate the paper at the acquirer and clear the transactions in electronic form, but this would be impossible if cardholders continued to demand the original drafts.

Neither Hock nor his staff at NBI, however, believed that all cardholders were actually "demanding" the original drafts; they were merely *accustomed* to receiving them. Although some cardholders were no doubt reassured by the original, most

---

[6]See the "Supporting Documents" section of IRS publication number 583, http://www.irs.gov/publications/p583/ar02.html (accessed on 18 December 2006). The difference between "proof" and "evidence" of payment is subtle—the former is a legal proof recognized by the courts, and supported by the Universal Commercial Code, while the latter is something that a particular party (e.g., an employer or the IRS) would accept as sufficient evidence.

[7]Dumler interview.

[8]For an explanation of descriptive billing and its benefits for the banks, see Magnis (1970).

[9]Some banks used a hybrid method, returning the physical drafts for on-us transactions, but providing a descriptive bill for interchange transactions (Dumler interview).

would probably not notice if they received something that merely *looked like* the original, as long as it contained the most important information: the merchant name and location; the date of the transaction; and the amount. In fact, cardholders already received on occasion a clone of the original draft if it was badly mangled by the merchant or the punch-card readers.[10] If the issuer could print what NBI called a *facsimile draft*, based upon transaction information electronically transmitted from the acquirer, most customers might not even notice the difference, and even if they did, the facsimile would still be an adequate evidence of payment. If the cardholders accepted the facsimile drafts without serious complaint, the bank was then one step closer to implementing descriptive billing.

To test this hypothesis, NBI conducted an experiment with six of its more technically-advanced banks starting in early 1973.[11] Acquirers of interchange drafts captured the descriptive billing information in electronic form, and then transmitted it to the issuer. The issuer then computer-printed the transaction information onto the punch-card layer of a new, blank sales draft and sent that to the cardholder with their summarized bill.[12] The facsimile looked nearly the same as the original, but did not contain any details of the purchased merchandise, nor the cardholder's signature. The lack of item detail actually posed little problem as most merchants neglected to write anything meaningful, and as long as the customer recognized the charge, their signature was superfluous. If the customer could not recognize the charge, or needed the original for some other purpose, the customer could still request it from their issuer. The issuer would then request it from the acquirer, who would send it through the mail. Effectively, the movement and return of physical sales drafts became the exception instead of the rule.

In October 1973, NBI announced that "neither its member banks nor cardholders have related any major problems or objections to the facsimile drafts..."[13] Again, it was not that cardholders were *delighted by* the facsimile drafts; they simply did not care enough to complain about them to any significant extent. After a few months, they also became accustomed to them, and requests for originals were infrequent. During the test, cardholders requested only 1 original for every 500 facsimiles. Forty-five percent of those were due to the cardholder not recognizing the acquirer's processing name for the merchant, which often differed from the merchant's trade name, but this could easily be adjusted. Nineteen percent were requested for business purposes, typically for employers who were wary of the facsimiles, and those cardholders quickly learned to keep the customer receipt layer of the original draft. The remaining 17 percent were requested by the issuer for fraud analysis and prosecution.[14]

---

[10]Dumler interview.

[11]'NBI finds no major problems with facsimile drafts', American Banker (10 October 1973), p. 81. Confirmed in Dumler, Derman, and Russell interviews.

[12]Note that this was not an exact, pixel-for-pixel copy of the original draft. The new draft was printed from discrete, alpha-numeric data.

[13]NBI finds no major problems.

[14]A later story from December quotes Hock as saying that 1 in 300 were requested, so either the ratio increased somewhat over the two-month period, or it was reported incorrectly. See 'NBI

In essence, this test was the key to determining if BASE II was *culturally* possible. NBI could engineer the computer systems and telecommunication networks, but if they could not also "engineer" the cardholder acceptance of facsimile drafts (which were just descriptive billing in a more recognizable form), cardholders would have demanded so many of their originals as to negate the benefits of an electronic clearing and settlement system.

As consumers used the card for more purchases, and descriptive billing became the norm, some cardholders did begin to complain, and in 1977, Rep. Frank Annunzio (D-Ill) proposed a bill that would have effectively outlawed descriptive billing.[15] This section was removed, however, from the final bill, as it was then too late to mandate a return to country-club billing, and the committee eventually realized that ensuring cardholder rights during charge disputes was the real issue. The 1973 test, however, showed that facsimile drafts would be acceptable to the current cardholder base, allowing NBI to continue with the design and implementation of BASE II.

Design of BASE II

The design of BASE II fell to a newly-hired employee named Win Derman.[16] A graduate of MIT and Stanford, Derman became NBI's 25th employee after a stint with the Stanford Research Institute, where he had specialized in management engineering and systems design. B Ray Traweek was also hired to manage the overall project. Traweek's extensive experience with computer systems began while earning a Masters in Mathematics from the University of Texas, and was honed while working for Convair (now part of General Dynamics) and TRW. While at TRW, he had worked on a banking system with Aram Tootelian, and when the BASE II project began, Tootelian convinced Traweek to come to NBI to lead it.

NBI had originally planned to use the same network of Sanders terminals developed for BASE (now renamed BASE I to avoid confusion) for the electronic clearing and settlement of interchange transactions. They assumed that acquirers could manually key the transactions into the terminal, sending each as a new type of message to the central switching computer. But Derman quickly realized that the growing number of transactions would ultimately make this approach impractical, so he convinced the NBI management that BASE II should use a batch transmission approach instead.

---

planning paperless card drafts', American Banker (18 December 1973), p. 1. Either way, the ratio was still small enough to justify building BASE II.

[15]The text of the original bill, HR 8753, and a transcript of the hearings is available in 'The Consumer Credit Protection Act Ammendments of 1977', 95th Congress, First Session (March 1977). See also Nilson (August 1977), Report No 169, p. 1.

[16]Details of the BASE II project primarily come from interviews with Derman, Traweek, Russell, Goldsmith, and Peirce.

In essence, the new BASE II design was a computerized version of the clearinghouse concept discussed in Chap. 1. Although BASE II was not the first implementation of this idea, commonly called an *automated clearinghouse* (ACH), it was by far the largest and most ambitious, the first with a national scope, and the first in the domain of bankcards.[17] With the BASE II system, NBI would act as the centralized clearinghouse of all BankAmericard interchange transactions, but instead of exchanging paper, the acquirers and issuers would exchange electronic records of those transactions. Instead of maintaining high-speed MICR readers and sorters, NBI would maintain one central mainframe computer to collect, sort, total, and distribute the transaction data. Furthermore, because the electronic transactions could be transmitted over telecommunication lines, all the BankAmericard processing centers in the entire nation could clear and settle through the clearinghouse every night.

Additionally, members would now also settle *with the clearinghouse* instead of each other. Prior to BASE II, the BankAmericard system performed *bilateral gross settlement*, meaning that each acquiring bank B1 collected from each issuing bank B2 the total amount (less interchange fees) of all transactions involving the issuer's cards. Since nearly every acquirer was also an issuer at this time, B2 might also collect roughly the same amount from B1 on the same day. In theory, this could result in $n(n-1)$ transfers of similar amounts between every pair of members every day. With BASE II, each member would settle only with the clearinghouse, resulting in just one value transfer per member per day. Furthermore, BASE II would perform *net settlement*, meaning that the amount each member owed the clearinghouse would be subtracted from the amount the clearinghouse owed the member, and the member would pay or receive only the difference.[18]

Data Capture

In order for all of this to work, however, the acquirers needed to encode the paper sales drafts into an electronic form that could be transmitted to NBI's data center. This process, known as *data capture*, could be accomplished either by manual entry, or by scanning the drafts using an Optical Character Recognition (OCR) device. The latter promised to be faster and more accurate than the former, but even in the ideal case, the OCR scanners of the early 1970s could capture only half of

---

[17] In the late 1960s, the California commercial banks organized the Special Committee on Paperless Entries (SCOPE), which resulted in the creation of the California Automated Clearinghouse Association (CACHA) (Yeatrakas interview). This organization, with the help of the Federal Reserve Bank of San Francisco, began operating what seems to be the first ACH in the US on 13 October 1972. See Brooke (4 June 1973), p. 13. This was only a regional system for direct deposit and pre-authorized debit transactions, whereas BASE II was a national system for bankcard transactions.

[18] Although this was new for the BankAmericard system, most other clearinghouses already used the net settlement technique to reduce the amount of funds transferred.

the information.[19] The card and merchant numbers were printed in a standard OCR font, but the transaction date and amount were typically hand-written on the draft by the merchant. Eventually imprinters with adjustable embossed wheels for the date and amount became available, allowing the OCR scanners to read the entire draft automatically. These imprinters were not widely adopted, however, as they were more expensive and consumed more counter space. Counter space is actually an often overlooked, yet critically-important dynamic in the history of payment systems. Many merchants have very limited counter space, and any system that requires a separate, large counter-top device faces a significant barrier to adoption. Additionally, the hype surrounding Electronic Funds Transfer Systems (EFTS) promised that all paper would soon be eliminated from all aspects of banking, so acquirers were not concentrating on how to make the processing of paper drafts more efficient.[20] In fact, many of the largest acquirers continued to use manual data capture until the widespread adoption of merchant point of sale terminals in the mid 1980s.

Although moving to a system of electronic data capture required an enormous amount of work and expense on the part of acquirers, they were, in many ways, eager to change. This is how Derman explained it:

> The reason that the member banks turned heaven and earth to do BASE II can be exemplified by one comment: a banker in New Jersey took me out in the hall and said, "look, you're going to make me do a tremendous amount of work to change ... but I'm going to do it. And you know why? Look up there on the wall; see that line? That's how high we stack the sales drafts that come in from our merchant banks when they process their Christmas volume, which is when we do half our business. And it takes us *four months* to work through that! And we're at risk for all those transactions and all that fraud during that four month period."[21]

Recall that acquirers credited a merchant's account upon deposit of the drafts, but the acquirer could not recover those funds until the drafts were processed, either by billing the cardholder for local transactions, or clearing and settling the non-local drafts through interchange. Any delays in processing resulted in increased float, and corresponding costs for the acquirer. Additionally, issuers were liable for any fraudulent transactions, and had no way to stop further purchases until they processed the drafts and detected that the card had been compromised. Thus, by shifting to semi- or fully-automated OCR data capture, acquirers could not only process their local transactions more quickly, they could also clear and settle their interchange transactions the same night through BASE II.

---

[19]What credit card executives should know about OCR readers, Nilson (November 1977), Report No 174, p. 1.

[20]Nilson rebuked this approach as myopic: "At this point in time, handling credit/debit transactions via electronic terminals in any volume is only a mirage. Except for automated teller machines and cash dispensers, EFTS is a bust! ... Banks, which until recent months had hoped EFTS would reduce the paper flow, must now find other ways to deal with the volume of sales slips which will increase at least 100% in the next five years as predicted in my last issue" (Nilson November 1977, Report No 174, p. 1).

[21]Derman interview.

Edit Package and TTUs

After acquirers captured the draft information in electronic form, they could then easily separate interchange transactions from local ones. They were, however, no longer required to sort and total the interchange transactions by issuer. Instead they simply submitted them in batch to the central clearing computer, which would sort and total all transactions submitted from all acquirers.

To get the transactions to the BASE II central computer, acquirers first needed to transform their data records into the BASE II format and validate them. The acquirers wrote their own software to convert formats, but validation was accomplished by running a program supplied by NBI, called the *edit package*.[22] This program ensured that all data were present, dates were in the correct format, card numbers were valid, and anything else that was necessary to ensure that all the transactions in the batch could be properly cleared and settled. The program also produced a number of reports that the member banks could use as a printed record of their outgoing transactions.

Although it was costly for NBI to maintain a version of the edit package for each kind of computer used by the processing centers, it was ultimately advantageous because they could clear and settle batches of transactions without having to handle individual exceptions. If the batch passed the edit package, every transaction could be cleared; if it did not, the acquirer had to correct the problematic transactions, or remove them from the batch. By making the batch the atomic unit, NBI greatly simplified the task of interchange accounting, as the amount submitted to interchange would always equal the amount credited, minus fees.[23]

After validating the interchange transactions using the edit package, acquirers copied them onto a magnetic tape, which was then mounted onto their *tape transmission unit* (TTU). The TTUs were custom-engineered DEC PDP-11/10 minicomputers equipped with a tape drive, modem, and a bell (explained later).[24] NBI contracted with DEC to install and maintain one of these devices in each of the 88 BankAmericard processing centers in the US.

Central Clearing Computer

At the core of the BASE II system was a large mainframe computer. Each night, starting at 5:00 PM Pacific Time, the central computer would begin calling each of the TTUs according to a schedule established with the processing centers. Because the TTU was a minicomputer, it could answer the call and establish communications automatically. For five hours, known as the *input phase*, the central computer

---

[22]Derman and Traweek interviews.

[23]Reportedly, Interbank's automated clearing and settlement system initially allowed individual exceptions, but they quickly moved to NBI's model as the exceptions were too difficult to manage (Derman and Powar interviews).

[24]Derman interview.

initiated connections to each TTU and read all the transactions contained on each tape. During the validation process, the edit package inserted verification amounts onto the tape so that the mainframe program could ensure that the information was transmitted accurately; if it had not, the TTU could automatically backup to the last checkpoint and resume transmission.[25] At the end of a successful transmission, the central mainframe then sent an instruction to the TTU that triggered it to ring the aforementioned bell. This bell told the operator in the processing center to un-mount the tape containing the outgoing transactions, and mount a new blank tape for the incoming transactions and summary reports.[26] Unfortunately, the tapes at this time did not contain enough capacity for both the outgoing and incoming trans-actions.

The central computer then moved into a two hour *sort and calculation phase*, during which it performed a number of tasks necessary for clearing and settlement. It first calculated the amount owed to each acquirer, which was the total of their submitted transactions, minus the interchange reimbursement and NBI's processing fees (1.95 percent and 2.5 cents per item respectively). It then sorted the transactions by issuer and calculated how much each issuer owed. Finally, it computed the net amount each member owed or was due from the clearinghouse. This information was then printed by NBI for use in the actual settlement, as well as auditing and accounting.

The final phase of the BASE II cycle was called the *output phase*. For five more hours, the mainframe again established connections with each of the TTUs, and streamed back all the interchange transactions for which that bank was the issuer. The member banks could then extract these transactions using the edit package, and incorporate them into their own billing systems. In addition to the incoming trans-actions, the central system also transmitted a full clearing report (which the member could use for bookkeeping and reconciliation), as well as the net settlement amount for that bank. By 5:00 AM Pacific Time the next morning, each bank had all the information they needed to bill their cardholders and settle with the clearinghouse.

The actual movement of "good and final funds" was still accomplished with clearing drafts, but now NBI completed these drafts on behalf of the members. Iron-ically, this last step in the process was not initially automated by BASE II, so after the drafts were prepared, an NBI employee literally got in her car and drove them to a BofA branch located just down the hill from NBI's data center.[27] This settlement process was eventually automated in the 1980s by transmitting the net settlement amounts electronically to a clearing bank.

Although 5:00 PM seems like an appropriate "close of business" time to begin the BASE II process, Derman explained that this start time was actually chosen for a more significant reason:

---

[25] Traweek interview. Confirmed in Brooke (6 November 1974), p. 1.

[26] Derman interview.

[27] Kollmann, Nordemann, and Harrison interviews.

We, even in those days, thought this was a worldwide system, so we ran everything worldwide. We didn't arbitrarily pick 5:00 PM. We said 5:00 PM is GMT 0:00.[28]

Although the original BASE II provided nightly clearing and settlement for the US
member banks only, as we shall see, it was eventually expanded to be the clearinghouse for all members worldwide.

Making Up With IBM

The original capacity target for BASE II was to clear one million transactions within
their allotted 12-hour processing window.[29] Considering the rate at which the system volume was increasing, it was also likely that they would need to expand their
capacity within just a few years. Unfortunately for Hock, the only mainframe computer capable of processing that kind of load and enabling seamless capacity up-
grades was made by IBM. Recall that Hock had previously sworn never to do business with IBM again, but the capacity requirements for BASE II made that pledge
difficult to maintain.

Fortunately, IBM had recently transferred the NBI account from the Banking to
the Manufacturing and Distribution Office, and it was now in the capable hands of
an IBM sales representative named Roger Peirce. Peirce had been with IBM since
1963, first as a systems engineer and later as a direct commissioned salesperson. He
had all the qualities that Hock respected: a sharp intellect, technical competence,
business savvy, and a direct, no-nonsense communication style. Additionally, while
developing numerous information systems, Peirce had learned not only what was
required for a successful project, but also how to handle difficult customers.

Traweek and Derman knew that BASE II required an IBM mainframe, but convincing Hock to buy one would be a challenge considering that Hock typically refused to talk with IBM sales representatives. They approached Peirce and asked him
to do something to soften Hock's temper. Peirce explained what they did:

> We arranged what we called "the pillow call." ... We got the highest ranking guy we could
> find in IBM... and we convinced him to come out. We said "look, this is going to be an
> unpleasant call—strap a pillow on your ass because you're going to get beaten!" So we
> went into this meeting and Dee basically railed and ranted at the guy for an hour and then
> went out, but after it was all done, it worked, and they decided they would do business with
> IBM.[30]

NBI ordered a System/370 model 145, and Peirce called in a number of favors to
advance its delivery so that it could be installed in time.[31]

---

[28] Derman interview.

[29] Derman interview.

[30] Peirce interview.

[31] Peirce interview. This was the first IBM mainframe to use silicon memory chips instead of a magnetic core. See http://www-03.ibm.com/ibm/history/exhibits/mainframe/mainframe_PP3145.html
(accessed on 15 December 2006).

Peirce personally oversaw the installation of the mainframe in April 1974, which no doubt endeared him to Hock. IBM, the most important computer company in the world, was now treating Hock as the important client he saw himself to be. As a result, Hock became more amenable to IBM, and Peirce in particular, which would eventually enable IBM to sell Hock on moving BASE I to their platform as well.[32] Peirce would also later join NBI and become Vice President of Systems Development, Operations, and Member Relations.

Final Development and Rollout

In addition to IBM, NBI contracted with a number of other vendors to construct the various pieces of BASE II. DEC built, installed, tested, and maintained the TTUs at the 88 BankAmericard processing centers. AT&T again supplied the telecommunications. Arthur Andersen designed the audit control system, and the Stanford Research Institute (SRI) performed the technical acceptance tests.[33] Compata, the organization that had written the BASE software, also returned to write the software for BASE II.[34] Using the same project management techniques they used for BASE, NBI completed the new system by November 1974, within its allocated budget of $7 million, and timeframe of 18 months.[35]

Some of the processing centers, however, still had not yet implemented their data capture systems by November. Thus all could *receive* interchange transactions from BASE II, but not all could *send* them. Therefore, NBI mandated that on 1 November 1974, every issuer had to receive electronic interchange transactions via BASE II, but the acquirers who had not yet automated could continue to mail paper drafts through the Christmas season; by 1 March 1975, all interchange transactions had to be cleared electronically. Both deadlines were met by the members, and the mailing of original drafts became the exception rather than the rule for the entire system.

It is important to note that on this latter date, the paper did not *entirely* disappear from the system. The paper was eliminated for the most part from interchange, but most merchants still completed and deposited paper drafts, and acquirers still handled that paper during data capture. The paper was not removed from this segment of the clearing path until Visa coordinated the development of small, inexpensive point of sale dial terminals. That story will be discussed in Chap. 7.

---

[32]Details of the BASE I port to IBM and the TPF operating system will be discussed in the next chapter.

[33]Although SRI had already separated from Stanford University in 1970, they did not formally change their name to SRI International until 1977. See http://www.sri.com/about/facts.html (accessed on 11 November 2010).

[34]Brooke (6 November 1974), p. 1.

[35]Hock (1974), p. 13.

Effects of the System

BASE II altered the BankAmericard system in five important ways. First, BASE II dramatically reduced the time it took to clear and settle interchange transactions. Under the manual system, it took an average of six to eight days for sales drafts to reach the issuer, where they often failed to reconcile with the already paid clearing draft; with BASE II, all sales drafts were now cleared and settled, in batch, overnight.[36]

Second, the reduction in clearing time resulted in a corresponding reduction in float, mostly for the acquirers, but also for the issuers. BASE II essentially forced the acquirers to implement an automated data capture system, enabling them to submit transactions to interchange much more quickly, and thus recover the funds they had already credited to their merchants. Issuers received the transaction details electronically at the same time they paid the acquirers, which not only eliminated the painful reconciliation process, but also provided an easy way to import the transactions into their billing systems in order to recover funds from the cardholder.

Third, automating the interchange process dramatically reduced the labor and postage costs associated with the clearing and settlement of interchange transactions. NBI estimated at the time that BASE II saved the members between $14 and $17 million in gross clearing costs during its first year of operation alone.[37] Although the exact amount would have been difficult to substantiate, as so many aspects of the business were in constant flux, there is no question that the labor costs alone would have made the existing manual process uneconomical as the number of interchange transactions increased.

Fourth, faster clearing also meant that issuers now received fraudulent interchange transactions in a more timely manner. Although BASE I stopped many fraudulent transactions, it only saw those that were over the merchant's floor limit. A compromised card number could still be used for numerous charges under the floor limit. The issuer would have no way of knowing that fraud was occurring until those transactions were cleared through interchange. The faster transactions were cleared, the faster the issuer could detect fraud, and take steps to cancel and recover the card.

Lastly, BASE II established a platform upon which NBI could offer other *batch-oriented* data transfer services between the members, just as BASE I provided a platform for *online* message exchange.[38] From its inception, BASE II allowed members to transmit other administrative transactions such as chargebacks, reversals, and requests for originals, in addition to interchange drafts.[39] BASE II was later extended

---

[36]Brooke (6 November 1974), p. 1.

[37]Brooke (6 November 1974), p. 1.

[38]The term "online" is often used in many different ways. Here I mean a system that maintains constant communication links between nodes, passing individual messages in a near-real-time manner. Some news accounts referred to BASE II as being "online" because it transmitted data over communication lines (as opposed to mailing magnetic tapes), but it is more appropriately described as a batch-oriented data exchange system.

[39]Brooke (6 November 1974), p. 1.

to include other kinds of clearing messages as well, such as rewards for recovering stolen cards, or reimbursements for telex costs incurred by foreign acquirers.[40] With the combination of BASE I and II, NBI could now facilitate any type of data exchange between its members. These two systems became the information processing backbone upon which Hock could eventually provide his "premier system for the exchange of value."

Losing Focus: BASE III

Shortly after NBI began the BASE II project, they also embarked on another system that has, so far, received almost no attention, perhaps because it was the organization's first significant failure.[41] While BASE I and II enabled data exchange *between* the member processing centers, this system, appropriately named BASE III, was designed to provide most of the necessary card-related data processing *within* a given center. It would replace the simple punched-card system originally developed by the BofA with a modern, on-line mainframe computer program that would provide all the functionality necessary for maintaining cardholder accounts. In essence, it was to provide "everything you needed to plug into Visa."[42]

NBI had two primary motivations for building such a system. First, in keeping with the general philosophy of networked payment card systems, NBI thought that if all members cooperated, they could build a better system than any one of the members could have built alone. At the time, Hock assumed that all the processing centers had more or less similar needs, so it made little sense to build 88 versions of the same software. NBI felt that they could manage the construction of a much more sophisticated, shared computer program for less money by combining all the members' resources. Once it was finished, those members that contributed the initial funding would receive the software, and as more members chose to adopt it, the original funders would receive a corresponding portion of the subsequent licensing fees.[43]

Second, if NBI developed a shared computer program, they could also enable a consistent and seamless integration with the BASE I and II systems. Recall that NBI wanted to enable fully-automated authorizations by connecting BASE I directly to each issuer's computer, and BASE III would provide them a perfect opportunity to deploy this functionality to a large number of processing centers. Additionally, once BASE II began sending incoming interchange transactions, BASE III could include the software necessary to import those easily into the cardholder files.[44]

---

[40] Kollmann interview.

[41] Hock's autobiography is the only published source that contains any mention of BASE III. See Hock (2005), pp. 241–243.

[42] Totten interview. Information on BASE III comes primarily from interviews with Totten, who managed the project in its later phases, as well as Fojtik, Peirce, and Russell.

[43] Hock (2005), p. 242.

[44] Totten interview.

NBI began this effort in mid 1973 with the ambitious intention of releasing it shortly before BASE II was put into production (November 1974). As opposed to their experience with the original BASE project, this time they found some existing software that they assumed could be expanded to meet the needs of all processing centers. This had been developed by the Centurex corporation of Los Angeles for the American Bank and Trust of Reading, Pennsylvania, which also happened to be an NBI member.[45] NBI hired Centurex in July of 1973 to help gather requirements from 80 other processing centers and extend their existing system accordingly.

Problems Begin to Emerge

It was during the requirements gathering phase of the project that the first problems began to emerge. Contrary to assumptions, the processing centers did have varying needs, and the larger centers required specific features that necessitated significant changes to the underlying data structures and logic. The most serious was what became known as the "multi-bank" feature—centers that processed for multiple member banks (e.g., the BofA) required the system to segregate cardholders and transactions according to issuing bank, something that the original single-bank system had never anticipated.

Instead of partitioning these more advanced requirements into processor-specific extensions, those gathering the requirements promised to include all these features in the main software. John Totten, who joined NBI in February of 1974 to lead the BASE III project, explained:

> Part of the problem with that was, many of the people that were on the project had never been in a credit card [processing] environment before, and so they would have these road shows and somebody would say "will it do X, will it do Y, will it jump over this and crawl under that?" And the typical answer was "yeah, if you sign up, we'll put that in."[46]

Because BASE III was entirely funded by license fees paid by advance subscribers, there was strong incentive to agree to any feature necessary to secure the sale. Members also had an incentive to subscribe early as the license fee was less for advance subscribers, and according to Hock, they would also receive a portion of the fees paid by future subscribers. As a result, the list of requirements grew far beyond what could reasonably be accomplished by a single, shared program to be delivered in November 1974.

In addition to a growing requirements list, the system was also being designed to the lowest common denominator of computer hardware. For example, many of the smaller centers were still using the simpler IBM 2260 video display terminals to interact with their mainframes, and were unwilling to upgrade to the more powerful,

---

[45] Brooke (1 August 1973), p. 1. See also 'NBI buys Centurex on-line card system', American Banker (2 January 1974), p. 5.

[46] Totten interview.

but expensive 3270. Thus BASE III was constrained to use the 2260 even though the larger and more innovative centers had already upgraded to the 3270. Roger Peirce noted that because NBI had little experience with the IBM environment, they did not yet understand how much of a constraint this would be. He described the BASE III design approach as "skating to where the puck is instead of where the puck is going to be." [47]

By the time Totten took control of the project, NBI had already spent all the money raised by selling advance licenses, and were still ten months away from their planned first release. [48] Furthermore, the first release was simply a more generic form of the original Centurex software. Most of the new features would not be available until the second release, which was planned for 90 days after the first, and the multi-bank capability would require yet another release, which was promised for 90 days after that. The project was clearly in trouble, and Hock was forced to ask the Board for additional funds. Hock later admitted that asking for more money was in actuality an unwillingness to recognize and admit failure, and only served to further compound the problems. [49]

BASE III encountered yet another problem during the development phase that is common in rapid parallel development. BASE III was supposed to import incoming interchange transactions from BASE II into the cardholder files, but BASE II itself was being developed at the same time and thus became a moving target. Totten explained:

> I can remember, my development team was in Los Angeles, and we'd be working on some sort of details about the transaction format, and I would walk down the hall and Win [Derman] or B Ray [Traweek] would say, "oh, we just changed the transaction format." I asked them, "How in the world am I going to have a system that's compatible with you if you guys are continually making these changes, which I have to accommodate, and I learn about it over the water fountain?" [50]

Problems Come to a Head

Centurex did eventually deliver the first version of BASE III in late 1974, but few centers chose to install it, as the new features were still to come 90 days later in the second version. When that second version became available, those that installed it found the performance to be somewhat less than satisfactory. Russell explained:

> ... we purchased a rotten piece of software, and proceeded to "improve" it. As you well know, improving rotten software only exacerbates the rotten aspects of it, and when we were finished we had a beautiful piece of garbage which had but one flaw—it required 25 hours to run! Now, even the genius of Dee couldn't figure out how to add another hour

---

[47] Peirce interview.

[48] Totten interview.

[49] Hock (2005), p. 242.

[50] Totten interview.

to every day, and so it failed, miserably. Unfortunately, four or five banks installed this software, and at least three of those plan managers were fired for their decisions.[51]

Unfortunately, NBI had promised to deliver a third version of BASE III in another 90 days, and this version would require substantial changes and additional code to accommodate the multi-bank feature, which would likely make the system even slower and less reliable. A number of key players including Traweek, Totten, and Peirce convinced Hock that BASE III was doomed, and that NBI should admit failure and cut their losses rather than waste even more money and time.

Success in Failure

Although admitting failure was difficult for Hock at the time, he was able to use the termination of BASE III to achieve a more important goal he had been pursuing for some time. When NBI was formed, the largest members had forced Hock to agree to a maximum cap on their quarterly service fees. These fees were based on the sales volume each member generated during the quarter, and were a key source of operating revenue for NBI. The larger issuers had already reached the cap, but NBI was still required to handle their ever-growing volume. Hock wanted to eliminate the cap, but since it was written into the bylaws, removing it required approval by a super-majority of the Board.[52]

Hock went to the Board with a plan about how to terminate BASE III, recoup the losses it had caused, and generally streamline NBI's operations. The plan had four points: The third version of BASE III would be abandoned, the entire project canceled, and the advance license fees refunded; NBI would layoff a third of its "nonessential" employees; member fees would be reduced overall; but the cap would be removed and replaced with a sliding fee to be phased in over five years. Hock persuaded enough of the Board members to adopt the plan, thereby removing the cap, but the victory was bittersweet. On 22 January 1976, thereafter referred to as "Black Thursday," a third of NBI's non-essential employees were laid off.[53]

Returning to Purpose and Principles

In retrospect, both Hock and Russell admit that the central mistake of the entire BASE III project was actually a loss of focus. Hock wrote:

> The lesson finally sank in. We had never gone back to our purpose and principles to ask what card processing software for bank use had to do with "creating the world's premier

---

[51]Russell correspondence. Confirmed by Totten.

[52]Cleveland (1999), pp. 11–12.

[53]Cleveland (1999), pp. 11–12.

system for the exchange of value." It had nothing to do with our purpose, or our belief about decentralization of function in pursuit of it. It was not a mistake of the people, it was a mistake of the leadership. We were extremely good at some things, we were very good at many things, but we were not good at everything. One of the principle arts of leadership is to make such distinctions and we failed to do so.[54]

Russell concurred:

...we tried to become all things to all people, instead of doing that for which we were created. Writing and selling file management software is a completely different bag from managing and operating online payment systems.[55]

Both Hock and Russell (as well as the rest of the early NBI leadership) believe that the primary purpose of a networked payment system is to provide a framework in which competitors can cooperate just enough in order to offer a service that no single member could have realistically offered alone. BASE I and II both supported that purpose, but BASE III did not. BASE I and II were simply coordination mechanisms, and neither constrained the members from adding proprietary features to their local systems in order to gain a competitive advantage. Although BASE III would have made it slightly easier for some members to coordinate with NBI's core systems, it also threatened to *homogenize* those members by supplying them with a single, common software program that would have been difficult or even impossible to augment with local innovations. Thus, BASE III upset the delicate balance between competition and cooperation that is so critical in a networked payment system.

More importantly, BASE III demonstrated that NBI had temporarily lost sight of what kind of system they were actually building. By developing BASE III, NBI was acting more like a computer systems vendor, a role for which they were neither created nor prepared. NBI was formed to build and operate an electronic payment system, not develop computer systems for their own sake. The latter was only a means to achieve the former.

NBI's leadership also learned a more general lesson from the BASE III project. Although there would be times when they needed to encourage the development of ancillary technologies to enhance the functionality of the network, they should constrain their input to only those mechanisms that enable *coordination* (e.g., data formats, communication protocols, and other standards). Construction of the actual technologies should then be left to firms that specialize in such devices, and they should enlist *multiple competing* firms so as to encourage further innovation. NBI applied this lesson well when they encouraged the development of inexpensive merchant dial terminals, the story of which will be discussed in Chap. 7.

---

[54] Hock (2005), p. 242.

[55] Russell correspondence.

Conclusion

In this chapter, we reviewed how NBI automated the clearing and settlement of interchange transactions, which was one of the key operational problems facing the BankAmericard system. We also discussed the BASE III project, which was an attempt to replace the punched-card accounting system developed by the BofA with a more modern mainframe computer program. This project ultimately failed, primarily because it was a significant departure from NBI's core purpose.

With the combination of BASE I and II, Hock was much closer to his dream of worldwide electronic value exchange. Nevertheless, there were still a number of areas in which the system needed to expand. Hock wanted to enable cardholders to access any kind of funds they might possess, including deposits and investments, which implied that the system needed to expand outside the credit departments of the member banks. He wanted cardholders to have access to those funds anywhere in the world, which implied that the cooperative organization needed to expand outside the US. It also implied a significant expansion of the computer systems and networks not only to handle the increased volume, but also to ensure a dependable service. These expansions, as well as others that were forced upon NBI, occurred throughout the 1970s, and it is to these that we now turn.

Chapter 6
Expanding the System: Organizational and Technical Growth

In the previous chapter, we reviewed the creation of NBI's BASE II, which automated the clearing and settlement of interchange transactions. With the combination of BASE I and II, NBI now had the necessary data processing infrastructure on which they could build Hock's worldwide electronic system for the exchange of value. To achieve this goal, however, the payment system needed to be expanded, both organizationally and technically.

In this chapter, we will examine the various ways in which the system was expanded throughout the rest of the 1970s, most of which were instigated by NBI, but some were also forced upon them. I will segment these expansions into two major sections: those involving the organization, and those involving the computer systems. In order to understand the explosive growth that occurred during the late 1970s, one must hold the organizational and technical aspects together. The organizational expansions certainly triggered much of the growth, but if the computer systems had not also been expanded during this same period, the payment system would have quickly contracted again, or at least grown far more slowly.

Expanding the Organization

From 1972 to 1976, the NBI organization experienced three fundamental changes that would significantly shape the payment system's evolution. First, Hock and his staff replicated the NBI organizational structure at the international level, forming a new organization called IBANCO, of which the entire NBI system was a member. Second, NBI's prohibition on participating in both their system and Interbank's was repealed after a lengthly legal battle and Department of Justice review, creating the condition known as "duality." Third, both of these changes were woven together when the organization adopted the name "Visa," an action that became the catalyst for a rapid expansion of the membership, cardholder base, and sales volume. We will now examine each of these in turn.

D.L. Stearns, *Electronic Value Exchange*, History of Computing,
DOI 10.1007/978-1-84996-139-4_6, © Springer-Verlag London Limited 2011

IBANCO

From its inception, the BankAmericard licensing program was international, at least to some extent. Barclays Bank, Ltd., in the UK became the first international licensee in 1966, and by late 1972, banks in 15 countries were participating in the program.[1] Although the BankAmericard Service Corporation (BASC, a wholly-owned subsidiary of BofA created to manage the card program) relinquished control of the domestic licensees to NBI in 1970, it still retained control over the international ones. Thus, the international organization remained roughly the same as the domestic one had been prior to NBI, and not surprisingly, experienced many of the same problems.

According to Hock, the international licensees attempted to break away from the BASC at the same time NBI was forming, but were unable to organize.[2] In 1972, after observing the initial successes of NBI, they made a second attempt, asking Hock to help create an international version of the organization. Hock was of course delighted, as this would further his ultimate agenda of creating a worldwide system for the exchange of value.

Determining the Structure

Creating an international organization, however, would be far more difficult than establishing NBI. Despite the differences between the US BankAmericard licensees, they still all spoke the same language, used the same currency, served a roughly similar culture, and participated in a common banking system. A global organization could assume none of those, and would thus need to separate the system elements that were truly universal from those that were specific to a particular region, country, or member. These universal elements were primarily Hock's set of principles discussed in Chap. 2, the rules governing international interchange, and the use of the worldwide marks.

Although every licensee had an economic interest in forming an international cooperative organization, they also feared that one country would amass too much political power, and thus control, over the system. The chairman of the international organizing committee explained that

> In structuring the new corporation, the committee sought to gain a balance between, on the one hand, equitable representation of all members and protection of the system from domination by a single member, country or region, and [on] the other, preservation of autonomy of each member's bank card program and each national bank card system, consistent with the interests of the worldwide system.[3]

---

[1]Brooke (20 September 1974), p. 1.

[2]Hock (2005), p. 196.

[3]Brooke (20 September 1974), p. 8.

This balance was obtained primarily by structuring the Board of Directors to ensure that no member, country or region had a majority of votes, but all had enough representation to block policy that was not in their best interest. Even the United States, which generated the vast majority of the system's volume, held a minority of seats on the Board. Unlike the NBI Board, the international licensees had less interest in controlling the daily operational details, leaving those decisions to the NBI staff.[4]

Studium ad Prosperandum, Voluntas in Conveniendum

After two years of negotiation, the structure of the new organization was established and nearly all the issues had been resolved. Nevertheless, there were some critical disagreements still, primarily centering around Hock's principle that any qualifying bank must be admitted to the system. The international licensees had enjoyed exclusive rights to their country or region for many years, and the prospect of allowing their competitors to become members of a system they had spent money and time developing was unacceptable to some.

Hock scheduled a final meeting in San Francisco where these last issues would be discussed, but he expected that little would change. To achieve consensus, Hock realized he would need a device to give the licensees some perspective.

Prior to the meeting, Hock had a set of custom-designed cufflinks made for each of the representatives. As expected, the meeting itself achieved little, and the effort appeared to be a lost cause. As a final tribute, Hock took the licensees to a restaurant in Sausalito, the same town where he had developed his principles for the NBI organization four years earlier. After dinner, he placed the cufflinks before each representative and began one of the most important speeches of his career. His recollection of it is so powerful, it is worth quoting in full:

> ... a small gift was placed before them as I concluded. "It is no failure to fall short of realizing such a dream. From the beginning it was apparent that forming such a complex, global organization was unlikely. We now know it is impossible, notwithstanding two years of exceptional effort. Not knowing with certainty how today's meeting might end, we felt compelled to do something that would be appropriate no matter what happened. Would you please open the small gift on the table before you?" As they each opened a small, beautifully wrapped box and began to examine the contents, I quietly continued.
>
> "We wanted to give you something that you could keep for the remainder of your life, as a reminder of this day. On one cufflink is half of the world surrounded by the Latin phrase, 'Studium ad prosperandum'—the will to succeed. On the second cufflink is the other half of the world surrounded with 'Voluntas in conveniendum'—the grace to compromise. We meet tomorrow for the final time to disband the effort after an arduous two years. There is no possibility of agreement. As organizing agent, we have one last request. Will you please bring your cufflinks to the meeting in the morning? When it ends, each of us will take them with us as a reminder for the remainder of our lives that the world can never be united through us because we lacked the will to succeed and the grace to compromise. But if, by some miracle, our differences dissolve before morning, this gift will remind us to the

---

[4]Russell interview.

day we die that the world *was* united because we *had* the will to succeed and the grace to compromise."

There was a moment of profound silence as they examined their gift. It was shattered by one of my more exuberant Canadian friends, may his soul rest in peace, who rose with a huge grin and exploded, "You miserable bastard!"[5]

The next morning, the licensees reached consensus on every outstanding issue, and they unanimously agreed to form the new organization.

Although this story sounds almost too good to be true, the cufflinks and the basic points were verified by other sources.[6] Nevertheless, it is uncertain what role the cufflinks actually played in encouraging compromise. Chuck Russell recalled that the licensees agreed to allow competitors to join only after it was decided that new members would pay higher fees to compensate the original licensees for their efforts in developing the system in their respective regions. The cufflinks and Hock's speech may have shamed the licensees into seeking a compromise solution, but the ultimate compromise was likely achieved only once economic incentives and protections for the existing licensees were added to the new international bylaws.

Formation

In June 1974, IBANCO was organized as a for-profit, non-stock Delaware corporation, just like NBI.[7] NBI continued to manage the US members, but became a member of Ibanco, along with other national associations and individual licensee banks. Hock became president of Ibanco as well as NBI, and Ibanco contracted with the NBI staff for the management of Ibanco's operations. A new set of international bylaws and operating regulations were created from those used by NBI, but individual regions and countries were free to enforce their own, additional rules, provided they did not contradict the international ones.

The creation of Ibanco was an important expansion towards achieving Hock's goal of a worldwide electronic value exchange system, primarily because it created a framework of rules in which all BankAmericard participants could both cooperate and compete. Under the BASC, each licensee negotiated their own terms, and there were no mechanisms to enforce the few rules that existed. Under Ibanco, there were clear and consistent rules as to the interchange reimbursement fee, dispute resolution, the use of marks, design of cards, format of the drafts, as well as penalties for violating the rules. These rules were necessary to provide a cohesive, networked, worldwide payment service.

---

[5]Hock (2005), pp. 210–211.

[6]The cufflinks themselves are pictured in Chutkow (2001), p. 138. Russell confirmed the dinner and the presentation.

[7]Brooke (20 September 1974), p. 1. IBANCO reportedly stood for "International Bankcard Company," but was commonly referred to only by the shortened name, and often in title case after first use (i.e., Ibanco).

Antitrust and Dual Membership

As the organization expanded internationally, it also expanded domestically, though not entirely by choice. Throughout the early 1970s, NBI was embroiled in an antitrust lawsuit brought by a bank that was both a member of NBI and Interbank. The case posed a question regarding this new type of organization that had no obvious answer: should banks be allowed to join multiple bankcard systems? Since the member banks actually own and govern these systems, would this lead to more or less competition?[8]

Historical Context

The answers to these questions were further complicated by a division of the membership originally created by the BASC licensing structure. Recall that when BofA franchised the program in 1966, it gave most banks exclusive licenses for their territory. These banks saw the exclusive right to issue the cards as a great benefit, as they typically considered the card program not as a profitable business venture of its own, but as a method for attracting new customers and thus deposits. But most banks, especially those in states with restrictive branching laws, often needed the help of other, smaller banks to enlist a sufficient number of merchants to make the system attractive and viable. Thus, the licensee banks contracted with these *agent* banks to sign up additional merchants and process their transactions. Many licensee banks also allowed non-competing agents to "re-issue" their cards to the agent's depositors, but the licensee held the receivables and thus enjoyed all the interest revenues.

When NBI formed, it maintained this distinction, labeling the issuing banks *Class A* members and the agents *Class B*. The 200-plus Class A members were full owner/members of NBI, while the thousands of Class B members were merely "sponsored" by their respective Class A member (by 1973, there were 250 Class A and 4,410 Class B members).[9] By the late 1970s this distinction had eroded and was formally eliminated, but during the first part of that decade, it was fundamental to understanding the issue of duality.

By the time NBI formed, a small number of Class A banks had also joined Interbank, primarily to hedge their bets on Hock's tenuous new organization. NBI immediately put a moratorium on this practice, fearing that Interbank would learn of NBI's plans through the dual members. One of the dual Class A members, Worthen Bank and Trust of Little Rock, Arkansas, warned NBI's management that they would challenge any attempt to make the ban permanent. Hock himself was adamant in his opposition, though the rest of his staff was actually divided on the

---

[8]Information on duality and the antitrust case comes from the following sources: Hock (2005), pp. 181–194; Wiegold (2 January 1973), p. 1 and other trade press articles; interviews with Katz, Honey, Russell, Powar, Conway, and Derman.

[9]Various articles in *American Banker*.

issue, and there was considerable internal debate.[10] Nevertheless, in October 1971 NBI adopted a new section into their bylaws, number 2.16, which prohibited any member that issued a BankAmericard (i.e., Class A member) from participating in any other bankcard association. As promised, Worthen quickly filed a private antitrust suit, claiming that the ban was a horizontal restraint on trade deserving an immediate injunction.

It is important to understand that although Worthen wanted to be a member of both systems, it was not as interested in *issuing* both types of cards as it was in *acquiring* both types of transactions. Worthen's primary complaint was that NBI's ban applied to Class A members only; Class B members were still allowed to acquire transactions for both systems. Because merchants wanted to deposit all their various bankcard transactions with the same institution, Worthen argued that Class B members had an unfair advantage in the acquiring business.

The Arguments

Whether the ban on dual membership would result in more or less competition was complex to answer because it depended on one's perspective. From the perspective of an individual bank, the ban seemed to restrict competition, as Class A members had less freedom than the Class B members. From the perspective of the entire payment system, however, the ban seemed to increase the potential for competition, as the two systems would need to offer competitive fees and develop innovations to attract and retain their members. If banks could be members of both systems, there would be less incentive for them to encourage competition at the system level, as they would be owners and tax-payers of both. Furthermore, Hock argued that there would eventually be enormous pressure to merge the two systems, and little incentive for banks to break away to form a new competitor. Thus, whether the ban encouraged competition depended largely on whether one wanted to optimize for competition between the individual banks, or between the systems themselves.

Hock was focused on the system as a whole, and as such, was strongly against duality. Furthermore, he also opposed the idea of any single agency or organization dictating what was in the best interest of the public. In a 1974 speech, he observed that

> The proponents of several views seem to make an assumption that such matters as the public interest and social cost can best be judged by whatever entity they deem suited to the task ahead. The real question is, who is best suited to judge such matters? Congress? The Executive Branch of Government? The Federal Reserve? Commercial Banks? Savings Banks? Bank Card Organizations? The Consumers Union? The Justice Department? Or is it the public? And if the public, how can it have any opportunity to exercise its judgement except by the only effective method which has ever been found; that is, by choosing freely among a variety of competing services with complete information about the costs, practices and benefits of each. My strong conviction is that the public should choose and my great

---

[10]See Hock (2005), pp. 182–183. Also confirmed in Katz and Russell interviews.

fear is that they may never have the opportunity. If solutions are forced upon them it matters little which organization does so, for ultimate abuse of such power will be inevitable.[11]

Although his general claims are certainly open to critique, this quote allows us to peer into Hock's way of thinking. One of the most salient features of natural systems for Hock is how they function so effectively without centralized control. Here he expresses the common libertarian belief that a free market is far more effective than myopic regulation, which is, for a libertarian, the most pernicious form of centralized control. Hock wanted to see many competing payment networks, and he feared that without a ban on dual membership, no new payment system would ever arise. Furthermore, NBI and Interbank would eventually be pressured to merge, and the resulting monopoly would ultimately abuse its power. In the end, consumer choice would be restricted, not enhanced.

Trials

On 19 July 1972, the district judge sided with Worthen, declaring the ban on dual membership to be a "group boycott" and thus a horizontal restraint of trade that was *per se* illegal under antitrust law.[12] By deeming it *"per se* illegal," the judge considered it to be so obviously anticompetitive that no detailed economic or business review of the system was necessary. The judge also granted an immediate injunction prohibiting NBI from enforcing the ban, but delayed the award of damages until after the appeal's process.

NBI immediately appealed the case, arguing that because this type of venture was so new and untested, the ban should be evaluated under the "rule of reason," meaning that the court should conduct a full business and economic analysis of the system in order to determine if the ban was indeed anticompetitive. In a friend of the court brief, the Department of Justice (DOJ) also encouraged a full trial to determine the merits of the policy.[13] In September 1973, the appellate court agreed, sending the case back to the district court for a full trial under the rule of reason.[14] Worthen appealed to the Supreme Court to uphold the *per se* ruling and injunction, but was denied a hearing.[15]

The costs of an extensive trial were unappealing to both sides, so NBI and Worthen eventually reached a settlement. NBI agreed to extend the dual membership ban to Class B banks as well as Class A, but wait to enforce it until they received a

---

[11] Hock (1974), p. 3.

[12] Wiegold (2 January 1973).

[13] Wiegold (12 July 1973), p. 1. For Worthen's response, see 'Worthen opposes call for full trial', American Banker (23 July 1973), p. 1.

[14] 'Court upsets ruling against NBI dual card ban', American Banker (25 September 1973).

[15] 'Plea for new hearing by Worthen is denied', American Banker (25 October 1973), p. 1, 'Worthen asks high court to review reversal', American Banker (11 December 1973), p. 1, 'High court refuses Worthen-NBI review', American Banker (20 February 1974), p. 1.

"business review" letter from the DOJ, stating their opinion and enforcement inten-tions.[16] Thus far, NBI's arguments had met with favorable responses from the DOJ, but the DOJ's head lawyer had recently stepped down, and the new leadership was far more skeptical. After a lengthy investigation, the DOJ issued a letter on 7 Octo-ber 1975 that was so carefully hedged "as to leave unresolved the legal permissibility of an effective prohibition against dual membership."[17] They neither explicitly con-demned nor condoned the ban, leaving NBI a target for further antitrust litigation.

Duality

Although NBI felt they could defend the ban in court, the costs of losing were enor-mous. Under US antitrust law, a convicted corporation was liable for treble damages, and its officers could face jail sentences. Hock had little chance of convincing the Board to enforce the ban, and as we shall see, eliminating it could help achieve another, perhaps more important goal. Thus, the bylaw was summarily removed in June 1976, ushering in a state known as "duality" in the US.[18] Banks were now free to join both NBI and Interbank, and most did. But this resulted in a larger and more important expansion for NBI than Interbank, as the latter's membership was not only significantly larger than the former's, it also comprised the largest and most important banks in any given area.

The subsequent history of bankcard systems has shown that Hock's predictions regarding the effects of duality were entirely correct. Most banks went dual within six months, no competing system arose, and dual members found little incentive to pay for innovations in one system that they would only have to pay for again in the other. Reflecting on it in 1979, Hock told an interviewer:

> It won't be until 1981 when banks can sit back and ask, 'What hath God wrought?' or more properly 'What hath the Department of Justice wrought?' But already you can see some changes. When banks were either Master Charge *or* Visa issuers, every time one card asso-ciation came up with an innovation, the members of the other would press their association to come up with a competitive answer. Now, rather than press the other association for inno-vation, some banks just criticize whichever is the innovator. As joint owners they can now solve competitive problems by inhibiting the innovator rather than by spurring the laggard. I have seen a lot more of this in the last year than I have in the past and it disturbs me.[19]

The ultimate irony came in 1998, when the DOJ sued both Visa USA and Master-Card, claiming that their common governance was creating anticompetitive effects. Additionally, the DOJ sought to eliminate rules that restricted members from issu-ing American Express, or any other proprietary card. The court sided with the DOJ

---

[16]Hock (2005), p. 190. See also 'NBI maps new rules banning dual membership', American Banker (17 September 1974), p. 1, Brooke (20 November 1974), p. 1.

[17]Baxter (1983), p. 587.

[18]'A second card in your future?', ABA Banking Journal (August 1976), p. 54. Other countries such as Spain and France did not allow such duality. The effects this had on the system evolution and competitive landscape in those countries would be an interesting focus for further research.

[19]Streeter (1979), p. 70.

on the latter issue, but not the former. In any case, it was too late to separate the two organizations.[20]

In recent years, both Visa and MasterCard have reorganized into publicly-traded, for-profit corporations. While these reorganizations did open up new sources of investment capital for the systems, analysts have mused as to whether they might also help stem further attempts at antitrust legislation, as ownership of the organizations would now, at least in principle, be open to the public. It is doubtful, however, that these reorganizations will make the antitrust concerns disappear entirely, as publicly-traded corporations may still be liable for antitrust violations if they use their market power to stifle competition within a defined industry.

Adopting the Name VISA

The final organizational expansion to discuss was the adoption of the name we know the system by today—VISA.[21] It might seem strange to refer to a name change as an "expansion," but the adoption of the Visa name not only ties together the two structural expansions already discussed (Ibanco and duality), it also became the catalyst for an explosive growth in the membership, cardholder base, merchant acceptance, and sales volume, all of which would quickly make Visa the dominant bankcard system in the world.

The Need for a New Name

When the BofA originally licensed the BankAmericard program, they insisted that the name and the blue-white-and-gold bands design (the BWG mark) be used on every card, regardless of issuer. This was necessary to build the universal recognition and acceptance needed by any payment system. The licensee banks, however, always resented having to use the name "BankAmericard," as it evoked the name of the largest and most powerful bank in the nation, and made their banks look subordinate to it. Although the BASC eventually allowed the licensees to add their own name to the card, the BASC still required the BankAmericard name to be in larger, more prominent type.

If the BankAmericard name was merely contentious for the domestic licensees, it was completely unacceptable for most of the international ones, as it evoked not only the name of a powerful multi-national bank, but also a powerful foreign country. Thus, most of the international licensees negotiated the use of an entirely different name on the card, though they retained the same BWG mark. As a result, the

---

[20]Evans and Schmalensee (2005), pp. 281–284.

[21]As we shall see, VISA is technically an acronym, but it is commonly written in title case after first use.

BankAmericard was known as "Barclaycard" in the UK, "Sumitomocard" in Japan, "Chargex" in Canada, and "Carte Bleue" in France.[22]

This confusing array of names inhibited the universal acceptance that Hock desired. Merchants who saw few international travelers were unsure if they were allowed to accept cards that looked similar but had different names. If Hock was to build the truly universal, worldwide value exchange system he envisioned, he needed to create a new name that would be acceptable and appealing to cardholders, merchants, and the entire Ibanco membership.

But there was another, perhaps more important reason to change the name. When Hock was forming Ibanco, he and NBI's general counsel, Bennett Katz, approached the BofA about transferring ownership of the BWG mark to the new organization. The BofA responded that although they would be happy to license the mark to Ibanco, transferring ownership would not be possible, as the mark was too closely associated with the name BankAmericard, which was in turn closely associated with the Bank of America. Hock and Katz countered by arguing that if Ibanco could associate a different name with the mark, BofA should then have no objections to transferring ownership. BofA concurred, and signed an agreement to relinquish ownership of the mark to Ibanco, without additional compensation, provided that 95 percent of the membership, comprising 95 percent of the volume, adopted a new name within five years (i.e., by 1979).[23] Note that, at the time, the BofA generated more than five percent of the total volume, so this agreement gave the BofA the right to block a new name and card design if it was contrary to their interests.

Although the reasons for a new name are generally acknowledged by all sources, the creation of that name is a matter of contention. According to Hock, he and his staff developed a set of principles the new name needed to embrace, and then held an internal, "self-organizing" naming contest. The name "Visa" was suggested many times, but, because there were dozens of different recollections as to who originally suggested it, everyone was given the credit.[24] Honey contends that he suggested the name to Hock for the original debit card, but Hock reserved it for the overall name of the product and organization.[25] The Hoefer, Dietrich, and Brown advertising agency of San Francisco sued NBI/Visa in 1977, claiming that they suggested the name during an advertising pitch, but settled out of court when documents produced during discovery showed that the name had been generated internally prior to their presentation.[26]

---

[22]Some international licensees followed the domestic model of merely adding the licensee bank's name (e.g., "Banco de Bilbao BankAmericard"). For a pictorial catalog of the various international cards, see Nilson (September 1976), Report No 147, p. 2. Also note that the domestic Carte Bleue card was a national debit card only, so they issued a separate BWG card for use outside France.

[23]Katz and Honey interviews. See also Hock (2005), p. 216.

[24]Hock (2005), pp. 217–219. Goldsmith claims that he was the one who originally suggested the name to Hock (Goldsmith interview).

[25]Honey interview.

[26]Visa concept stolen by NBI says creative agency, Nilson (May 1977), Report No 163, p. 1; Nilson (March 1979), Report No 208, p. 2. NBI actually compensated a number of financial institutions

Redesigning the Card

Regardless of how the name was generated, NBI faced the arduous task of convincing the membership to adopt it. The domestic members would generally welcome it, but convincing BofA and the international members would be particularly difficult, as those banks currently had names on their cards that were strongly identified with their own organizations or services. To accommodate their concerns, Hock proposed what was known as the "tri-level marks" concept, described here in a speech from 1976:

> Card designs are ... self-limiting. They do not accommodate evolving services or equitably balance the legitimate needs of involved parties. The ideal design would accommodate marks owned by an individual bank, representing services available only from it. It would accommodate marks owned by an association of banks within a country, representing services good only in that country. It would accommodate marks owned by an international organization representing services which are universal throughout the world.[27]

With this new concept, Hock made an important philosophical shift regarding the nature of the card. He now saw it as a substrate that could carry any number of marks identifying not only the issuer, but also a range of services available to the cardholder. It was still an identity device, but it would now identify the cardholder to not only the BankAmericard service, but also any of the other services advertised upon it.

The task of redesigning the card and implementing the name change fell to a product developer named Tom Honey. While pursuing a graduate degree, Honey had been fascinated by an article on the future of electronic funds transfer (EFT) written by John Fisher of City National Bank and Trust (Columbus, OH), the same bank that conducted the full EFT test discussed in Chap. 4. Honey went to work for Wells Fargo Bank and the Bank of California, installing one of the first ATMs in the US in late 1971, and becoming generally acquainted with all the new banking technologies. He eventually interviewed with Hock, who saw in Honey a kindred passion and vision. Honey joined NBI in 1973 and developed their first debit card, named Entrée, which will be discussed in detail in Chap. 8.

In keeping with the tri-level marks concept, Honey and his team developed a new design for the card and merchant signs:

> We kicked around various design options until it became clear: we would put the VISA name in the middle white band of both the card and merchant decal and allow every issuer to use the top blue band of the card for their own name and service indicia. That solved both our international issuer problem and the Bank of America problem. We just added VISA to the card name.[28]

---

that had already used the Visa name in one way or the other. See Chutkow (2001), p. 217; and Nilson (March 1977), Report No 160, p. 1.

[27] Hock (1976), p. 9.

Fig. 6.1 A redesigned Visa card from Bank of America. BofA was allowed to retain their BankAmericard mark in the *top blue band*, but the new Visa name was added to the *center white band*. Other banks would include their own names or marks in the *blue band* (author's personal collection)

This solution not only placated BofA and the international members, it also solved a nagging problem that had existed from the early days of the licensing program. For reasons unknown, merchant signs had always featured the BankAmericard name in the white band, rather than in the blue band as it was on the card. With the new design, the merchant signs and cards were now identical.

More importantly, Honey's new design also included a phased reduction in the size of the marks so that the issuing organization could control more of the front of the card. The first phase would simply add the Visa name to the white band, but the second phase would reduce the colored bands and Visa name to a small rectangle either in the center or the lower-right corner of the card.[29] In a proposed third phase, which has not yet occurred, the entire mark would be moved to the back of the card where the various ATM network marks appear today.[30]

With these phases, Honey was making a subtle but important distinction between *brand* and *mark*, asserting that Visa was actually the latter and not the former. The issuing organization established the brand, and Visa was simply a mark that was

---

[28]Honey correspondence.

[29]It was first moved to the center, and then to the lower-right where it remains today, though Visa has recently removed the colored bands from the mark. Pictures of the centered placement can be seen in Chutkow (2001), p. 215.

[30]This was one of the key reasons cited by Citibank for leaving the Visa system in 1998. See Evans and Schmalensee (2005), p. 171.

added to identify an available service. This allowed banks to issue locally-branded cards that could access a number of different financial service networks. In many ways, the Visa mark is similar to other so-called "ingredient brands," such as Intel Inside®, or Dolby® sound.[31]

Furthermore, the tri-level marks concept also allowed for a compromise that would eventually entice most of America's major retailers to accept the card. Recall that the large-scale merchants had always resisted bankcards because they threatened the loyalty gained through the merchant's proprietary card. But since those merchant-specific cards were rarely profitable, a bankcard that allowed merchants to sell off their receivables to a bank, while retaining their identity on the card, would be an acceptable compromise. The new card design allowed for just that; Visa members could offer merchants a card with the merchant's name in the blue band, and enable any set of incentives the merchant wanted to offer customers. Once the Visa marks were reduced in size, the merchant could further customize the look of the card, making it appear like they simply added the Visa marks to their original, proprietary card.[32]

Implementing the Name

Redesigning the card and merchant signs was relatively easy, but getting the members to implement these changes would be much more difficult. Every merchant acquirer had to replace every sign and decal at each of their merchant locations, and in Japan this included thousands of expensive, lighted "Sumitomocard" signs. Every issuer had to print and distribute new cards to every cardholder. All the members had to replace all their paper forms, and run advertisements informing the public that the name was changing. All of this implied a significant cost that created a natural incentive for the members to resist a rapid changeover. NBI's management realized that they needed a catalyst that would push at least the domestic members to implement the change quickly.

Although I have presented the duality issue and the name change in separate sections, they were actually occurring at the same time and must be understood in relation. When the DOJ issued the review letter, NBI's management knew that they must remove the ban on dual membership. But they also saw the opportunity to create the catalyst they needed for a rapid implementation of the Visa name, and set about mixing the ingredients.

In May 1976, the NBI Board approved the name change to Visa, and the Ibanco Board followed suit in August. In June of the same year, NBI lifted the ban on dual membership and approached a few strategic Interbank members, inviting them to join NBI. In September, NBI formally announced the new Visa name.[33] In March

---

[31] Honey interview.

[32] For a report on the card done for the Woolworth Company, then the fourth largest retailer in America, see Nilson (August 1981), Report No 266, p. 1.

[33] Nilson (September 1976), Report No 147, p. 2.

1977, Ibanco was renamed to Visa International Services Association (creating the recursive acronym VISA), and NBI was renamed to Visa USA. The membership was then given six months to replace their merchant signs, and an ample two years after that to reissue the new cards. Visa USA then began a multi-million dollar national advertising campaign, supported by additional local member advertising, informing the public that BankAmericard was now becoming Visa.

What happened next is the key to understanding the reaction. Those few strategic Interbank members, now Visa USA members as well, then began sending out applications to consumers in their area, including those holding BankAmericards issued by their local competitors, offering to convert consumers to this new Visa card they were hearing so much about. One of those new members was Citibank, then the second largest bank in the nation, and they went one step further by sending out applications across the *entire nation* starting in the fall of 1977.[34] Consumers, who were being barraged with ads promoting the new name, were expecting something related to the new card, and typically did not notice that the offer came from a different bank, nor did the applications make that particularly obvious. Even if they did, it is doubtful that most Americans would have noticed—*Business Week* reported a couple of years earlier that "an estimated 60% of the 55 million holders of national bank cards do not know which bank issued their cards or processes their accounts."[35] The old BankAmericard issuers, who were planning to phase in their new Visa cards slowly over two years, saw what was happening, realized they could lose their cardholder base, and rushed to re-issue the new Visa cards. Meanwhile, they had little time to apply for membership in Interbank, much less think about issuing Master Charge cards.

The strategy was highly effective, simultaneously forcing a rapid implementation of the new name, and delaying the Visa USA members from joining Interbank and issuing Master Charge cards. The number of card-issuing banks in the Visa system increased from 8,983 at the beginning of 1977 to 10,836 in 1978, a 20% increase in one year, and the number of active accounts jumped by 45% during the same period.[36] Soon afterward, a consumer opinion survey found that the sample not only understood that BankAmericard had become Visa, but a large portion of respondents also thought that *Master Charge* had become Visa as well.[37]

The creation of Ibanco, the establishment of duality, and the name change to Visa all combined to create an explosive growth that quickly made Visa the dominant card system in the world. By the first quarter of 1978, Visa had surpassed Interbank's sales volume both in the US and worldwide.[38]

---

[34] 'A Visa-card offensive angers the opposition', Business Week (5 September 1977), p. 31. See also Nilson (February 1977), Report No 157, p. 2; and for Nilson's accusation that Citibank was sending out applications indiscriminately, see Nilson (February 1978), Report No 180, p. 1.

[35] 'Bank cards take over the country', Business Week (4 August 1975), p. 53. See also, 'Visa-card offensive angers the opposition', Business Week (5 September 1977), p. 31.

[36] Nilson (July 1980), Report No 240, p. 1.

[37] Honey interview.

[38] 'Visa's climb to No. 1 in cards', Business Week (17 July 1978), p. 26.

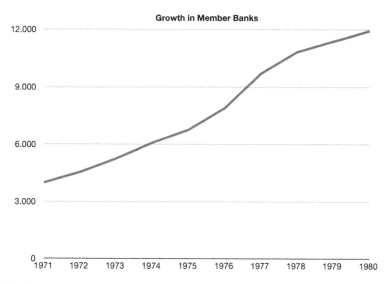

Fig. 6.2 Growth in Member Banks, 1971–1980 (*source*: Dougherty). For more system statistics, see Appendix

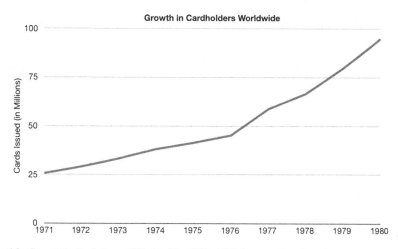

Fig. 6.3 Growth in Cards Issued Worldwide, 1971–1980 (*source*: Dougherty)

Expanding the Computer Systems

As the organization expanded, so did the computer systems, and these two developments must be understood in relation. Although the organizational changes just discussed contributed to Visa's explosive growth during the latter 1970s, the critical changes made to BASE I and II during this same period allowed them to *handle* that growth, and ultimately led to even further expansion of the payment system.

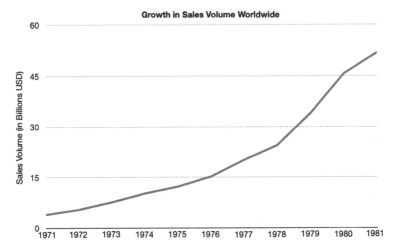

Fig. 6.4 Growth in Worldwide Sales Volume, 1971–1980 (source: Dougherty)

These changes can be grouped into three principal areas. First, BASE I's capacity was significantly increased by re-implementing it on IBM hardware and the Airline Control Program (ACP) originally developed for the Sabre airline reservation system. Second, another data center was opened on the East Coast, running in parallel with the one in San Mateo. Third, the computer systems were extended internationally to provide automated authorizations, and eventually clearing and settlement, to all Visa International members. We will now examine each of these in turn.

Expanding BASE I's Capacity

The dependability of BASE I has always been a top priority for Visa's computer systems staff. Visa's existence largely depends on their ability to offer a payment service upon which cardholders, merchants, and members can rely, and the authorization service is the primary and most common point of contact for those groups. If BASE I is unavailable, or misbehaves in some way, customer confidence can quickly erode, devaluing the card as a payment device. Visa employees call this the "back of the wallet" effect—if a cardholder is improperly denied an authorization, the cardholder typically moves that card to the back of the wallet, and will choose other methods of payment for future transactions.[39]

---

[39] Elliott interview.

Capacity in Real-Time Systems

As discussed in Chap. 4, the design of the original BASE I included a few key mechanisms to ensure the availability of the authorization service. All critical telecommunications and computer hardware had redundant backups. The central switch also had the ability to stand-in and approve transactions when the issuer's host computer or personnel did not respond. NBI could also stand-in for the acquirers, answering authorization calls after the acquiring centers closed for the night.

There was another threat to availability, however, against which redundant hardware and logic could not guard—overwhelming the system's *capacity*. In any real-time, transaction-processing system, there is a somewhat fixed number of transactions the system can process at any given time. Once the concurrent transaction load reaches this amount, the system cannot accept more, and becomes unavailable until the existing transactions are processed. Often a queuing mechanism is used to hold new transactions until they can be processed, but eventually the CPU spends so much of its time switching between tasks and managing the queue that it simply cannot accept more transactions. If the software developers anticipate this condition, the system will gracefully reject new transactions, asking the sender to try again later; if they do not, the system often crashes.

For BASE I in particular, the floor limits provided a crude but effective mechanism for tempering the transaction load. Each merchant had a limit under which the transaction was automatically authorized. NBI also established interchange floor limits for the acquirers, under which the acquirer could authorize the transaction without contacting the issuer. But the interchange floor limits were removed shortly after BASE I was put into production, and the merchant floor limits were reduced in an effort to stem fraud. Thus, the transaction load began to increase.

It is important to emphasize, however, that the main threat to capacity is not the aggregate transaction load experienced over a given period, but the peak. Authorizations in particular have a more or less predictable ebb and flow cycle, with dramatic peaks occurring at certain times, and on certain days. But how high those peaks will reach can only be estimated, and if the estimates are too low, the system will become unavailable at the most inopportune time.

BASE I was just over a year old when the system capacity was exceeded by an unexpectedly large peak:

> ... the day after Thanksgiving [1974] was the biggest shopping day of the year. Now over time that's changed a little, but for many years, the Friday after Thanksgiving was *the* volume day. Well anyway, BASE I died a horrible death; several times ... they would have an [acquirer] that would choke them to death and cause it to crash. Well instead of shutting down the big users, bringing it back up and letting it start to breathe again, they just brought it all back up and guess what? It went right back down again. That day was one of the most horrible in Visa.[40]

An experienced systems developer named Frank Fojtik led a team to expand BASE I's capacity. Fojtik was exactly the sort of technical person Hock admired.

---

[40]Fojtik interview.

Speaking with a no-nonsense Texan drawl, Fojtik remarked that his technical expertise was the result of "a whole lot of scars I got on my ass" while working with cutting-edge technology, and he summarized the entire Visa mission by saying, "if you can't recognize [the card], it ain't worth much; if it don't work, it's worth even less." Fojtik had been recently hired from Singer, where he had worked on electronic cash registers, and developed a number of networked, transaction-processing computer systems.

DEC or IBM?

Fojtik and his team were able to reorganize the structure of BASE I to achieve enough capacity to survive the 1975 Christmas shopping season, but they all knew it was merely a temporary solution. After the ban on dual membership was lifted in 1976, both the aggregate and peak volumes dramatically increased, and the systems group was now faced with a difficult decision: should they upgrade to the new DEC PDP-11/70; or should they switch over to the IBM System/370 mainframe line? Hock, in his usual style, declared that the decision would be made by all the key technical staff after considering the arguments presented from both sides. But instead of letting the IBM and DEC sales people in the room, he assigned members of his own technical staff to make the case for each alternative, arguing that his own staff would think in terms of what was best for Visa, and would ultimately need to believe in the solution. Fojtik served as DEC's champion, and Derman pitched IBM.[41]

The argument for upgrading to the next PDP-11 was relatively easy to make, as it featured the same type of architecture and thus required little change to the BASE I software. DEC, however, was suspiciously vague about when another, more powerful PDP-11 might be available, leading the technical staff to wonder about the long-term prospects of that platform.

The argument for moving to the IBM System/370 line rested primarily on their seamless upgradability. If their current mainframe ran out of capacity, it could be replaced with another more powerful one without any changes to the application software. IBM had a number of 370s already in production, and more planned for the future. More importantly, IBM had become the standard in the banking world, and would thus be easier to sell to the Board of Directors. But this approach also required a re-implementation of the BASE I system, as the IBM environment was completely different.

Hock held a lengthy meeting, listening to the arguments, pitting his staff against one another, and challenging all their assumptions. But it was mostly a charade—Hock had already made up his mind earlier, but wanted his staff to come to the same conclusion. Chuck Russell conveyed how the decision was actually made:

---

[41] Information on the DEC vs. IBM decision comes from interviews with Derman, Fojtik, Peirce, Schramm, and Russell. There is some disagreement as to who voted for which alternative, but as we shall see, it mattered little in the end.

Dee was leaning toward re-upping with DEC, but before so doing, decided to give IBM one more shot. He asked the SFO [San Francisco] IBM chief, Bob Irwin, to come in with his right hand man, Roger Peirce, and meet with him and me to tell us why we should go with IBM.

Now you have to understand that, at that time, SFO was considered *Siberia* by IBM ... Bob no longer "fit in" at IBM because he was considered "uncouth" by the then button-down culture, which prevailed during the 70's and 80's at IBM ... [So] Bob was banished to SFO ... [but Bob and Roger] were/are two of the brightest individuals I've ever worked with.

Get this picture. Bob and Roger walk into Dee's office. Bob is reasonably well dressed, but he's wearing well-polished *GI paratrooper boots*! Roger has a button-down shirt on, but it looks like he slept in it, and his hair apparently hadn't seen a comb in weeks! This duet put on a presentation right out of Tom [Watson] Sr.'s book. Blunt, honest, brief and to the point, and not one ounce of BS or political correctness. It would have curdled the button-down set's milk!

At the end of their presentation, Dee, in his usual fashion, commenced hassling them. After two or three minutes, Bob got up and said, "Look Dee, if you're too f—— dumb to understand the difference between what IBM brings to the table, vs. what DEC can do, you're wasting my time," whereupon both he and Roger walked out of Dee's office and slammed the door behind themselves.

Dee, rarely at a loss for words, was speechless for a few moments, then he turned to me, and said, "Hell, chief, if they feel that strongly, they are the people to go with." And that's how the decision was made.[42]

Airline Control Program

Thus it was decided to re-implement BASE I on the IBM hardware platform, but this resulted in a new dilemma: which operating system should they use? IBM offered a few choices at this time, the most common being MVS, but this was designed primarily for controlling batch-oriented applications, not real-time systems. In 1969, IBM had released what became their most well-known transaction processing monitor, called the Customer Information Control System (CICS).[43] But Peirce thought that it was not reliable enough at the time for Visa's needs. It was also relatively inefficient, and would have required an excess of powerful and expensive hardware to achieve the necessary capacity.[44]

There was, however, another less well-known operating system offered by IBM that Peirce thought would be perfect: the Airline Control Program (ACP). The design of ACP was originally developed for the Sabre airline reservation system, which was a joint project between IBM and American Airlines in the early 1960s.[45]

---

[42]Russell correspondence.

[43]This was actually one of IBM's first software "products" sold independently of the hardware. See Ceruzzi (1998), p. 106. Note that CICS is actually a subsystem designed to run on MVS, not a full operating system itself.

[44]Peirce interview.

[45]For information on Sabre, see Copeland et al. (1995), Knight (1972), Head (2002), and Campbell-Kelly (2003), pp. 41–45. For a detailed review of ACP/TPF, see Siwiec (1977), pp. 169–195, and Scrutchin (1987), pp. 158–160. Additional information on ACP comes from interviews with Peirce, Fojtik, Totten, Reid, vonGillern, and Boston. Although the name "Sabre" is often written in all capitals, it was never an acronym, and was actually derived from the Buick LeSabre.

After Sabre went into full production, IBM enhanced the system based on their initial experience, and repackaged it in a more generic form, known as Programmed Airline Reservation System (PARS). PARS was adopted by most of the major US airlines, and further enhanced based on its observed performance. The operating system that controlled the PARS application programs, which comprised most of the code base, was broken out and licensed separately as ACP beginning in 1972.[46] It was eventually renamed Transaction Processing Facility (TPF), and it is still the heart of most airline, hotel, and car rental reservation systems.

ACP is a rather unique operating system and database in one. It was specifically designed for the airline reservation environment, meaning that it is extremely adept at processing an unpredictably-large number of simultaneous transactions, each of which require little CPU time and limited but specialized operating system services. The goal of ACP was to enable the applications to process most transactions within just a few seconds, allowing the reservations clerk to keep up a normal flow of conversation with the customer.[47] In fact, the ACP designers considered the reservations clerk, as well as the system operators, to be crucial elements of an overall system comprised of both humans and machines.[48] This view led to a number of features not commonly observed in other 1970s-era operating systems, nor even in those existing today.

To ensure that the system met the needs of the reservations agent, it was designed to do a few specific things as quickly as possible. The operating system itself was small and light-weight, consuming little memory and CPU cycles for its own work. Its network control routines were highly-tuned, imposing less than five percent overhead on the CPU, compared to over 30 percent in other operating systems.[49] It also processed transactions in parallel using a cooperative "multiprogramming" approach.[50] This was a kind of non-preemptive multitasking, which is usually quite dangerous, as programs only yield when they need data from a peripheral device, but since PARS and BASE I transactions are of short duration and always need to access peripherals, this approach was satisfactory for the time. Whenever an existing transaction needed data from a file or the network, ACP suspended that transaction and began processing new ones until the requested data were fully read and available in memory. This allowed ACP to process a large number of transactions simultaneously.

ACP was also designed to help the operators keep the system up and running. All normal maintenance could be performed while the system was still online. New versions of the application programs could be loaded dynamically without shutting down. All key system metrics could be constantly monitored, and all significant

---

[46]Siwiec (1977), p. 173.

[47]Knight (1972), pp. 1424–1425.

[48]Siwiec (1977), pp. 171–172.

[49]Knight (1972), p. 1426. One IBM developer noted that this came with a certain risk—the system was not terribly protected, and one could easily write code that could bypass safeguards in order to obtain the necessary performance.

[50]Knight (1972), p. 1427.

activity was both logged and streamed to a printer or terminal.[51] Most ACP installations used multiple, redundant CPUs, and ACP could automatically switch to the secondary when the primary failed or needed maintenance. The database could also be mirrored onto redundant disks, allowing quick recovery. And since no system is ever perfect, ACP was designed to restart after a crash in just a few seconds, as opposed to the multiple minutes required by other operating systems.[52]

These technical features were no doubt appealing, but perhaps the main selling point of ACP was that PARS provided a clear example of a working ACP system that was already operating at a scale far beyond BASE I. The original capacity requirement for BASE I was 3,500 authorizations per hour, and by 1976 this had climbed to 50,000, or nearly 14 per second; in contrast, the existing PARS installations were processing 50 to 75 transactions per second.[53] Furthermore, IBM's testing had shown that the transaction throughput was more or less linear with the CPU speed, suggesting that capacity would continue to grow as IBM developed faster processors.[54] BASE I was also much simpler than PARS, and required far less disk access per transaction.

The actual re-implementation of BASE I was accomplished by an IBM programming team familiar with ACP, and was completed in less than a year.[55] Fojtik stressed that this was almost an entire re-design of the system, as there was little documentation on the existing BASE I, and the ACP environment required a completely different approach. Once the software was ready, Peirce installed two IBM System/370 model 138 mainframes in the San Mateo center, one being a redundant backup for the other. The authorization messages were cutover to the new IBM system in late 1977, resulting in an estimated three-fold increase in capacity.[56]

Beyond the initial increases, moving to the IBM platform also allowed Visa to continue expanding their capacity without adjusting the software. The instruction set for the IBM System/370 mainframes remained backwards compatible, allowing one to run software developed for an earlier model on a later, more powerful model without modification.

---

[51]This was also necessary in order to debug the system, as some logic errors may only occur under certain timing-dependent conditions. The logged information could also be analyzed to determine the actual usage of the system and tune it accordingly.

[52]Siwiec (1977), pp. 171–172.

[53]BASE I numbers come from Tootelian and Peirce interviews. PARS numbers come from Siwiec (1977), p. 172. For comparison, Visa claims that their average peak in February 2007 was 6,800 per second, and their peak capacity was 13,000 per second. See http://corporate.visa.com/md/fs/corporate/visanet.jsp (accessed on 12 February 2007).

[54]Siwiec (1977), p. 174.

[55]Peirce interview.

[56]Peirce and Schramm interviews.

Multiple Data Centers

Although moving to IBM and ACP would greatly enhance the capacity and dependability of the BASE I installation at San Mateo, there was still only one data center, and all interchange authorization traffic flowed through it. While BASE I was being re-implemented on ACP, John Totten, who transferred to BASE I after BASE III was canceled, expressed concern to Hock and Russell about this single point of failure:

> I remember going in for some work on the budgeting numbers in December 1976, and I said, "… here we are, providing the service off of one computer in one data center, which is made out of wood, combustible wood, on a hillside that has dry grass, above a road where a car could catch on fire; we're right below a parking lot where kids are parking their cars, and the cars could come off the edge and drop into the building; and not only that, we're a mile from the San Andreas fault! How many more threats could you take on? If your goal is to run the credit card industry of the world, we really should have some sort of redundant, parallel site."
>
> I went back in [on Monday] and Dee said, "you know, we thought about what you said, and you're right. You have a new job. Your new job is to go somewhere on the East Coast, find a site and build a center." Nothing more. No papers. Nothing more than, "we thought about it, now let's do it." … and Dee said, "Oh, and by the way, this has to be up by July 1977." So we had six months to find a site, build it, and staff it.[57]

Selecting the Site

Totten returned to the San Mateo center and set about establishing the criteria by which he would choose the site. First and foremost, they needed a highly-reliable and secure telecommunications service, so the new site had to be wired for the new digital communications system recently offered from AT&T. The new site also needed to be in a location where a suitable workforce would want to live. Totten toured the East Coast and came back with a recommendation. Unfortunately, he neglected to consider the criteria that would be most important to Hock:

> The city we recommended was Charlotte, North Carolina, not McLean. Because McLean was much more expensive … so we came back and made the recommendation to Dee … and he said "Charlotte—who knows about that kind of place? I'm in the process of making a major move to take electronic banking into Europe, and I want to have the letter head, when someone in Europe sees it, to know that it's an important place. Now McLean, Virginia, is that near DC?" And I said, "yeah, it's right across the river." He said, "could we use a Washington DC address on our letterhead?" and Dave Hall [who joined Totten's team] said, "yes, I've already checked it out and there's a box, we've already signed up for, out at Dulles airport, which has a Washington DC address." And Dee said, "well that's it!"[58]

Hock was always conscious of Visa's image, not only with the public, but also within the banking industry. At this time, Visa's headquarters were in San Francisco, the banking capital of the West Coast, and Hock wanted Visa's presence on the East

---

[57] Totten interview. Information on the creation of the East Coast data center comes from interviews with Totten, Peirce, Derman, and Fojtik.

[58] Totten interview.

Coast to be in a similarly important place (presumably New York was not an option). Although Visa eventually moved its headquarters to San Mateo and then Foster City (smaller towns south of San Francisco), they still maintained a San Francisco mailing address by renting a post office box at the nearby San Francisco Airport.[59]

Totten selected a site in McLean that was on the same telephone grid as the CIA, something he felt would provide the security and reliability he wanted. He chose a steel-framed building that was still under construction, and leased the top two floors, which were then finished before the lower floors. When they moved in, the elevators were not even working yet, so the employees had to climb the exposed stairs. Totten remarked, "That was the typical way of Visa: we figured out every way to skin the cat to get it done quicker."

The new center was built and staffed by the July 1977 deadline, but Totten and his staff were still awaiting their redundant pair of IBM mainframes as well as the new BASE I software. Since they had a robust telecommunication system, they established a merchant authorization call center, similar to the one in San Mateo, providing backup and off-hours coverage for the acquirers in the eastern half of the country. Soon afterwards, the computers and the BASE I software arrived, and they set about installing the first dual-site ACP system.[60]

Designing a Dual-Switch ACP System

The main goal of creating the second data center was to provide a full, redundant backup system in another location. It would be somewhat wasteful, however, to leave that system dormant until the primary system failed, which was the common practice for redundant mainframes within a single center. Instead, while the IBM programming team was re-implementing BASE I on ACP, they also added the features necessary to run multiple, cooperative systems in parallel. This was rather innovative at the time, as none of the airlines had ever run more than one concurrent ACP installation.

To accomplish this, a new telecommunication circuit was run from the McLean center to each end-point on the existing BASE I network. Each end-point had an affinity to a primary data center where it sent all of its outgoing authorization requests, but it could receive incoming authorizations from either center. If the primary center stopped responding, the end-point would automatically begin sending requests to the secondary center.

Running parallel authorization systems, however, required more than just switching the network. Recall that BASE I has the ability to stand-in for issuers and authorize transactions on their behalf when their systems are unavailable. The policies that dictate how much BASE I may approve over how long a period, the authorizations it approves under these conditions, as well as the card numbers that should be automatically denied, are all kept in the ACP database. These data, and changes to

---

[59]Cleveland (1999), p. 47.

[60]Totten and Fojtik interviews.

them, also needed to be replicated between the centers to ensure that no information was lost during an outage. To accommodate this, BASE I was enhanced to send data change notification messages between the various installations.

The dual-switch approach provided Visa with not only some added protection against regional threats, but also a convenient way to conduct major maintenance on a center without shutting off the entire service. If they needed to shut down the San Mateo center for any reason, all traffic could be switched to the McLean center in a matter of minutes. Either center was capable of handling the entire load on its own.

The dual-switch concept proved to be so successful that Visa eventually added major centers in England and Japan as well. All four centers run simultaneously, handling the authorizations for their given area, but the centers in the US and England can handle the entire world's traffic alone if needed.[61]

Expanding Internationally

International Authorizations

Moving BASE I to IBM/ACP and opening the second data center gave Visa the capacity it needed to handle the growing volume of domestic interchange authorizations. *International* authorizations, however, were still quite slow and cumbersome. If a US cardholder made purchases in a foreign country, the acquirer needed to telex the issuing bank to obtain an authorization. The process was just as inefficient as domestic authorizations prior to BASE I, but suffered further due to the greater difference in time zones.

The ultimate goal was to expand the online computer network internationally, but in the 1970s this was not entirely practical, so Fojtik developed a rather ingenious stopgap. Building on a similar system he had done for Singer, Fojtik wrote some software that emulated a telex and provided a bridge to BASE I. When a foreign bank needed an authorization on a US card, they telexed a new number in San Mateo, which corresponded to a modem connected to one of the old PDP-11s. Fojtik's software then read the request, parsed it, reformatted it into a BASE I authorization request message, and submitted it to the switch. A few seconds later, his program received the response, which it then reformatted into a telex reply message. Because the operating regulations stipulated the proper ordering of the telexed information, it was rather easy to write the parsing software, and Fojtik remarked that it was actually quite forgiving. Because card numbers, expiration dates, and amounts were all distinctly recognizable, the software allowed them to be in almost any order with any amount of whitespace in between. Using this system, foreign acquirers could now obtain international authorizations within a few seconds, at any time.[62]

---

[61] Sources indicated that a fifth center has been added in the US, but it is unclear if this new center will replace one of the existing ones.

[62] Fojtik interview.

This "auto-telex" system was eventually replaced when the online computer network was expanded into other countries. The first links were to the UK and Canada in 1977, and within a decade, Visa had amassed enough leased lines and satellite links to connect every member bank and processor on the planet.[63]

Multi-Currency Clearing and Settlement

BASE II also expanded outside the US, though it was not until the mid 1980s that transactions were settled in multiple currencies, a necessary feature for the payment system to be considered truly "international."[64] From the early days of the BankAmericard licensing program, it was agreed that foreign transactions would be cleared and settled in US dollars only. The currency conversion was done by the acquirer, and although the operating regulations established certain limits on how and when this should be accomplished, most acquirers used this system to their own advantage.

In the late 1970s, the international members began using BASE II for electronic clearing and settlement, but transactions were still converted to US dollars by the acquirer, who chose the most opportune time to perform the conversion. They also typically increased the rate by a few percentage points in their favor to cover their conversion costs. For highly-volatile currencies, this could result in substantial profits for the acquirer. Cardholders were also confused when they received their bills, as the amount was not expressed in the local currency, and the dollar amount was converted at a different rate from the one in effect when the purchase was made.

The Eurocard system, which was affiliated with MasterCard in the US, began offering multi-currency settlement to their European members in the early 1980s, and MasterCard had announced that their US dollar members would also participate in that scheme starting in 1986. A team at Visa, headed by a foreign exchange expert named David Nordemann, was charged with developing a similar feature.

Nordemann devised an approach that would allow all members to clear and settle with the Visa system in one of many supported currencies.[65] Visa, as the central clearinghouse, would then perform all currency conversions using the wholesale exchange rates, plus a percentage fee that could be divided between the acquiring and issuing regions. This fee was primarily designed to compensate the acquirers who would now lose the income they gained from controlling the conversion rate. Issuers were also allowed to add a few percentage points to foreign transactions, provided it was allowed under local law. Many issuers today charge between one and three percent for foreign currency transactions, and recent laws in the US now

---

[63] 'Visa verification net reaches UK, Canada', American Banker (22 July 1977), p. 1.

[64] Information on multi-currency clearing and settlement comes from interviews with Nordemann and Schonheyder.

[65] As of 2007, Visa clears in 172 currencies and settles in 16 (http://corporate.visa.com/md/fs/corporate/visanet.jsp, accessed on 12 February 2007).

require that this be made explicit, as it was previously buried in the exchange rate reported on the bill.

The Board accepted the proposal, and multi-currency settlement began in 1986. Implementing this in the BASE II software posed certain challenges, but finding a bank that would commit to fixed currency exchange rates each day was even more difficult. In order for multi-currency clearing and settlement to work, BASE II needed a set of conversion rates that would remain constant from the moment the data collection began to the final transfer of funds several hours later. During that time, the currency exchange rates continued to fluctuate, so any bank willing to act as Visa's currency trader would be taking a significant risk. Eventually Barclay's, which had a large foreign exchange department, agreed to play this role, and was able to mitigate the risk by closely monitoring the markets and quoting rates based on their projections.

Multi-currency clearing and settlement is one of those quiet features that does not get the appreciation it truly deserves. Extending the authorization network internationally was certainly important, but allowing members to clear and settle in their own native currency established Visa as *the* premier worldwide payment system. With the addition of this feature, Hock's original vision of a global system for the exchange of value was nearly fulfilled.

Conclusion

In this chapter, we examined the various ways in which the payment system was expanded, both organizationally and technically, throughout the latter 1970s. The organizational expansions touched off an explosive period of growth for Visa, establishing them as the dominant bankcard system. To understand this period correctly, however, one must consider the changes to the organization and the computer systems together. The enhanced computer systems not only enabled Visa to handle the dramatic growth, they also made the entire payment system even more attractive to prospective members.

Nevertheless, there was one aspect of the payment system that still fell short of Hock's expectations: the point of sale. Most merchants were still grappling with cumbersome hot card lists, paper sales drafts, and card imprinters. In order to make the Visa system a common, and ultimately preferred method of payment, they needed to eliminate the paper entirely, and capture the transaction electronically at the point of sale, even at the smallest of merchants. It is to this story that we now turn.

Chapter 7
Automating the Point of Sale: Encoding Standards and Merchant Dial Terminals

In the previous chapter, we saw how NBI/Visa expanded during the 1970s to become the dominant worldwide bankcard system. This was accomplished through a number of changes, both to the organization and the computer systems, which ignited an explosive period of growth for Visa, both in terms of sales volume and capacity.

In this chapter, we will examine the last area of the payment system to become fully automated: the point of sale (POS). Although a few banks began deploying POS terminals in the early 1970s, most merchants were still referencing dense lists of invalid card numbers, telephoning for verbal authorization, and manually completing paper sales drafts. Floor limits reduced the number of transactions requiring authorization, but they also allowed too much undetectable fraud and credit losses: an estimated one billion USD each year.[1] If the Visa payment system was ever to become a true replacement for cash and checks, this first link in the payment chain needed to be automated fully, even at the smallest of merchants.

Hock's philosophy typically dictated that what happened between the merchant and the acquirer was their business, and Visa's influence on that relationship should be limited only to those aspects necessary to ensure the health and stability of the overall system. For most of the 1970s, Visa stayed out of the point of sale, concentrating instead on automating the exchange of information between members. This allowed the innovative banks to experiment with various kinds of POS terminals and card-encoding methods. As the banks committed significant amounts of time and money to their various solutions, intense debates broke out regarding which should become the national, and ultimately international, standard.

At the turn of the 1980s, Visa decided it was time to intervene, and forced a certain amount of closure to these debates through two important actions. First, they mandated that all Visa cards issued after 1980 include a magnetic stripe encoded to their standard, effectively ending the card-encoding debate. Second, they encouraged the widespread use of POS terminals by stimulating equipment manufacturers to build inexpensive devices that used standard voice telephone lines, and providing

---

[1] 'Visa dial terminal pilot project final report' (April 1982), p. 1.

D.L. Stearns, *Electronic Value Exchange*, History of Computing,
DOI 10.1007/978-1-84996-139-4_7, © Springer-Verlag London Limited 2011

the economic incentives necessary for merchants to adopt them. These actions created the conditions by which full POS automation could be achieved at the national, and eventually international, level.

Before we examine these two moves in detail, however, we must first briefly discuss the technical vision that informed them. This vision, and the various steps needed to achieve it, were developed during a project known as BASE IV.

Dreaming the Future: BASE IV

In 1974, after BASE II was put into production and the first version of BASE III was nearing completion, Hock began another systems development project that was his most ambitious yet. It was duly named BASE IV, but it also went by another name that was perhaps more descriptive for Hock: Electronic Value Exchange (EVE).

Electronic Value Exchange

Throughout the mid-1970s, the American banking industry was preoccupied with the possibilities of electronic funds transfer (EFT). Bankers were eager to replace cash and checks with seemingly less expensive cards, terminals, and automated clearing houses (ACHs). ATMs also promised to reduce the need for tellers and their corresponding labor costs. From Hock's perspective however, the bankers were simply trying to automate the existing forms of banking rather than re-imagining how banking's central function, value exchange, should occur in an entirely electronic world. In his speeches, he exhorted bankers to think not just of EFT, but also the broader concept of EVE, lest they "may swiftly be hooting in the commercial graveyard where the ghosts of form, which did not follow function, are buried."[2]

BASE IV was Hock's own attempt at imagining a world in which every financial transaction was completed entirely in electronic form. In this world, transactions could originate from any device, be it a POS terminal, a cash dispensing machine, a pre-authorized transfer, or even a telephone banking interface.[3] Those transactions might access any asset the payor owns: not just a credit line, but also deposits, or even liquid investments. Similarly, those transactions might credit any asset the payee owns. In the middle would be a switching system that has connections to all the devices and all the assets, or at least to other networks that can reach those assets. This switching system, which would of course be built and operated by NBI/Visa,

---

[2]Hock (1974), p. 8.

[3]In the 1970s, the word "terminal" was often used for any kind of origination device. In order to avoid confusion, I will use the more distinctive terms employed today. By "POS terminal," I mean a device used to authorize (and possibly capture) transactions at the point of sale, and by "ATM" or "cash dispenser," I mean a device used primarily to obtain currency.

would connect everyone's assets together, making them accessible from any device, at any time. This, for Hock, was the essence of electronic value exchange.

IBM and Compata were hired to write the functional specifications for a system that could bring Hock's vision of EVE to life, and by 1975, their work filled a number of large binders. But that was as concrete as the system ever became. When BASE III was canceled, BASE IV met a similar demise, for three principal reasons. First, most of BASE IV's components were intended to run in the member processing centers, and BASE III had demonstrated that NBI should not be in that business. Second, the necessary technologies were either unavailable at that time, or were far too expensive for the system to be economically feasible. Third, it was unclear whether the public was actually ready to abandon cash and checks for electronic transactions. Peirce counseled Hock and Russell to "stick [the design] on the shelf and go on with something else, because you'll never be able to build this system. The world's not ready for this."[4]

Gems in the Rubble

Although BASE IV was never built, it still had a profound influence on the evolution of the core payment system. Peirce explained:

> The value of BASE IV was that it defined an end point and identified the building blocks and standards required to reach that end point. Almost everything we did subsequent to BASE IV was consistent with it.[5]

Two of Visa's subsequent actions—standardizing how the cards should be encoded, and stimulating the development and adoption of affordable POS terminals—will be discussed in detail in the following sections. But there was another key idea generated during the BASE IV design that is worth mentioning here: a new kind of extensible message format. The original BASE I message format was fixed both in length and content, containing only the few fields necessary for credit authorization. This would simply not suffice in the all-electronic world envisioned for BASE IV. Multiple transaction types were already needed, and the payment and banking industries were still experiencing profound change, making it likely that entirely new, unforeseen products and services might arise in the future, requiring completely new types of transactions and message fields. As with any large, decentralized system, changes to the messages would need to occur gradually, and the format had to allow for some messages to include new fields while others omitted them.

To accommodate these requirements, IBM developed a dynamic format that could be extended gradually over time without significant changes to the switching software. Each message began with a type indicator that distinguished between

---

[4]Peirce interview. Peirce stressed that as an IBM salesperson, he had every incentive to encourage NBI to pursue the plan, but he knew that it would end in disaster, and thus was unwilling to risk the long-term relationship between the two organizations.

[5]Peirce correspondence.

authorization requests, financial transfers, reversals, administrative messages, or any other kind of transaction that might be needed in the future. Following the type were eight bytes treated as a bitmap: each of the 64 bits corresponded to a data field defined in an external dictionary, and the value of the bit indicated if that field was present or absent in the message. To enable more than 64 fields, one of the bits was eventually reserved to indicate whether another bitmap and set of fields followed the current one.[6] Thus, messages could contain only the necessary and relevant fields, densely packed, with a relatively small eight-byte overhead per fieldset to indicate which fields were present.

As new fields were defined, the only change necessary to the switching software was a new entry in a field definition table. Although the standard allowed for variable-length fields, the values of such fields were always prefixed by their actual length, enabling the switching and logging systems to handle them opaquely. Issuers could also take advantage of new field values when present, or safely ignore them.

After a battle with the airline industry, which is unfortunately too detailed to cover here, this format was eventually ratified as the standard for all electronic financial messages by the ANSI and ISO banking industry committees. The format, known as ISO 8583, allowed Visa to not only support new types of transactions over time, such as single-message debit, but also add new fields incrementally to existing transactions, such as the Card Verification Value (CVV) or the related three-digit number in the signature panel used when the card is not swiped through a terminal (CVV2).[7]

Encoding the Card: Magnetic Stripes and Magic Middles

One of BASE IV's key design goals was to remove the paper sales drafts entirely from the system. All transactions were to be originated in electronic form at the point of sale, and that implied not only some sort of counter-top electronic device, but also a *machine-readable card*. A POS terminal that required manual entry of the card details would suffer from the same data entry errors that occurred before the use of embossed cards and imprinters discussed in Chap. 1. Thus, the POS terminals needed to "read" the card directly, and that implied a mechanism for encoding the account details onto the card itself in some sort of machine-readable form.

The BASE IV design did not specify any particular method for encoding the card, primarily because there was considerable debate at the time within the banking and airline industries as to how this should be done. Visa would eventually force a temporary closure of this debate, but to understand the issue fully, we must first review the various encoding options and the ways in which certain groups made claims about the superiority of their technique over others.

---

[6] According to Derman, this chaining of bitmaps and fields was added during the ANSI standards process and was not part of the original IBM design.

[7] For a description of single-message debit transactions, see Chap. 8.

Encoding Options and Standards

In the early 1970s, there were two general approaches to making the card machine-readable: optics and magnetics. Within these two approaches, issuers experimented with various techniques, but they eventually standardized on Optical Character Recognition (OCR) and the magnetic stripe (often abbreviated as "magstripe"). The approach used generally depended upon the issuer's industry; the oil and retail industries normally preferred OCR, while the banking and airline industries typically favored the magstripe. This was not entirely universal, however, and as we shall see, one powerful bank developed and promoted its own unique optical technique.

Simply defined, an OCR system "reads" alpha-numeric characters printed in specific fonts (or encoded in variable-width bars) using optical sensors and shape-detecting algorithms. The retail and oil industries both made early commitments to this technology. Standard Oil of California installed what seems to be the first OCR-based data capture system for card sales drafts in 1956.[8] The National Retail Merchants Association formed an optical scanning standards committee in the late 1950s, which subsequently recommended the use of a similar system that could read product identifiers printed on labels.[9] In the 1960s, Addressograph-Multigraph perfected their "barcode" technique, which encoded the characters into a series of parallel vertical bars, and these proved easier for the machines to read reliably.[10] Most of the retail industry eventually adopted the barcode technique, especially the supermarkets, and electronic cash register manufactures began to build-in scanning wands to read them.[11]

Because the oil and retail industries were already using OCR to capture their payment card drafts, it was a relatively easy step to propose reading the card directly at the point of sale using a similar technique. The embossed characters on the card were already printed in an OCR-readable font so that they could be read from the imprinted draft, and the OCR sensors were beginning to reduce in size and cost.

The Data Source Corporation seems to be the first vendor to have developed an OCR-based, card-reading POS terminal. NDC, the large processor discussed in Chap. 4, installed these terminals at numerous service stations and retail locations in 1971, and the first unit installed reportedly caught an unauthorized card on its 14th transaction.[12] Data Source and NDC claimed that OCR was the best technique for POS terminals, as issuers did not need to add anything to their cards. They often neglected, however, to mention that although the POS terminals could read the account number, which was embossed in the standard IMR-7B OCR font, they

---

[8]Schantz (1982), p. 11.

[9]Schantz (1982), p. 13.

[10]Schantz (1982), pp. 15–16.

[11]Campbell-Kelly and Aspray (1996), pp. 176–180. In the early 1980s, Visa considered requiring a barcode on their debit card, which they were trying to sell to the supermarkets, but decided against it because it lacked the necessary capacity.

[12]'NDC credit authorization pilot underway', Payment Systems Newsletter (July 1971), p. 7, 'Operations and systems notes' American Banker (16 February 1972), p. 6.

could not yet read the expiration date, which was inexplicably printed in a different font.

The banking and airline industries also made early commitments, but to magnetics instead of OCR. As noted in Chap. 1, the banks standardized on the Magnetic Ink Character Recognition (MICR) technique in 1957 for automating the processing of checks and other bank drafts. MICR was never considered as a candidate for card encoding, but in the late 1960s, the airlines and IBM developed another magnetic technique that seemed promising: the magnetic stripe.[13]

The magstripe is essentially a piece of magnetic tape, similar to that used for computer data storage or audio recording, affixed by heat to a paper ticket or plastic card. Just like a computer storage tape, the magstripe can be encoded with binary data, which can then be extracted by passing the tape over a relatively inexpensive reader head. The airlines used this technique for their automated ticket vending systems, and adopted it as a standard for their own, privately-issued payment cards in 1969. The various cash dispenser manufacturers also adopted this technique for their access cards in the early 1970s.

As discussed in Chap. 4, many banks conducted POS terminal tests using the magstripe during 1971. When plans for these tests became known, the American Bankers Association (ABA) formed a task force to develop standards for card encoding, hoping to avoid unnecessary duplication and fragmentation in the marketplace.

The ABA task force evaluated a few different encoding techniques according to four basic criteria: availability, reliability, cost, and security.[14] In MacKenzie's terms, these criteria were four "properties" of the artifact, about which the task force would construct knowledge and disseminate it via the authority of the ABA.[15]

In their report, they concluded that the magstripe "offered the greatest opportunity to satisfy a wide variety of requirements for both present and future needs."[16] In many ways, their conclusion was entirely expected, as most of the task force members came from those banks already planning POS terminal tests using magstripes. Later critics would question whether the task force members recommended the magstripe primarily because the members had already made large investments in it.[17] But this accusation had an obvious defense: those who had already made investments in the magstripe would have done so only after their own investigations,

---

[13]It may be surprising that MICR was never considered, but Perry Hudson, who served as chairman of the ABA card standardization task force, remarked that it was simply never suggested (Hudson interview).

[14]Hudson noted that OCR was the only serious competitor to the stripe, but at the time of their investigation (1970), OCR POS terminals were not yet available. Additionally, Magtek was already selling a magstripe POS reader that was being used by the airlines.

[15]MacKenzie argues that we construct knowledge about the properties of artifacts according to four methods: testimony of authority; induction through testing; induction through use; and deduction. Each of these methods involves a social dynamic, even deduction, which is typically thought to be asocial. See MacKenzie (1996).

[16]'Magnetic stripe for credit cards urged by ABA unit', American Banker (16 February 1971), p. 1.

[17]For example, see Brooke (3 November 1971), p. 6.

and their conclusions were unlikely to change when they made the same investigation as a member of the task force just a few months later. Not enough time had passed yet for them to discover the various problems that would eventually surface after the magstripe was used in production with payment cards.

The report offered several reasons why the magstripe was recommended over other techniques. It was already widely available, and, as an established technology, had proven its reliability and durability in the field. Although adding the stripe virtually doubled the cost of the card, the reader heads were less expensive, simpler, and more reliable than OCR sensors. The stripe also offered a large capacity, allowing the inclusion of data beyond the basic account information visible on the card. Finally, the stripe was volatile, allowing for the possibility of devices that could write back to the stripe, which the task force thought might be desirable for off-line systems.

In terms of availability, reliability, and cost, the magstripe genuinely seemed to be the best option, and in the subsequent debates, these points remained largely uncontested. The final criterion of security, however, was not so straightforward. Regarding this property, the task force originally wrote:

> While no encoding technology was thought to be foolproof against fraud, the magnetic stripe was thought to have the greatest security against casual fraud because it is difficult to alter, the data is not visible, and it requires a fairly high level of sophistication and collusion to counterfeit.[18]

As we shall see, all of these claims, as well as the understanding of *where* security should be evaluated, would soon be contested.

Magstripe Tracks

Although the airlines and the ABA recommended the magstripe for their cards, they did not agree as to how the card information should be encoded upon it. Of central concern was the density at which the data should be recorded. Magnetic tape contains a large number of contiguous ferrite-oxide particles, and it is somewhat arbitrary as to how one divides them into discrete segments representing binary values. The technology in general use at the time was able to read reliably at a density of 75 bits per inch (bpi), but newer equipment in testing promised to read just as reliably at 210 bpi.

The ABA wanted to establish a standard quickly because the various pilot tests were scheduled to begin in the near future. Because the POS terminals being used in these tests would perform online authorization only, the banks needed only two fairly short fields on the magstripe: a 13-digit account number and a four-digit expiration date.[19] Using a 5-bit per character encoding at 75 bpi would provide the

---

[18]Quoted in 'Magnetic stripe for credit cards urged by ABA unit' American Banker (16 February 1971).

[19]At this time, the account number was actually variable in length, but tended to be around 13 digits. Sixteen-digit numbers were not used until later.

banks with space for 40 numeric characters, which was more than enough for their needs.[20] Additionally, they felt that the lower density would be more durable, as the lighter packing created a lower potential for bit-dropout, a condition often caused from damage incurred by the many unorthodox activities for which the cards were often used, such as scraping ice off windshields or opening locked doors.[21]

The airlines, however, required more than the account number and expiration date. To enable fully-automated ticketing, the magstripe also needed to carry the cardholder's name. Names require alpha-numeric characters, which implied at least a 7-bit per character encoding. A density of 75 bpi simply did not provide enough characters, so the airlines were willing to wait until 210 bpi readers were commercially available.[22]

The issue was eventually resolved by subdividing the stripe into two tracks, the first recorded at 210 bpi and the second at 75. The airlines claimed the first track and defined a field layout that included the cardholder name, account number, expiration, and a few airline-specific fields. The ABA took the second track and defined a field layout that included only the account number and expiration. The magstripe on all cards would contain both tracks, and devices could read either or both. To this day, payment card magstripes still contain two tracks, encoded at different densities, containing roughly the same information.[23]

Soon after this compromise, a third track at 210 bpi was also defined. Recall that one of the benefits of the magstripe cited by the ABA task force was its changeability. The ABA allocated this track primarily for read/write scenarios, where terminals and cash dispensing units would alter the contents based on the last transaction. The definition of the track was given over to the thrift industry, and although they recognized the value of writability, they saw it more as a chance to encode sophisticated personal identification data, such as a digitized finger or voice print.[24] The third track was briefly used in a read/write mode for off-line cash dispensing units, but was quickly abandoned after bankers realized just how easily it could be read and altered using widely-available audio equipment. As telecommunication costs in the US dropped, and ATMs and other terminal devices became strictly online, most issuers removed the third track in order to reduce the height of the stripe.

---

[20] The encoding scheme used four data bits plus one parity bit per character, allowing for 16 distinct values. This was enough for the digits 0 through 9, plus a few special values used as field separators and begin/end markers.

[21] This point was made by Bertram Tobin of Chase Manhattan Bank, quoted in 'Standards are the glue', Payment Systems Newsletter (July 1972), p. 1.

[22] The airline encoding scheme used 6 data bits plus one parity bit per character, providing a maximum of 79 alpha-numeric characters on the stripe.

[23] Derman interview.

[24] Brooke (14 September 1973), p. 6.

Magstripe Security

Shortly after the ABA task force defined the encoding standards for the second track, George Warfel from the Western States Bankcard Association began questioning its security, pitting his authority as a trained engineer against that of the ABA. He did not mince words: "Upon encodement with the American Bankers Association-proposed format, you create a fraudable document that can plague the entire credit card community..."[25] He revealed that for about $150, an amateur can build a fairly simple device using widely-available audio parts and transistors that could copy the contents of one ABA-encoded stripe to another. He called it a "skimmer," and noted that "It is just like the tape-dubbing machine used by college students to copy tape cassettes—except it works for cards."

Playing on the fear of the counter-culture, he presented a scenario where a young gas station attendant could use one of these devices to copy the data from the stripe of a legitimate card to the stripe of a stolen one. Because POS terminals read only the stripe on the stolen card, and not the embossed numbers on the front, any typical transaction the thief made with the stolen card would be authorized. But sales drafts generated using a card imprinter would pick up the embossed numbers, which were for an account that was no longer valid.[26] At this pre-BASE II time, it might take weeks before that draft reached the issuer, and only then would the issuer realize that the stolen card now had a new stripe. By the time the issuer could determine which account had been skimmed, the attendant could easily skim a different card, creating a near endless cycle of unstoppable fraud. Furthermore, if the stripes and terminals were shared between the different payment networks, one could easily skim the stripe from a BankAmericard and copy it to a Master Charge or American Express; it would likely take months for the card organizations to determine what had happened.

To be clear, Warfel's concern was not with the magstripe itself, but with the way the ABA proposed to encode it, and the environment in which it would be used. Warfel observed that the only environment in which the magstripe was currently used was cash dispensing. The access cards for these devices employed magstripes, but they were encoded and used in much more secure ways. For example, Docutel used four tracks to hold a "deviously scrambled code" that must be input by the cardholder to complete the transaction. Burroughs included a second, unalterable stripe that was encoded at the time of manufacture. IBM used a 45-degree rotation on their more sophisticated reader heads. The cash dispenser manufacturers could do all this because their devices were used under controlled conditions, and the added encoding security contributed little to the $15,000 to $25,000 cost of a dispenser.

---

[25]Brooke (3 November 1971), p. 1. This article is an edited version of Warfel's speech to the Data Processing Supplies Association.

[26]Recall that these early POS terminals performed authorization only. Merchants still completed a paper sales draft for each transaction, and it was these paper drafts that would be cleared and settled.

In contrast, the ABA-encoded stripe would be included on millions of cards and used in hundreds of thousands of POS terminals that need to be purchased by relatively low-volume merchants. In order for this to be economically feasible, the ABA proposed a format that was much simpler and did not require any additional user input. But Warfel felt that the ABA went too far, suggesting that their format was the "extreme in simplicity" and was thus vulnerable to unimaginable amounts of fraud. Although the format may have been adequate a few years earlier, technology had developed in the meantime to the point where any hobbyist could build a skimmer:

> Today you can buy transistors like gum-drops, in plastic bags by the dozen. The radio catalogs list 'credit card reader heads' along with hi-fi components. Thus, what was secret in '67 is common knowledge today. What was secure in '67 is vulnerable today.[27]

Given the vulnerability of the ABA-proposed stripe, Warfel questioned whether the banking industry should adopt OCR instead. By this time, Data Source was offering their OCR terminal, and since it read the embossed numbers on the front, the authorization and sales draft would always refer to the same account. This was not completely secure though, as the numbers could be cut off and re-arranged, or melted down and re-embossed, but it would be easier to detect than a skimmed magstripe. Nevertheless, Warfel realized that switching to OCR may not be possible given the existing investments in magstripes, so he also suggested that the ABA at least require the use of high-coercivity materials. Once encoded, this kind of stripe was essentially unalterable by a hobbyist, as changing it required special writing heads and high amounts of magnetic energy.

The ABA task force quickly responded to Warfel's criticisms by acknowledging the vulnerabilities of the magstripe, but arguing that with some minor adjustments, such as the use of high-coercivity materials, the magstripe was still more secure than any other available option.[28] They urged the banking industry to wait for the results of the various POS terminal tests being conducted by the banks, as these would reveal not only how secure the stripe was in practice, but also ways in which it could be made more secure.

This was a subtle but important shift in the task force's approach. They now asserted that the proper level at which security should be discussed is the *entire payment system*, not just the particular card-encoding technique. In this way, they were redefining the locus of the security property, focusing the participants away from the magstripe artifact toward the system as a whole. The task force was envisioning a future environment where the POS terminals would not only authorize transactions, but also capture and transmit them electronically for clearing. Thus the stripe would become the sole location of account data, eliminating the central problem Warfel described. Even if a card was skimmed, the task force believed that fraud detection algorithms running at the issuer or on the switches would quickly detect it, and a simple examination of the transaction logs for the affected accounts would reveal the merchant location where the skimming occurred.

---

[27]Warfel quoted in Brooke (3 November 1971), p. 1.

[28]Brooke (3 November 1971), p. 1.

The debate subsided for nearly two years as various issuers conducted their POS terminal tests, but it resurfaced again in April 1973. Jack Scantlin, chairman of Transaction Technology Incorporated (TTI), a subsidiary of Citicorp, had been "suspicious of magnetics technology for quite some time," and decided to see just how easy it was to compromise the ABA-encoded stripe. Scantlin invited 22 students from the California Institute of Technology (Cal Tech) to design devices that posed a serious fraud potential, promising an attractive $5,000, $2,500, and $1,000 for the three best entries. Each team submitted their devices, along with a detailed report, and although TTI refused to discuss the devices for fear of giving criminals too many good ideas, *Business Week* described two types of skimmers built for as little as $25.[29] Scantlin then issued a press release announcing that he had discovered a "cheap and easy way to defraud the magnetic stripe," and called into question the ABA's commitment to the technique.[30]

The ABA's response to Scatlin was the same as their response to Warfel. This time, however, the ABA questioned the actions of TTI, as its sibling Citibank was already represented on the ABA task force. If TTI or Citibank had any exceptions to the magstripe, or any suggestions for improving it, they could have raised them at one of the task force meetings. Instead, they chose to issue a press release designed to characterize the magstripe as the "Achilles heel of the whole credit card system."[31] In response, Citicorp attempted to distance themselves from TTI's actions, stating that corporate management was unaware of the contest and would have never condoned it.

When asked why they encouraged students to develop devices capable of generating fraud, John Reed, the Executive Vice President of Operations for Citibank replied "we simply wanted to know about card-reading technology." Unlike Warfel, however, TTI and Citibank had an economic motivation for questioning the security of the magstripe. They had recently invested more than $30 million developing a different kind of proprietary, non-magnetic encoding technique. They were also just about to use it for nearly a million Citicards, and would soon offer it to other banks on a licensing basis. They called it the "Magic Middle."

The Magic Middle

Citibank and TTI never publicly revealed the technical details about the Magic Middle, but much can be deduced from the patents granted to TTI in 1972 and 1973.[32] The Magic Middle was essentially an optical form of a computer punch-card. As the name indicates, a payment card using this technique contained a special middle

---

[29] 'Beating the new credit cards', Business Week (11 August 1973), pp. 120–122.

[30] Brooke (9 April 1973), p. 1.

[31] Brooke (13 April 1973), p. 1.

[32] For the basic concept, see United States Patent number 3819910. For details of the actual encoding method, see numbers 3775755 and 3858032.

layer, sandwiched between the normal top and bottom layers of plastic. The outer layers were opaque to the human eye, but infrared light could shine through them. The middle layer was made of a material that would reflect infrared light, except for the places where holes were punched through it. Thus, a reader could shine infrared light from one side, and a sensor on the other side could detect light coming through the holes, determining which were punched and which were not.

The middle layer contained four horizontal data tracks and one clocking track in the center. The clocking track had every other row punched, providing a simple means for ensuring proper alignment. The tracks were read vertically, one column per character, allowing for a 4-bit encoding scheme. The width of the tracks, and thus the maximum capacity on a standard payment card, was not disclosed, but since it was used by Citibank for many years, it was likely as much as the lower-density ABA track on the magstripe. The tracks ran across the width of the card, below the magnetic stripe and embossed account numbers, allowing it to coexist with the other encoding methods.

Armed with the results of their Cal Tech contest, Citibank and TTI claimed that the Magic Middle was far more secure than the magstripe for two reasons. First, the encoding technology was not even visible to the human eye, so it had a measure of security through obscurity. Second, even if the technique became well-known, it could not be copied without highly-specialized equipment. A Magic Middle skimmer would require an infrared light emitter and sensor, devices that were harder to obtain in the early 1970s than a magnetic tape reader head. Of course, this also implied that the card was far more expensive to manufacture, but Citibank argued that this was a small price to pay for a completely secure encoding technique.

Citibank and TTI christened the Magic Middle in October 1973, after they had already issued nearly a million Citicards containing it and installed terminals at 1,200 merchants that could read it.[33] Customers could use their Citicards for purchases at those merchant locations, in Citibank ATMs, and for identification and checkcashing at any of Citibank's 226 branches. Two years later, Citibank would also install special interactive terminals, called "Citicard Centers," in their branches that would enable cardholders to complete basic account management tasks without waiting for, or speaking to, a teller. Interestingly, they admitted the Citicard Centers were "designed to begin conditioning customers to use the terminals and to allay their fears of computer technology."[34]

When the Magic Middle was announced in 1973, Citibank articulated a non-confrontational strategy regarding industry standards. Their spokesperson said:

> Realistically, it is not within our plans to convert the whole industry. We feel we have a better mousetrap than the mag stripe and embossed systems. We honestly feel this is a better way. Whether our technology dominates is not relevant to us. It was developed for our own use.[35]

---

[33]Tyson (25 October 1973), p. 1.

[34]Brooke (8 May 1975), p. 1.

[35]Mark Ponton, VP of Marketing, Personal Banking Group, quoted in Tyson (25 October 1973), p. 1.

Citibank changed its position less than a year later, however, announcing that they would make the Magic Middle available for licensing nationwide.[36] Furthermore, they began working with National Cash Register (NCR) and Docutel to add Magic Middle readers to their electronic registers and cash dispensing machines. Citibank was now directly challenging the *de jure* ABA magstripe standard, hoping to establish their own proprietary technology as the new *de facto* standard.

In a somewhat cheeky move, the ABA responded to Citibank and the Magic Middle by simply adjusting the card-encoding requirements to exclude proprietary technologies.[37] In a new amendment to their report, they required that any encoding technique proposed as a standard must not incur licensing fees; have sufficient capacity for recording all necessary information; and be available to any card issuer regardless of industry. The ABA spokesperson admitted that these requirements effectively disqualified both the Magic Middle and OCR, but assured that they were in the best interest of all issuers.

Citibank continued with its licensing plan, but was unable to sign enough banks to pose a serious threat. In many ways, this was not surprising, as few banks would be willing to pay the licensing fees and higher manufacturing costs, not to mention trusting what Spencer Nilson called "the world's most hated bank" with their encoding technology.[38] When the major West Coast banks, such as BofA and Wells Fargo, ventured into POS terminals, they chose the new devices from Data Source instead, which could read both the magstripe and the embossed account numbers and compare them to detect skimming.

Visa and the Magstripe

Throughout all of these debates, NBI/Visa remained mostly a passive observer, occasionally commenting that although the magstripe seemed likely to become the accepted standard, they would not rule out the emergence of a better encoding technique.[39] As the 1970s drew to a close, Hock decided that it was time to encourage full automation of the point of sale. This would not only bring Visa one step closer to the all-electronic value-exchange system he envisioned in BASE IV, it would also enable a zero floor limit environment, which would dramatically reduce the effects of fraud (in a zero floor limit environment, every transaction is authorized, which allows issuers to identify and stem fraud quickly). But this also implied that Visa needed to mandate a standard encoding technique for all cards bearing their mark, both domestically and internationally.

---

[36] Brooke (11 September 1974), p. 1.

[37] American Banker (14 November 1973), p. 1.

[38] Nilson (March 1978), Report No 182, p. 1.

[39] For example, see Brooke (18 October 1972), p. 1.

The task of establishing Visa's encoding standard fell to Win Derman, who had already been working with the various standards groups on the bitmap message format.[40] In addition to the basic ABA-defined fields, Derman defined two new ones that would be needed in the Visa context. The first was a three-digit "service code," which at the time, merely indicated if the card could be used in international interchange, domestic interchange, or no interchange at all. Some members of Visa International operated in non-exchangeable currencies, so the magstripe needed to include information that would prohibit use outside the country of issue. Although one digit would have sufficed at the time, Derman argued that they should reserve two more for future needs, and today, these are used to indicate what kind of authorization is required, and what services the card supports. The second field was a PIN verification value (PVV), which is generated through a one-way encryption algorithm. The PVV allows a terminal or ATM to verify a PIN in an off-line environment.

Although these two fields were small-enough to fit into the remaining space on the ABA-defined second track, Derman also wanted to take advantage of the larger capacity of the first track. By this time, 210 bpi magnetic reader heads had become standard, and the ABA, wanting to take advantage of the larger capacity, had unfortunately established a banking-specific format for the first track that differed from that used by the airlines. To distinguish the two, both industries agreed to add a single-character format code to the front of the stripe: A for airline and B for banking.

Derman wanted to build upon the airline's format so that Visa cards could be read easily by airline POS terminals. During this period, Visa was also concentrating on improving their presence in the T&E market, so compatibility with the airlines' systems, which American Express already had, was paramount. But convincing the member banks to switch to the airline format for the first track would be difficult, as many were already issuing cards using the banking format.

His solution was to recast the debate as a domestic versus international one, knowing that Visa was now an international organization, and any standard they proposed would need to be seen as international as well. Fortunately for Derman, when the ABA defined their format for the first track, they encoded the expiration date in the American MMYY format (that is, a two-digit month followed by a two-digit year). The airline format, which was established through the International Air Transport Association (IATA), used the more international form of YYMM. Since the ABA recommended standards only for the US, international banks also tended to use IATA's YYMM format.

Derman presented his case to the US banks, arguing that the ABA format for the first track was US-centric, and since Visa was an international organization, their encoding standard should use an international date layout. Since the airline format already expressed the expiration date in an international manner, it would make sense to build upon that. The existing format code would then allow the US banks

---

[40]Information on the Visa magstripe standard comes from interviews with Derman.

to gradually transition to the airline format, as the POS terminals could still read the banking format during the changeover.

The US banks eventually agreed, and Derman got the standard ratified by Interbank, the ABA, ANSI and ISO. The banks and the airlines were now finally on a common standard for the first track, although Visa cards would also continue to carry the now-extended second track. In 1979, Visa adopted a bylaw requiring all cards bearing their mark issued after 1980 to include a magnetic stripe, encoded according to the Visa standard.[41] Citibank, which had joined Visa after the ban on dual membership was lifted, threatened to sue Visa for effectively destroying their potential licensing market. They ultimately capitulated, however, in exchange for a three month extension of the magstripe deadline.

Visa's mandate of the magstripe forced a temporary closure to the card-encoding debate. It would resurface again when card manufacturers perfected the embedding of a computer chip in plastic, but for now, the path toward the development and mass-adoption of inexpensive POS terminals was paved.

Dialing for Dollars: The Merchant Dial Terminal Project

Now that all Visa cards would carry a standardized magstripe, the next step was to create the right incentives for the mass-adoption of POS terminals. As already discussed, a few different manufacturers were offering authorization terminals at this time, but these devices reportedly cost between $1,000 and $2,000 each, making them far too expensive for low-volume merchants.[42]

Although the unit costs were high, the real expense was in the way these early terminals communicated with the acquiring processor, as they required separate, dedicated leased data lines, which incurred hefty monthly fees. For merchants who processed only a few card transactions a day, the fixed-price of the leased line combined with the merchant discount seriously reduced their profit margins. If Visa was to bring about the all-electronic BASE IV world, they needed to stimulate the development of a new kind of terminal that every merchant could afford to purchase and use, and then provide the right economic incentives to encourage merchants to adopt them.

Dial Terminals

In 1979, Visa started a new project to define the requirements and functional specifications for these affordable terminals. Technical leadership of the project fell to

---

[41] Kutler (6 February 1979), p. 1. See also Kutler (12 June 1979), p. 3.

[42] Information on the Dial Terminal Project comes from interviews with Fojtik, Harrison, Derman, Powar, Peirce, and Pittenger, as well as the 'Visa dial terminal pilot project final report' produced by Visa USA (April 1982).

Frank Fojtik, who had previously spent time thinking about terminals when he joined NBI in 1974. Given his prior experience in telecommunications and electronic cash registers, Fojtik realized that the best option for low-volume merchants would be a terminal that could use their existing voice telephone lines. Any merchant accepting cards for transactions over the floor limit was already using that line to call for authorizations, and if the terminal dialed a similar local number, it would incur no additional cost. In fact, the terminal should obtain the authorization more quickly, resulting in a shorter call time.

Visa briefly considered producing the dial terminals themselves, but ultimately realized that they lacked the necessary expertise. Furthermore, manufacturing POS terminals was not what they considered their core purpose to be, and their foray into writing card processing software (BASE III) had convinced them not to stray from that again. Instead, they decided to develop the devices in cooperation with multiple vendors. Visa would establish the requirements and write the detailed functional specifications, and the assorted vendors would design and build compliant terminals, competing with one another for what promised to be a sizable market.

The requirements and specifications were kept rather simple. The terminals would perform authorization only, so there was no requirement for internal data storage or an integrated printer. The terminal must have a small keypad with which the merchant can enter the purchase amount and send the authorization request. It must have some method for displaying the response and authorization code to the merchant. It needed to be as small as possible, as merchant counter space is precious, and it needed to run on a conventional power supply. Lastly, and most importantly, merchants must be able to obtain the resulting device for less than $500.

The Pilot Test

Visa found four manufacturers willing to build such terminals for a pilot test: GTE, Northern Telecom, Sweda International, and Taltek Electronics.[43] By the end of the pilot test, several more manufacturers had developed terminals based on Visa's specifications, including the now famous Verifone. A total of 800 units were ordered from these vendors, and Visa USA members installed them at various types of merchants in disparate geographical regions. Besides making standard local calls to an acquiring processor, some terminals were configured to call a machine in Visa's San Mateo data center to test inbound Wide Area Telephone Service (WATS) lines, and others called local access nodes for the relatively new GTE Telenet packet switching network.[44]

IBM developed the software to answer calls placed to the San Mateo center and transform the terminal requests into BASE I authorization messages. This software

---

[43] 'Visa dial terminal pilot project final report' (April 1982), p. 3.

[44] Although the final report mentions local calls to acquirers as one of the telecommunication paths, Powar recalled that all calls during the test actually came to San Mateo.

ran on IBM Series/1 computers, which would soon be deployed at the member processing centers to replace the DEC Tape Transmission Units used by BASE II. These powerful minicomputers, known at the time as "Member Interface Processors" (MIPs), were also employed as gateways to BASE I, so it was relatively easy to interface the dial terminals to the authorization system through those machines.[45] After the pilot test, this software was made available as a standard package on the MIP, enabling the POS terminals to call the local acquiring processor rather than the San Mateo data center.

The pilot test ran from June 1980 to December 1981, and it proved to be a success on nearly every front. From a technical standpoint, the terminals worked exceedingly well, and merchants reported that they were almost never inoperative. Visa's requirements stipulated a minimum mean time to failure of 18 months, but the average in practice was nearly 36 months. The telecommunication performance was more mixed: terminals that made local and intrastate WATS calls were reliable and cost effective, but interstate WATS was too expensive due to tariff increases, and the GTE Telenet service experienced operational problems. The final report noted the need for interstate WATS would be eliminated once the answering software was made available on the MIP, and GTE was steadily improving their reliability. Despite using dial-up connections, the speed of the system was also adequate. An authorization made through the terminals typically took 20 seconds, which was at least twice as fast as one obtained verbally. It also involved less manual data entry, and thus allowed fewer opportunity for errors.

Interestingly, Visa later used the CompuServe network as an inexpensive way to route authorizations from the dial terminals to BASE I. CompuServe had spent large amounts of time and money building local network access points in nearly every US city to facilitate a consumer-oriented online service, but they often had more capacity than they needed, and thus made their infrastructure available to organizations like Visa. Using the CompuServe network quickly became the preferred option for Visa, as the merchant could dial a local number that did not incur additional costs, and CompuServe maintained all the local telecommunications infrastructure.[46]

From a business and fraud-control perspective, the pilot test results were even more impressive. The creation of BASE I had helped limit fraudulent transactions, but even as late as 1980, only 12 to 15 percent of interchange transactions were actually authorized—the rest fell under the merchant's floor limit. In contrast, merchants participating in the pilot test authorized every transaction, and within the first few days, the number of recovered cards rose sharply. Over the duration of the test, more than 3,000 cards were recovered by participating merchants, and over 10,000 transactions were declined that would have been allowed under the existing procedures.[47] The terminals also served as a powerful deterrent; one member bank reported that

---

[45]The MIPs were later renamed "Visa Access Points" (VAPs). Powar noted that they used the limited number of MIPs available that year as an incentive for terminal adoption; to get a MIP, the member had to purchase 200 terminals.

[46]Pittenger and Powar interviews.

[47]'Visa dial terminal pilot project final report' (April 1982), p. 3.

"... incidents have already occurred in which a thief, upon seeing his stolen card being put through the terminal, has turned and literally run from the store."[48]

The terminal's ability to deter fraud benefited not only the issuers, but also the merchants. For transactions under the floor limit, merchants were supposed to check the card number against a large, dense list printed in a warning bulletin, but many found this arduous, time-consuming, and potentially insulting to the customer. If the number was in the warning bulletin and the transaction proved to be fraudulent, the issuer could levy a chargeback against the merchant, resulting in a deduction from the merchant's account for the transaction amount plus a ten dollar penalty fee. Merchants participating in the pilot test simply swiped every card through the terminal, resulting in an 82 percent decrease in their chargebacks.

Adoption Incentives

Although a promised reduction in chargebacks might have been attractive enough, Visa USA realized that they needed to offer merchants a stronger, positive incentive to adopt the terminals. Their solution was a reduction in the interchange reimbursement fee, the powerful economic setting used to balance the issuing and acquiring sides of the system.[49] Transactions authorized through POS terminals would qualify for a special Terminal Interchange Reimbursement Fee (TIRF) of one percent, which was 20 percent less than the current average. Since this is the fee acquirers pay issuers, the TIRF provided an incentive for acquirers to push the terminals, which they did by reducing the merchant discount fee by a similar (though perhaps not equal) amount. For merchants, the lower discount fee, reduction in chargebacks, increase in authorization speed, and inexpensive unit price, all combined to make the terminals a net benefit.[50]

The TIRF provided the economic incentive necessary for mass-adoption of the terminals, but obtaining Board approval for such a reduction would be difficult. The interchange fee was an important source of revenue for issuers and the large banks were reluctant to fund automation that would primarily help acquirers and merchants more than them. For these larger issuers, the warning bulletin was sufficient, as it provided a convenient way to justify chargebacks.

Hock was especially critical of this attitude in his speeches. At the American Bankers Association's national bankcard conference, he denounced the way the bulletins were being used in practice:

---

[48] 'Visa dial terminal pilot project final report' (April 1982), p. 37.

[49] The importance of this fee is discussed in Chap. 3.

[50] The TIRF was not the first time Visa USA had offered a special incentive rate. In 1979, they offered an Electronic Interchange Reimbursement Fee (EIRF) to merchants who used their electronic cash register systems to authorize all transactions and submit them electronically to their processor within three days. This rate was originally developed to entice JC Penney, one of the three largest retail chains in America, to accept Visa cards. The details of this deal, which became highly controversial, will be discussed in Chap. 9.

> If you think carefully about warning bulletins, their functioning becomes apparent. They permit a card issuing bank, for a small fee, to employ the collective power of Visa or Interbank to force the merchant signing bank or the merchant to accept all losses which result from failure to follow an impossible procedure, which, in turn, was imposed by the collective power of the organization.

Hock argued that, in the long run, this practice would ultimately hurt those it was currently serving. Eventually, the promise of a guaranteed transaction would be undermined, and merchants would begin to question why they were paying a discount to accept something that was no better than a check. Consumers were also starting to think twice about using their cards, as merchants tired of chargebacks were requiring personal information such as phone numbers and home addresses from the cardholders.

This difference in perspectives created a palpable tension. Hock saw terminals as an important step toward a totally electronic value-exchange system, but the large issuers were focusing on their individual programs. Visa's CFO recalled that

> Dee wanted to increase the Visa momentum and deliver the "knock out punch" to all of his competitors and detractors ... Dee had the industry lead, but he wanted everyone else to believe that Visa had all of the answers, to choose anyone else would be suicidal.
> But others were growing tired of Dee's ... big ideas ... As for the typical banker stereotype of the period, they were happy the system was "fixed," they were all making money, they all wished deregulation and competition would go away, and now they wanted to get back to playing golf, not embark on the next grand plan that Dee had devised.[51]

This seems to have been a common theme throughout Visa's early history: Hock often had to resort to manipulation or tricks to get Board members to put aside their own self-interests in order to improve the overall system. Although these improvements invariably benefited those who initially opposed them, it was difficult to convince those members of such ahead of time.

Resolutions

Hock's plan was to introduce a resolution that would commit the Visa USA members to authorizing 80 percent of all interchange transactions within five years. Achieving such a goal would require the mass-adoption of terminals, which in turn would require the TIRF. Hock knew this would be a controversial proposal, so he purposely omitted it from the proposed agenda mailed to the Directors before the Board meeting.[52]

The meeting for that year, 1982, was held in Bermuda, and in keeping with previous years, Visa invited and paid for spouses to attend. This was advantageous for a number of reasons. First, and most important, the spouses were actually invited to attend the Board meetings, primarily because, as Visa's CFO put it, the Directors

---

[51]Cleveland (1999), p. 20.

[52]Cleveland (1999), p. 22.

"would be more inclined to act civil, consider the good of Visa over their bank's self interest, and in other words, vote for whatever Dee wanted."[53] Second, the members would also have an incentive to cooperate in order to end the meetings early so they could spend time with their families. Third, with their spouses there, the Directors would also have less time to meet with one another and discuss any opposition they might have to Hock's proposals.

Hock also knew that most Directors tended to leave the meetings early if they felt that the final day's topics were unimportant, so he kept the 80-percent authorization goal off the agenda. Hock had learned the time of every Director's return flight, and as those who would oppose the resolution drifted out, he adjusted his mental vote tally accordingly. After enough Directors had left, Hock switched topics and introduced the resolution, which was well-received by those remaining, and unanimously adopted. The larger issuers always wondered when they had ever voted for such a goal, but as the terminals were installed by most merchants, the reduction in their fraud losses convinced them that it was perhaps the right idea after all.[54]

Adoption and Consequences

Although the Board adopted the resolution, it actually took seven years to reach the 80-percent authorization goal. Despite a set of economic incentives that enabled the terminals to pay for themselves within weeks or months, the merchants did not rush to install them. Bill Powar, who took over the POS business unit in 1982, explained that medium- and large-scale merchants formulate and implement their technical plans according to a multi-year cycle, and will not consider the adoption of a new technology until the next planning stage. Although Visa members could demonstrate that the terminals would provide a net benefit for their merchants, it often took several years before the merchants were ready to purchase and install the terminals in their stores.[55]

During this elongated adoption period, the terminal manufacturers continued to enhance their devices. As noted earlier, the first dial terminals performed authorization only; merchants were still required to complete and deposit paper sales drafts. By the mid-1980s, most terminals also supported data capture, meaning they could store the details of each transaction and transmit them electronically to the acquiring processor each night. These types of terminals also featured printers that could automatically dispense cardholder and merchant receipts, completely eliminating the need for the old multi-part paper sales drafts and card imprinters.[56]

---

[53]Cleveland (1999), p. 20.

[54]Cleveland (1999), pp. 22–23.

[55]Powar interview.

[56]Powar, Derman, and Fojtik interviews.

When manufacturers began offering these data capture terminals, Visa USA again offered a special Terminal Interchange Reimbursement Fee (TIRF) for transactions that were not only authorized through the terminal, but also cleared electronically within three days. Like the original TIRF, this new rate provided enough incentive for acquirers and merchants to mass-adopt the data capture terminals, although the pace was again gated by technology planning and implementation cycles.[57]

As these terminals were installed, the paper largely disappeared from the system. Merchants still retain the paper receipts printed by the terminals, but they no longer deposit them with their acquiring bank. Just as with BASE II, the only time a merchant is required to produce the paper is during a dispute, making the exchange of paper the exception rather than the rule.[58]

But the adoption of data capture terminals altered the system in a more profound and fundamental way than simply eliminating the paper. It transformed the way the banks viewed the acquiring business, which now resembled data processing far more than that it did banking. Banks had always justified their merchant discount fees based on the costs of supplying sales drafts, imprinters, training, and draft processing. The terminals reduced or eliminated most of these costs, and the TIRF resulted in further downward pressure on the discount fees, changing the business model into one completely based on scale. To survive, a merchant processor needed to acquire as many transactions as possible, and by the mid to late 1980s, banks found themselves either incapable or uninterested in providing the necessary computing infrastructure. As a result, many banks decided to outsource this function to more specialized firms such as First Data Resources (FDR), or exit the merchant side of the business entirely. Throughout the 1970s and early 1980s, nearly every bank was both an issuer and an acquirer, but by the late 1980s, members tended to specialize in one function or another.

Conclusion

In this chapter, we reviewed how Visa fully automated the last, but perhaps most important, area of the payment system: the point of sale. They accomplished this by not only stimulating the development and adoption of inexpensive POS dial terminals, but also establishing a common standard for encoding the card. With the mass-adoption of data capture terminals in the mid-1980s, the Visa system was capable of processing transactions entirely in electronic form, a dream envisioned by Hock when he was forming NBI, and expressed in the BASE IV design.

I have yet to discuss perhaps the most important element in Hock's electronic value-exchange system: access to deposits through the debit card. In Hock's world of EVE, cardholders should be able to access any pool of value they possessed, and

---

[57] Powar interview.

[58] Derman interview.

his debit card was the key to accessing not only deposits, but also liquid funds in investment accounts. Although this seemed a natural step to Hock, the debit card was highly controversial for the larger banks, as they saw it as a threat to their own ATM and EFT plans. It is to this story of the debit card that we now turn.

Chapter 8
Challenging Conceptual Barriers: EFT and the Debit Card

In the previous chapter, we saw how Visa fully automated the point of sale (POS) by establishing a common standard for encoding the card, stimulating the development of inexpensive POS dial terminals, and encouraging their widespread adoption. Once this occurred, Visa transactions could be processed entirely in electronic form, and the Visa system began to resemble the electronic value exchange system Hock had always desired.

While all this automation of credit card transactions was taking place, NBI/Visa was also working to expand the kinds of assets the system could reach. Key to Hock's vision of electronic value exchange was the ability for cardholders to access any pool of funds they might possess, including deposits, and liquid investments. As early as 1973, Hock began talking publicly about a card that could directly access deposits, and the organization's first debit card, called Entrée, was launched in 1975. Contrary to expectations, however, the card was issued by only a handful of member banks during the 1970s, and it was not until the 1990s that it became widely adopted.

Why did it take so long for the issuing banks to become interested in Visa's debit card? Considering that most banks were dreaming at this time of the "cashless-checkless society," where sleek electronic messages would replace costly and cumbersome paper payment instruments, why did they not eagerly embrace a card with established recognition, acceptance, and electronic processing? The commonly-assumed answer is that bankers did not want to give up their highly-profitable credit cards, but I will argue in this chapter that the complete answer is much more complicated and nuanced than that. Although concerns over losing credit card profits were certainly at work, to focus solely on this reason would be to ignore the highly significant relationship between the Entrée card and the various electronic funds transfer (EFT) plans being formed, discussed, and executed upon by the member banks during this same period. As we shall see, the bankers, retailers, and regulators all had different understandings of and expectations for what EFT would entail, and most of these were substantively different from the Entrée card, as well as Hock's broader concept of electronic value exchange (EVE). Not surprisingly, these disagreements combined to impede acceptance of the Entrée card throughout the 1970s and early 1980s.

D.L. Stearns, *Electronic Value Exchange*, History of Computing,
DOI 10.1007/978-1-84996-139-4_8, © Springer-Verlag London Limited 2011

Visa Synonymous with Credit, Debt, and Financial Distress?

We should pause at this point and address the fact that many readers may be surprised to learn that NBI/Visa has been offering a debit card since the mid-1970s, as consumers and the popular press more commonly associate the Visa brand with buying on credit, mounting consumer debt, and increasing rates of financial distress. Although Visa's centralized marketing efforts focus on payments in general and never mention the word "credit," most American and UK consumers continue to think of Visa as a "credit card company," primarily because debit cards were more slowly adopted in these countries than elsewhere, and their reliance on consumer credit is also much higher than the rest of the world.[1]

This association between Visa and rising levels of credit, debt, and bankruptcy in the US and UK has also caused many politicians, journalists, and even a few academics to lump the central Visa organization and the issuing banks together in their critiques.[2] Their accusations of predatory lending practices, confusing fees, and misleading marketing are certainly justified, but their articulation rarely makes a distinction between the core organization and its member banks, nor between the practices of issuers in the US and UK and those in other parts of the world.

I have no wish to dispute the claims of these critics, but I do find their lack of distinctions to be historically misleading. In order to understand the history of Visa's debit card, it is important to make a distinction between the interests and motivations of the *central Visa organization* and those of the *member banks* who issue cards and establish the terms by which transactions are settled with the cardholder. As we shall see in this chapter and the next, these interests and motivations *were not always aligned*, and in many cases, *were in direct conflict* during this period.

Although the accusations of these critics may certainly be applied to some of the larger American and UK issuers, I find it difficult to maintain them against the rest of the system participants, and especially against the central organization and its founders. It should be apparent after reading the proceeding chapters that Hock did not intend to create a more efficient means of entrapping consumers in uncontrollable levels of debt, nor did he have a particular motivation to do so. Hock's desire was to build a system that enabled consumers to electronically access any pool of funds those consumers might possess, allowing them to choose for themselves wether a particular transaction should be funded with deposits, a line of credit, or any other form of monetary value. There is little about the Visa payment system, both technically and organizationally, that assumes the value being exchanged comes from a line of credit, and the banks in other countries such as France, Norway, New Zealand, and Japan have always used cardholder deposits to settle Visa transactions. The penchant for consumer credit in the US and UK has more to do with historical contingency and consumer preference than system design, but even this has changed in recent years. In 2002, the total number of US debit card transactions processed by Visa exceeded those from credit cards, and in 2008, the total dollar

---

[1] Mann (2006).

[2] For example, see Manning (2000).

volume did so as well.[3] Worldwide, debit transactions surpassed credit transactions in 2003, both in terms of number and dollar volume, and that ratio has continued to rise.[4]

All of this should be good news for the critics of credit cards, but it naturally raises an important historical question: why did it take so long? If NBI's first debit card was released in 1975, why did it take over 30 years for American consumers to use debit cards more than credit cards? The purpose of this chapter to help answer this question, but in order to do so, we must first take a look at the specific historical context surrounding the launch of NBI's Entrée card, and how that influenced its initial reception and rate of adoption.

EFT Utopia, Dystopia and Reality

It would have been difficult for a banker in the early 1970s to miss that something significant was happening. As soon as banks began to adopt digital computers and telecommunications in the 1960s, futurists began dreaming and talking about the inevitable "checkless society," or when they were feeling particular bold, the "cashless-checkless society."[5] By the early 1970s, the various banking trade journals were filled with articles about the possibilities of "Electronic Funds Transfer (EFT)," where checks would be replaced by electronic messages sent by various kinds of terminals and cleared through centralized computer systems. Many banks were already experimenting with ATMs and POS terminals, and several regional automated clearinghouses (ACHs) had been established to facilitate the electronic processing of payroll and benefit deposits, as well as the payment of recurring mortgage, utility, insurance bills. Rafts of books were published promising to explain this new alphabet soup of banking-related technologies and urging bankers to join the electronic banking "revolution" or be left behind.

These authors typically portrayed the possibilities of EFT as a kind of bankers utopia, where self-service customers would interact directly with the bank's computers, transferring electronic money effortlessly between accounts, largely without any human intervention. Deposits would stream directly into consumer accounts, and recurring bill payments would automatically disperse it back out again. The physical handling of payment instruments would be limited to cash, and even most of that could be handled by the ATM. In time, banks could even move their operations to areas with cheaper labor and property costs, yet still be accessible by

---

[3] 'Total US Visa Debit Volume Surpasses Credit for First Time', http://corporate.visa.com/media-center/press-releases/press950.jsp (accessed on 22 June 2010).

[4] Lee (21 April 2004), p. 11.

[5] For early articulations of this see Mitchell (1966) and Carter (1967). Most bankers and serious analysts acknowledged that cash would always remain, but the popular press often predicted the "death of cash."

customers via telephone, ATMs, unmanned kiosks, POS terminals, and other such devices. Labor costs would plummet, and profits would abound.[6]

There was, of course, a real and pressing motivation behind these utopian visions. At this time, the Federal Reserve and the major US banks were processing an estimated 60 million checks *each day*, and each one had to be physically transported from the bank of deposit to the bank of issue, and sorted against the other checks at each step along the way. Magnetic Ink Character Recognition (MICR) sorters had automated the sorting process by the early 1970s, but the costs of physically handling and moving that much paper around the nation were still astounding; Ronald Mann recently estimated that it costs about seven dollars to process each check that passes through the Federal Reserve, which when totaled over a year, amounts to one half of one percent of the nation's entire gross domestic product.[7]

When talk of this "cashless-checkless society" reached the general public, it was greeted not so much with excitement as with confusion and anxiety, especially amongst those over 35.[8] Instead of a banking utopia, it sounded to consumers much more like a Orwellian dystopia. The unsolicited mass-mailing of credit cards in the mid 1960s had already damaged whatever trust consumers had in the banking industry, and phrases like the "cashless-checkless society" made those who had so far avoided credit cards wonder whether they would be forced to use one. Many felt that all this automation would make their bank "impersonal" and reduce them to simply "a number." Those who had concerns about the reliability and accuracy of computers understandably expressed unease over plans to remove the paper trail from the system. Those who typically received cash for their wages or benefits were apprehensive about the need to obtain a bank account to receive electronic credits, and worried about being cheated when the money no longer flowed physically through their hands. Those concerned with privacy issues were naturally nervous about the loss of anonymous instruments like cash, not to mention a system that would make it easy to record and analyze every purchase made. Religious groups preoccupied with the apocalypse saw it as fulfillment of the prophesy in the book of Revelation that the mark of the beast (in this case, the credit card) would be required in order to purchase basic goods and services. Under pressure to protect consumers, the US Senate's Banking Committee eventually put forward tentative bills to establish a moratorium on further EFT development, and established a commission to research the issues and report on recommendations.[9]

Much of the public's negative reaction actually seemed to stem from an unclear understanding what "EFT" actually was, but this is not surprising given that there

---

[6]Like many other cases, these futurists failed to see how these computer systems would also incur significant costs of their own, especially in terms of a new skilled labor force to maintain them. See Noble (1984).

[7]Mann (2006), p. 11. Note that with the passage of the "Check 21" act in 2003, checks may now be truncated at the bank of deposit and cleared electronically, which should reduce their costs considerably.

[8]For an early review of these sentiments, see Riday (1968).

[9]See 'Federal legislation is introduced to establish electronic fund transfer systems commission and study', Payment Systems Newsletter (April 1974), p. 1.

was also little agreement amongst bankers as to what EFT would actually entail, much less when it could reasonably be achieved. As bankers began investigating the possibilities in the early 1970s, a number of important questions arose. Should EFT services be thought of as competitive weapons between the banks, or should they be conceived as a public utility run by the government? If it was to be shared, who should have access: just commercial banks, or the thrifts and investment banks as well? And how would large retailers gain access: through a participating bank or directly? How should it be funded and what should be the pricing model for the various services? Should there be only one type of POS terminal, or should each network develop their own? Did all of this require the establishment of several ANSI or ISO standards before any real implementation could occur? And was any of this really possible, or would it be better to concentrate instead on making cash and paper checks more convenient through the use of ATMs and check guarantee systems? What EFT should be, it seemed, was open to interpretation, and the ultimate solution (or solutions) would require negotiation and cooperation amongst several interested groups.[10]

As one might expect, different groups had very different answers to these questions.[11] The Federal Reserve saw EFT as simply the electronic version of their current check clearing services, and thus argued for a single monolithic system, funded by taxes, that would clear electronic transactions at par. From the Fed's perspective, it made little sense to build multiple competing systems, as the significant investment in computers and telecommunications would be best recouped by funneling as many transactions as possible through a single system.

The more technically-advanced commercial banks tended to disagree. They saw EFT as a competitive banking service, something that would differentiate them from their rivals. Most of these banks were already experimenting with ATMs, and they tended to think of an ATM as a special kind of "branch," that is, a competitive presence in a given service area, and thus not shared with other banks. When some of these banks began to experiment with POS terminals and machine-readable cards, they continued their logic, arguing that the terminals should not be shared either.[12] These banks were willing, however, to *sell* access to their EFT services, hoping to establish a nationwide acceptance through their correspondent banks in other states.

The less technically-sophisticated banks typically favored a shared solution, operated either by the Fed or by an association of regional banks. These banks were often too small to fund competitive systems of their own, and paying to access an EFT system owned and controlled by a competitor was understandably less than ideal.

The credit unions, savings and loan, and mutual savings banks (collectively known as the "thrifts") were also interested in EFT, but for slightly different reasons. American banking regulations had traditionally denied these banks any kind

---

[10]This concept of "interpretive flexibility" comes form Pinch and Bijker (1984).

[11]The following positions were articulated during a 1974 roundtable discussion. See 'When we achieve a nationwide electronic funds transfer system', Banking (May 1974).

[12]See Reed (October 1972), p. 20+.

of third-party payment device; customers of these banks could not write a check to a merchant, but instead were required to visit the branch to withdraw funds in person and then deliver those funds to the merchant themselves. Ostensibly this was meant to enforce the stated purpose of these kinds of banks (savings in the form of time deposits), but it also effectively kept these banks from competing with the commercial banks for demand deposits. Although the thrifts were allowed to receive payroll and benefit deposits in electronic form, they hoped that national EFT would also enable them to offer some form of third-party payments to their customers.

Three developments in the early 1970s moved the thrifts closer to this goal. The first was the development of Negotiable Order of Withdrawal (NOW) accounts, which once blessed by the various state regulators, gave the savings and loans a payment instrument that looked and functioned almost exactly like a check from a commercial bank. The second was the decision by the Comptroller of the Currency and the Federal Home Loan Bank Board, both of which regulated the thrifts, that an ATM or unmanned kiosk did not constitute a "branch," and thus did not violate branching restrictions.[13] The third was the admission of the thrifts to NBI, which provided them with a national credit card with electronic authorization and clearing.

The thrifts typically favored a national system run by the Fed, primarily because their initial attempts to gain access to the early automated clearing house in California were blocked until the Fed intervened.[14] The thrifts feared that if the large commercial banks developed competitive EFT systems, they would be denied access outright or effectively denied access through high fees. Although the thrifts were capable of building and operating their own ATM networks for cash withdrawals, they still needed access to a national automated clearinghouse in order to clear and settle interchange payment transactions.

The large national retailers, such as Sears, Montgomery Wards, and JC Penney, also had strong opinions, but they often found themselves articulating those from the sidelines. When bankers met to discuss their desires for EFT, the retailers were rarely invited, and their compliance with whatever solution would come to pass was generally assumed. The trouble was, the large national retailers were already in a position whereby they might not need banks at all to usher in the era of EFT. Most had already developed their own internal EFT systems by the early 1970s, and were beginning to make those services available to their customers. These retailers already cashed payroll and benefit checks from their customers, maintained their charge card accounts, and issued branded cards that could be read by any of their electronic cash registers (ECRs). Most importantly, these ECRs could electronically credit or debit centrally-maintained accounts from any of their stores, *without paying any merchant discount fee*. Gordon Worley, the Vice President of Finance for Wards commented that it would be relatively trivial for them "to accept deposits and make withdrawals through our electronic cash registers ... and I think the banks

---

[13]This decision was challenged in the courts, but was ultimately upheld. See *Independent Bankers Association of America v. Smith, Comptroller of the Currency of the United States*, No. 75-1786, United States Court of Appeals For the District of Columbia Circuit 175, decided 23 March 1976.

[14]'When we achieve a nationwide electronic funds transfer system', Banking (May 1974).

should co-operate with us on this because, if they force us to go our own way, they could find themselves locked out."[15]

Electronic Funds Transfer or Electronic Value Exchange?

When NBI entered into this fray over EFT, Hock quickly became frustrated with bankers who seemed to be thinking of EFT as simply a way to make their existing practices more efficient, and not an opportunity to radically reshape the way financial services were made available to consumers and merchants. In a 1974 speech at a Federal Reserve conference, he said:

> Of considerable concern is the basic context in which electronic funds transfer is usually discussed. That it is strongly tied to the traditional structure of bank clearings, to reliance upon Federal Reserve assistance in automated clearinghouses, and to the present function of checks, is considerable evidence that banking may be in danger of a course of conduct which has caused many industries to become anachronisms in the marketplace; that is to forget the essence of their business and thus confuse form with substance and cause with effect.
>
> ... It is perhaps understandable that the massive, somewhat preemptory, check clearing activities of the Federal Reserve should have evolved. It is less understandable they be electronically perpetuated. For if an industry uses radically new technology in a manner that perpetuates existing form rather than enhancing function, it may swiftly be hooting in the commercial graveyard where the ghosts of form, which did not follow function, are buried.
>
> It makes no more sense for electronic value exchange to be patterned after the present Federal Reserve check clearing system, and managed, owned or subsidized by the Fed, than it would had the airlines put steel wheels on 747's and jetted them down the Penn Central tracks.[16]

During this speech, he encouraged his audience to abandon the term "electronic funds transfer" for the broader, more encompassing term "electronic value exchange" (EVE), because the former was limiting their thinking about what might be possible now that money had assumed electronic form. Hock was concerned that while his member banks were haggling over the specific form of a national EFT system, they were missing the broader shifts that were already occurring around them, as well as the corresponding opportunities. He argued that consumers and merchants wanted more convenient access to financial services, and there was no particular reason why they would continue to use the existing banking system if another, more attractive option was presented to them.

In fact, there were several other non-bank organizations that were already poised to do exactly this. As mentioned earlier, the large national chain retailers already had charge card plans with electronic processing, and most already owned, or were in partnership with, financial institutions that could provide more complete services to

---

[15] 'Banking at the chain store—closer that you think', US News and World Report (16 September 1974), p. 77.

[16] Hock (1974).

their customers, including deposits, loans, insurance, and real estate.[17] These chains already had a "branch" in every city and most small towns across America, and they had a long history of interacting with more far-flung customers via telephone and mail-order. In many ways, the large retailers were more already adept at being "banks" than the banks were.

Regional chain retailers such as Fred Meyer in the Northwest were also providing complete financial services to their customers, most of whom did not maintain a bank account at all. By 1974, Fred Meyer stores were cashing upwards of 450,000 payroll and benefit checks a month, and if customers had any cash remaining after their purchases, they could deposit it into an interest-bearing account for future use.[18] The account was actually maintained by a state-chartered savings and loan recently purchased by Fred Meyer and electronically linked to their mainframe computer, but from the customer's perspective, the store was acting as their "bank." It was also less intimidating and far more convenient than a traditional bank: a typical bank at this time was open for only four to five hours during the middle of the workday, whereas Fred Meyer stores were open 18 hours a day, seven days a week.

Investment banks were also taking steps to provide better banking services to the more affluent. In the early 1970s, several investment firms began offering what became known as "money market funds," which pooled together customer deposits and invested them into relatively safe, short-term securities, such as Treasury bills.[19] These funds differed from ordinary investments, however, in that customers could withdraw their capital incrementally, on demand. When Fidelity introduced their version in 1974, they completed the service by issuing checks, just as the thrifts had done with NOW accounts. In 1977, Merrill Lynch took this one step further when they unveiled their new "Cash Management Account" (CMA), which came with not only checks but also a Visa card. These types of accounts were highly attractive at the time, as well as threatening to the banks, as they could pay market-rate interest on those "deposits" during a time of high inflation. Banking regulations at this time dictated the relatively low rate of interest commercial banks were allowed to pay on savings accounts, and prohibited them outright from offering any interest on demand accounts.

In addition to retailers and investment banks, several other non-bank institutions were already engaging in activities that closely resembled the core services of banking. The telephone companies were issuing "calling cards," most of which were pre-paid, requiring advance "deposits" from which one could make purchases of telephony services. The postal systems in many European countries were offering

---

[17]Sears owned Sears Bank and Trust Company as well as Allstate Savings and Loan in California, and was investigating a merger with Red Carpet, a real-estate brokerage franchiser; JC Penney had "large insurance and real-estate operations"; and Wards owned Pioneer Trust and Savings Bank. See 'Banking at the chain store—closer that you think', US News and World Report (16 September 1974).

[18]'Banking at the chain store—closer that you think', US News and World Report (16 September 1974), p. 79.

[19]Nocera (1994), pp. 75–88.

savings accounts and national giro payment services, practices that could easily be imitated by the US Postal Service. Non-bank financial service companies such as American Express were also selling travelers cheques, which were international payment instruments that debited advance deposits held by American Express, deposits which could easily be loaned to others for short terms. Hock relished in citing these kinds of examples and then rhetorically asking his audience, which one of these is not a "bank?"

In this new world of electronic value exchange, Hock argued, consumers would move their electronic money to whichever organization provided them with the best return, access, convenience, and customer service, be they retailers, investment banks, thrifts, or otherwise. Banking regulations, which had so far protected commercial banks from this kind of competition, were lagging behind the possibilities created by electronic money, and unless the banks moved quickly to improve and expand their services, they would find themselves no longer in control of the nation's money and payments.

The "Asset Card" Concept

For Hock, the key mechanism for maintaining that control was what he called the "asset card."[20] As early as 1973, he began speaking about a card-based payment service that could access not only a line for credit, but also deposits, investments, or any other pool of funds the cardholder might possess. He used the term "asset card" instead of "credit card" purposefully:

> In the context of customer use, "credit card" has always been a misnomer. Certainly from the user viewpoint, a bank card is solely used to create debits. That is, to dispose of value owned by or to be earned by the user. The term "credit card" is ... a classic example of naming and marketing the product from the perspective of the supplier rather than the user, thus making it unacceptable to a large number of prospective customers.[21]

Hock understood that the names we assign to things tend to influence the way we think about them. This is why the new name for his organization ("Visa") had to be free of any geographic ("American"), service ("Credit or Charge"), or form ("Card") connotations. Similarly, he wanted the bankers to speak about "asset cards" instead of "credit cards" because the latter tended not only to repel those averse to the idea of buying things on credit, but also to limit the ways in which the bankers thought about what the card could do.

In fact, limiting payment cards to credit lines actually made no sense to Hock, as he saw very little difference between credit lines and deposit accounts:

> Bank card accounts, savings accounts and checking accounts have only two substantive differences: First, the time at which the bank requires the customer to make credits—deposits

---

[20]Information on the asset card concept comes from interviews with Honey, Derman, and Russell, as well published sources cited later.

[21]Hock (1973), p. 4.

or payments—to balance the ledger, and second, the party to receive interest and at what rate depending on the balance struck.[22]

In other words, credit lines and deposits are actually two different sides of the same phenomenon: an "account." That account can contain funds loaned to the customer by the bank, or funds loaned to the bank by the customer. In fact, a single account can oscillate between the two states. If you overpay your credit account, the bank will happily hold on to the money, express your balance as positive, and apply those credits to your next statement. If you overdraw your deposit account, the bank can extend you temporary credit, express your balance as negative, and apply your next deposit as repayment of the credit plus interest. Hock argued that this separation between deposits and credit lines was more of a historical accident than a natural distinction, and there was no need to perpetuate it as banks moved into the world of electronic value exchange.

If there is little difference between credit and deposit accounts, Hock continued, then the mechanisms for exchanging the value contained in those accounts must also be essentially the same:

> Checks, like bank cards, are simply mechanical devices for exchanging value by debiting accounts. It is only by custom that credits are required in advance, that third-party acceptance carries no assurance of payment and that MICR encoding on paper governs the mechanics of clearings. In short, that checking accounts are designed more for the convenience of banks in acquiring funds than for customer convenience in the market place.[23]

Hock proclaimed that his asset card could do everything a check could do, and do it *better*, at least from the perspective of consumers, who were quickly becoming the most important customer segment for the future of banking. The checks issued to the increasingly mobile American consumer were unhelpful, as they were not typically accepted outside the issuer's local area, primarily because they were not guaranteed. The BankAmericard had demonstrated that transactions could be guaranteed on a national, and even international scale, and the asset card would be built upon the same organizational and technical infrastructure.

Furthermore, because bankers made an artificial distinction between deposit and credit accounts, their checks were unnecessarily inflexible. Checks required customers to make deposits in advance of their needs, but to do so, customers had to visit a branch—which Hock noted was inaccessible 82 percent of the time—and stand in time-consuming lines.[24] Why, Hock asked, were banks willing to extend their customers ample credit on their BankAmericards, yet not connect that credit to their customers' demand deposit accounts to cover overdrafts? He suggested:

> Bank card accounts could quickly be converted to banking accounts by revising software to carry either credit or debit balances, and marketing the service as a value exchange device with an optional credit feature.[25]

---

[22] Hock (1973), p. 4.

[23] Hock (1973), p. 4.

[24] Hock (1973), p. 4.

[25] Hock (1973), p. 4.

Not surprisingly, this new service would be accessed by Hock's asset card, which would enjoy the same nationwide (and eventually worldwide) acceptance as the BankAmericard. This was the essence of electronic value exchange, and by implication, the future of banking.

NBI's Asset Card

The task of turning this concept into an NBI product was given to Tom Honey, the product developer already introduced in Chap. 6. Although Honey could not control how the banks managed the relationship between their deposit and credit accounts, he could easily design and market a new kind of card that would primarily access funds in a demand deposit account rather than a credit line.

He designed the new card to be a companion to the existing BankAmericard. From an operational perspective, it would look and function almost identically to its elder: it would feature the same blue, white, and gold bands design; would identify the cardholder to the merchant and the system; and would be accepted at any location that currently honored the BankAmericard. When used for purchases, merchants would process the transaction in exactly the same manner: they would call for authorization if necessary; complete a paper sales draft; and deposit it at their acquiring bank. A draft produced from this card would also clear and settle electronically through BASE II just like a credit sales draft. Once it reached the issuer, however, instead of adding the draft to an existing credit account, the issuer would handle it more like a check, directly debiting the cardholder's deposit account. No further billing or collection would be necessary.[26]

The asset card was similar in many ways to an electronic check, but with four important differences. First, the asset card separated account identity from the payment instrument, allowing the card to be used in multiple contexts and devices. Banks were already issuing cards for use in their ATMs, and Hock wanted to replace those special-purpose cards with the more general-purpose asset card, which could also be used at any BankAmericard merchant. He was also thinking ahead to his BASE IV world, where the card could be used in electronic POS terminals, or any transaction origination device.

The second, and perhaps most critical difference was that asset card transactions would be *guaranteed*. In the check payment system, issuing banks could simply return a check to the merchant if the account had insufficient funds, but asset card transactions would be subject to the same payment rules as BankAmericard transactions. If the merchant followed the authorization rules, the merchant was guaranteed payment, even if the source account did not have enough funds. Because floor limits were still in place at this time, overdrafts were thus a distinct possibility, implying that issuers would sometimes be forced to extend temporary credit to cardholders.

The third difference was the scope of acceptance. Because asset card transactions were guaranteed, merchants could accept cards issued from any bank, even if

[26]Honey interview.

it was outside the local area. In fact, Hock's principle of "universality," which was canonized in the bylaws, operating regulations, and merchant contracts, specifically required merchants to accept *any* card with the blue, white, and gold bands design, regardless of who issued it or how that organization settled with the cardholder. While checks eliminated the need to carry large amounts of cash, they were essentially useless outside the issuer's area or at stores where the customer was unknown and thus untrusted. The asset card promised to blend the best of cash and checks: it would be accepted almost as readily as cash, yet be as convenient and safe as a check.[27]

The last critical difference was in the pricing of the service. As discussed in Chap. 1, one of the goals of the new Federal Reserve System was to eliminate the practice of discounting checks cleared through interchange. By the early 1970s, the Fed and State legislatures had enforced par clearing between all banks, and merchants had come to expect full payment for the checks they deposited. Although NBI considered the asset card as a replacement for checks, it was priced in the same way as existing BankAmericard transactions: merchants paid a two to six percent discount fee to acquirers, and acquirers paid the standard interchange reimbursement fee to the issuers. These fees offered a significant benefit to acquirers and issuers, but merchants objected, arguing that they had signed up to accept a credit card, not a discounted replacement for checks.

NBI justified this pricing by appealing to the guaranteed payment feature, and noting that they did not benefit from the same government subsidies enjoyed by the Federal Reserve. But a few merchants considered it an attempt to reintroduce a non-par check, and refused to accept the asset card when it was first issued.[28] Unfortunately for them, their contracts specifically required them to accept all cards bearing the blue, white, and gold bands design, and most merchants eventually capitulated, primarily because volumes remained quite low during the 1970s.

Once ratio of debit to check purchases became significant, several merchants led by Wal-Mart sued Visa and MasterCard, demanding the right to accept the credit but not the debit card. Visa and MasterCard eventually settled, allowing merchants to accept one type of card without having to accept the other, but they also lowered the interchange reimbursement fees for debit cards, which allowed acquirers to offer lower merchant discounts, and thus keep most merchants accepting the debit cards.[29]

"Credit Paranoia"

Based on his experience at Wells Fargo, as well as prior consumer research done by NBI, Honey surmised that the asset card would be most attractive to a segment

---

[27]This is not to say that checks are somehow less prone to fraud than credit card transactions. The point was that asset card transactions should be no more dangerous than a check.

[28]Kutler (9 June 1977), p. 1.

[29]Evans and Schmalensee (2005), pp. 291–294.

of the population that he described as having "credit paranoia." This group was not opposed to payment cards *per se*, but was reticent to adopt a card that accessed a line of *revolving credit*.[30]

Consumer credit has always been a rather emotional subject in the US and the public discourse surrounding it has often been at odds with the actual practices of Americans. Nocera explained this well:

> Consumer credit ... has always occupied a peculiar place in the American psyche. On the one hand, there is no aspect of personal finance more likely to inspire anxiety and even fear. At any moment in our history, one can find ringing denunciations of consumer credit and "usurious" interest rates, calls for reform, worries that things have finally gotten out of hand. "Rather go to Bed supperless than rise in Debt," wrote Ben Franklin, and Americans have been echoing that sentiment ever since...
> On the other hand ... despite the denunciation, despite the free-floating anxiety, Americans have always borrowed money to buy things—if not from a bank, then from *somebody*...There isn't another Western country that has relied so heavily on consumer credit; between 1958 and 1990, there was never a year when the amount of outstanding consumer debt wasn't higher than it had been the year before.[31]

Bank-issued credit cards, which made consumer credit even more widely available, met with a similar response. Despite vituperative condemnation from political officials and stinging articles in the popular press, many Americans still chose to adopt them. More than 38.7 million Americans carried at least one bank-issued credit card by 1974 and that number was steadily increasing.[32]

Nevertheless, Americans were often conflicted about the proper use of bank-issued credit cards. Professional organizations, most notably the American Medical Association (AMA), passed resolutions in the late 1960s prohibiting their members from accepting credit cards for their services.[33] Although the AMA did eventually allow doctors to accept credit cards in 1971, they were still forbidden to advertise the fact outside of their offices.[34] Several states, such as New York, also passed laws prohibiting medical professionals from accepting credit cards for payment. There was just something unseemly about allowing consumers to finance their health care on credit.

There were also categories of purchases for which Americans in the 1970s would never dream of using a credit card. Cultural norms dictated that certain types of goods and services could be purchased with a credit card, but anything else should be budgeted for, and purchased with cash.[35] Today we commonly use credit cards to buy basic necessities such as groceries in order to earn "air miles" or some other

---

[30] Honey interview.

[31] Nocera (1994), p. 20. For a detailed history of consumer credit in the United States, see Calder (1999).

[32] Hock (1976), p. 18. For a classic critical article from the popular press, see O'Neil (1970), pp. 48–50.

[33] Stallwitz (1968), p. 56.

[34] 'Card may be solution to unpaid doctor's bills', American Banker (26 January 1971), p. 1.

[35] Mathews and Slucum (1972), pp. 21–27.

type of rebate, but in the 1970s, buying these types of items on credit was a sign of financial desperation. It communicated something tragic about one's social position, and was thus something to be avoided.[36]

This cultural "working-out" of the proper use of credit cards is referred to by technology and media researchers as the process of "domestication."[37] When a new device is introduced to a culture, firms typically attempt to construct a particular meaning and purpose for that new device through advertising, but consumers then tend to adjust that meaning as they make the device a part of their everyday lives. In the case of credit cards, their initial meaning was tied to consumer credit, which had specific acceptable uses, and thus so did the card. NBI's national advertising had been attempting to change that association, telling consumers to "think of it as money," but by 1974, this message had made little headway. Consumers still tended to think of plastic cards strictly as vehicles for consumer credit, but a debit card might challenge that association in a much more profound way.

In previous research, NBI had determined that about half of all Americans who had demand deposit accounts did not carry any kind of bank-issued credit card.[38] When asked why, the most common response by far was that credit cards tempted one to overspend and incur unmanageable debt. This group was unlikely to ever adopt a credit card, but a card that settled against their deposit account might be attractive.

Honey expected that the asset card would appeal strongly to those concerned about overspending, and would ultimately been seen as acceptable for any purchase currently made with cash or checks. To test the idea, he hired the Field Research Corporation to conduct 1,675 in-depth interviews in various US metropolitan areas across the nation.[39] The results confirmed many of his suspicions, but also revealed some interesting surprises.

First, over 60 percent of those surveyed showed some interest in the asset card. Interest came both from those who had a credit card and those who did not. Those who paid their bill in full each month were interested because it would eliminate the bill, but surprisingly, the strongest interest came from those who financed at least some of their purchases. When asked why, these cardholders responded that they saw it as a convenient replacement for cash and checks, not as a replacement for their credit card, indicating that they wanted to carry both and choose when to pay with deposits, and when to pay with credit.[40]

Second, those interested in the card were actually willing to pay for the privilege of using it. Honey had expected this given his experience helping to develop the Wells Fargo Gold Account (which offered a suite of consumer banking services for

---

[36]This is also similar to Zelizer's observation that we often treat money earned from different pursuits in different ways. See Zelizer (1994), p. 3.

[37]Hartmann et al. (2005).

[38]'Visa debit card service: a digest of key research findings' (March 1977).

[39]'Visa debit card service: a digest of key research findings' (March 1977); 'Visa debit card services' (March 1977).

[40]'Visa debit card services' (March 1977).

a flat monthly fee), but the member bankers in the advisory group were shocked. They had always assumed that payment services such as checks had to be given away free in order to entice deposits. A cardholder fee combined with the merchant discount or interchange fee would likely make the service at least self-supporting, if not outright profitable.

Member Reactions

Although consumers seemed to like the asset card concept, Honey encountered significant resistance when he began pitching it to many of the member banks. This may seem surprising as the asset card itself had a rather attractive value proposition: it was a fairly simple extension of the BankAmericard system; would reintroduce the revenue stream banks used to receive from non-par checks; and might even generate new monthly cardholder fees. Nevertheless, many of the card managers worried that the asset card might "cannibalize" their existing BankAmericard programs, many of which were just starting to become profitable. Honey tried to use the consumer research to show that cardholders would use the asset card as a companion to their BankAmericard, and not as a replacement, but most members remained unconvinced.

But there was another important and deeper reason why these banks resisted the asset card. Many of these banks were not against the idea of a debit card *per se*, but they were against the idea of a debit card controlled by NBI. They saw the asset card as a challenge to their own EFT plans, most of which had different assumptions about the required technological infrastructure and how that infrastructure should be shared with other banks.

Although most of these planned EFT systems faced the same kind of operational issues the credit card programs had already overcome, these banks did not consider the card associations to be the proper foundation upon which to implement their EFT plans. This was due at least in part to a particular social dynamic that was operating in most US banks at this time.

Credit Cards vs. "Real" Banking

Several interview sources commented that during the 1970s and early 1980s, there was a deep cultural and political divide between the credit card operations and what they called the "deposit side" of the bank. Hock lamented in a 1974 speech that "In the minds of the executive management of most banks, bank cards are little understood and rarely thought of as a real part of the bank."[41] Tom Cleveland, Visa's treasurer and CFO, also pointed out this attitude:

---

[41] 'Banking lacks national structures to deal adequately with change', American Banker (25 September 1974), p. 1.

In bad economic times, the Visa portfolio could deliver 70–80% of a bank's bottom-line profits, 10–15% was normal, but the card operations were never given the respect they deserved. They were not viewed as banking. They were the new stepchildren in the family of banking that everyone wished would stay quiet and unseen, but would keep working harder than ever.[42]

Of course, this was not completely universal; a few progressive or innovative banks did view the cards as critical to their future, but these banks were the exceptions, not the rule.

While bank presidents and directors often recognized the potential profits to be made from the credit card, the deposit side of the bank still considered it a somewhat questionable venture: something that might be useful in attracting new consumer deposits, but not something the bank should ever focus upon or integrate as a core function. For them, the credit card was just a new form of unsecured consumer lending, which was an activity more commonly associated with disreputable finance companies, corner pawn shops, and loan sharks. The high fraud losses resulting from the unsolicited mass-issuance of cards in the late 1960s, only further reinforced this view.

For these bankers, *real* banking consisted of two primary activities: taking in more and more deposits, so that you could make larger and larger commercial loans. This is how banks traditionally made their profits, and as such, those involved with deposits and commercial lending tended to have more political power within the bank than those involved with consumer lending and credit cards.

This power differential often took a physical form as well. The card operations center was commonly housed in the least desirable location of the bank building, often in the basement or attic. This was partly due to the noisy, finicky computing and sorting equipment, but card managers also felt an unspoken desire to keep them far away from the stately lobbies and offices where the "real" banking took place. Don Jutilla, the BankAmericard program manager for Puget Sound National Bank recalled his department's accommodations:

[the bank] never really thought we'd make it. They started out by putting us on the 17th floor of a 16-story building. We had a gold spire on the top of the building ... they put us up in there, thinking that we were probably just going to fade away and they wouldn't have to build a building for us or anything.[43]

Entrée vs. EFT

Because of this cultural and political divide within the banks, it was typically those on the deposit side who formulated and controlled the bank's EFT plans, not those on the credit card side. Instead of rethinking their assumptions and practices in light

---

[42]Cleveland (1999), p. 21.

[43]Jutilla interview. Jutilla noted that because his bank did embrace consumer lending more than others, he was actually treated better than most.

of the new technology and consumer needs, the deposit bankers tended to develop their EFT plans as extensions of their current practices, which were quite different from those of the credit card associations. As a result, their plans tended to differ from the asset card in at least three important ways.

First, bankers on the deposit side were typically much more conservative and cautious, so many of these banks opted for an incremental approach toward EFT involving ATMs and check authorization or guarantee systems.[44] Instead of replacing cash and checks with a debit card, these banks sought to make it easier for customers to obtain cash, and safer for merchants to accept checks. Any card they issued merely served as an additional form of identification, or the mechanism for accessing a check authorization service, which simply compared the account against a negative list. Some banks did go a step further by providing special terminals that transformed the check into a guaranteed payment instrument, but only in particular stores within a limited area.[45]

Second, for those that did plan to offer a point of sale debit card, they often required a different technical infrastructure from what NBI was proposing for the asset card. This is best explained by realizing that these bankers tended to see the point of sale as a special kind of ATM, while NBI typically viewed an ATM as a special kind of merchant. As a result, these bankers wanted a similar operational environment at the point of sale as they had for ATMs: electronic terminals; supporting the entry of a Personal Identification Number (PIN) for cardholder authentication; authorizing and clearing every transaction at the time of sale with a single message. In contrast, NBI's Entrée card was designed to operate in the same environment as the BankAmericard: accepted worldwide; at merchants with or without terminals; authenticated only by a signature; authorized only when the transaction exceeds the merchant's floor limit; and cleared at a later time with a separate message.

The key concern these banks had with the Entrée card's technical infrastructure was its potential for uncontrollable overdrafts. Since not all transactions were authorized at this time, it was distinctly possible that a given customer's account might not have funds to cover all their transactions received from clearing. This was of course common with checks as well, but checks with insufficient funds could be returned to the merchant, whereas Entrée transactions could not because they were guaranteed. This meant that banks would be required to extend temporary overdraft credit to Entrée cardholders, and although this would have resulted in a new lucrative source of revenue for these banks, they were nonetheless unwilling to entertain the idea. For them, "EFT" meant the instant electronic transfer of funds between accounts, which did not introduce the potential for overdrafts. Unfortunately, it would take many years for most merchants to adopt the technical infrastructure necessary

---

[44]For example, see 'Nashville Banks Cautious on EFT', American Banker (11 December 1975), p. 1.

[45]'Security Pacific, California, contracts for POS system for merchants', American Banker (7 October 1976), p. 2. Interestingly, the Nashville banks did not offer a guarantee because they were concerned that doing so would turn the merchant into a potentially illegal "branch," as checks were not guaranteed by law until they were presented to, and accepted by, the issuing bank.

to support these ATM-like transactions at the point of sale, but these banks felt that it was necessary to wait for that to occur.

Third, their plans often embodied a different model of competition and cooperation from NBI's. As already noted, the deposit side of these banks viewed the point of sale as a special kind of ATM, and they also viewed the ATM as a special kind of branch. Branches provided a competitive presence in a service area, and as such, were not shared with rival banks. Similarly, ATMs were not typically shared with rivals because they too provided a competitive presence. EFT devices and services at the point of sale were treated the same way; these banks were often willing to co-operate with their correspondent banks far away, but wanted a way to deny access to their competitors down the street. NBI's principles of universality and open membership would have made that impossible, so these banks formed new associations with different rules, or simply kept their technology proprietary, licensing it to selected correspondent banks.

This was quite common in the regional ATM networks that would eventually consolidate into the PLUS, Cirrus, and STAR networks, but one example in the world of debit cards was Worthen Bank and Trust's "Moneycard" service, which it began licensing in 1975.[46] Their Chairman and CEO described their strategy:

> Worthen believes that the best avenue for development of electronic funds transfer technology is a joint approach involving regional money-center banks, such as Worthen, in harmonious cooperation with correspondent banks located in towns and cities of all sizes throughout the state.[47]

Despite rhetoric such as "joint approach" and "harmonious cooperation," the operative phrase in this quote is "correspondent banks." Worthen was willing to share their debit card service with other banks, but only those with which they had a non-competitive relationship. They also wanted to retain complete ownership over the technology and marks, merely licensing them to their correspondents much like the BofA licensed the BankAmericard prior to NBI.

In many ways, NBI's asset card was a collision of social worlds. It looked and acted like a credit card, but it directly accessed consumer deposits. It was controlled by a card association, and promoted internally by the credit card department, and as such, threatened to upset the balance of power between the consumer credit and deposit sides of the bank. It brought with it a certain operating environment that was substantively different from that of checks and ATMs, and many of the banks were uncomfortable with the possibility of increased or uncontrollable overdrafts. It brought with it a particular set of rules that required the banks to co-operate with their direct competitors. But perhaps the worst part was that it would allow Dee Hock to dictate how the banks would enable electronic access to their deposits. Ken Larkin, the BofA executive who managed the BankAmericard licensing program before NBI, put it bluntly:

---

[46] For a review of ATM network sharing policies up until 1984, see Felgran (1984), p. 27.

[47] Penick (12 September 1975), p. 1. Worthen is the same bank that challenged NBI's dual membership ban. See the section beginning on p. 113.

As long as [Hock] kept to credit cards, banks were willing to give him leeway. The moment you get into the debit card, you're talking about more than $1 trillion [in deposits]. You're hitting bankers where they live. They weren't going to let anybody, *especially* Dee Hock, tell them how to manage their deposit stream.[48]

Enter Entrée

Although the number of potential issuers looked to be small, NBI announced in August 1975 that its new asset card, now named Entrée, would be available to issuers starting in October.[49] Initially, Hock wanted the asset card to look exactly the same as the BankAmericard, as he considered the manner in which cardholders settle with their banks to be a matter of privacy. But since electronic POS terminals with credit/debit options were not yet widely available, cardholders needed a way to distinguish between the two types of cards, so the separate name Entrée was used. Unfortunately for NBI, the separate name also had the side effect of providing merchants with an easy way to identify, and potentially refuse, what they considered to be the reintroduction of a non-par check. When NBI adopted the name Visa in 1977, they dropped the name Entrée from the asset card and let issuers put their own name in the blue band, making it much more difficult to distinguish from the credit card.

When the service officially launched in October 1975, about 15 banks promised to issue the Entrée card, but the rest remained uncommitted.[50] One of the first to issue was City National Bank and Trust of Columbus, Ohio, the same bank who tested a similar type of card back in 1971.[51] They were soon joined by Pittsburgh National Bank, as well as banks in Colorado, Arizona, and Louisiana.[52] As Honey had predicted, these early adopters found that the Entrée card did not cannibalize their credit card volumes, and at least one bank was able to charge a monthly cardholder fee.[53] They also discovered that their Entrée cards were used far more often than their BankAmericards, yet they experienced less fraud, primarily because cardholders were more careful with what they regarded as their own money.[54]

The card was renamed "Visa Debit" after the organization changed its name, but number of issuers still grew slowly throughout the 1970s, reaching only 90 by the end of the decade, causing the press to comment on the "disappointing acceptance

---

[48] Ken Larkin quoted in Nocera (1994), p. 308.

[49] Brouillette (28 April 1975), p. 1, Brooke (22 August 1975), p. 1.

[50] 'Visa debit card service: a digest of key research findings' (March 1977), p. 1, 'NBI announces Entree card', Payment Systems Newsletter (September 1975), p. 1.

[51] See p. 74.

[52] American Banker (3 March 1976), p. 6, American Banker (23 April 1976), p. 2.

[53] 'Visa debit card service: a digest of key research findings' (March 1977), p. 2. Louisiana National charged one dollar a month after the first six months, which was just enough to weed out the inactive cardholders.

[54] Honey interview.

of the concept over the past five years."[55] The adoption rate began to increase at the start of the 1980s, growing to 306 by the end of 1981. The widespread adoption of POS terminals helped matters a bit, as most transactions could now be authorized, and overdrawn accounts could be shut off quickly.[56] Throughout the 1980s, however, most banks continued to issue ATM and debit cards that carried one of the marks from the other PIN-based, single-message networks, such as PLUS, Cirrus, or Interlink, and not Visa.[57]

Several factors then combined to significantly escalate the rate of adoption in the US during the 1990s. First, Visa's technological infrastructure was expanded to support the single-message, PIN-based transactions that banks felt were necessary. This system was originally developed in 1985 for the Interlink POS debit card network, for which Visa USA provided the processing, and after Visa acquired Interlink in 1987, as well as the national ATM network PLUS, it was able to offer single-message, PIN-based transaction processing to all its US members.[58]

Second, Visa was able to convince a number of influential, money-center banks to convert their proprietary ATM cards to Visa Debit cards in the early 1990s. For example, Chase Manhattan converted their 800,000 "Money Cards" to Visa Debit in 1991, and their commitment influenced several other banks to follow suit, resulting in a 21 percent increase in cards issued that year.[59] These banks were now more receptive to the Visa Debit card not only because of the improved technological infrastructure and worldwide acceptance, but also because a new generation of management had ascended since the 1970s. These bankers saw less of a distinction between their card programs and deposit banking activities, and were thus less hostile to a debit card controlled by the card associations.

Third, Visa embarked on a national advertising campaign to promote the card amongst consumers, at which time they also renamed the card "Visa Check." The new name was intended to emphasize that the card was a more convenient replacement of checks at the point of sale, and distance it from the word "debit," which many consumers associated too closely with "debt." Visa's strategy was to increase overall consumer demand for the card, which would in turn push more member banks to issue them to their customers.

Fourth, the most important merchant class of all began to accept debit cards in the early 1990s: the supermarkets. Americans wrote the majority of their checks in

---

[55] 'NCNB to become biggest bank in Visa debit card program', American Banker (8 March 1979), p. 3. Confusingly, after the card was renamed Visa Debit, the name Entrée was reused for a separate joint venture between Visa/PLUS and MasterCard/Cirrus in the 1980s (Derman and Harrison interviews).

[56] Kutler (9 March 1981), p. 1. 'Debit card volume rises 187% at Visa', American Banker (14 December 1981), p. 9.

[57] As late as 1994, only eleven percent of US ATM/debit cards carried the Visa mark (Evans and Schmalensee 2005, p. 206). Honey believes that Hock mistakenly ignored the growing threat posed by these networks, favoring instead to focus on building his international organization (discussed in Chap. 9).

[58] Peirce, Loftesness, and Harrison interviews; see also Modi (October 1987), pp. 68–72.

[59] 'Fee income spurs new debit strategies', Banking (September 1991), pp. 92–94.

the supermarket checkout line, but the supermarkets had traditionally resisted accepting any kind of bank card because the standard merchant discount fees would have consumed most of their already narrow margins. Supermarkets began accepting PIN-based ATM cards initially, as those networks charged only a flat fee per transaction, and Visa responded by offering a specific merchant discount rate for supermarkets on their signature-based debit cards that on average was close to what the ATM networks were charging. This was enough to convince a few supermarket chains to accept Visa debit cards, and the others soon followed suit.

All of these factors combined throughout the 1990s to create a veritable explosion in American debit card volume: the number of transaction per year on Visa USA's debit cards rose from 87 million in 1990 to 6.5 billion by 2002.[60] As already noted, Visa USA has processed more debit transactions than credit since 2002, and debit card dollar volume eclipsed that of credit in 2008.

Conclusion

Since the debit card was ultimately adopted by the vast majority of US members, it is tempting to think of it as simply a product ahead of its time. That may have been true to some extent, but it is also helpful to view it as the locus of a power struggle between the central Visa organization and its members over what it should and should not be doing. From Hock's perspective, the debit card was simply the next logical step in creating his system for electronic value exchange, but from the membership's perspective, the debit card was a break from NBI's past activities, and an attempt to control their EFT plans. In their minds, NBI existed to coordinate their credit card programs, not compete with their EFT offerings.

To be clear, Hock did not wish to control the members' EFT plans as much as he wanted a chance to offer consumers what he thought was a truly better option. He was concerned that member banks would repeat the early history of bank credit cards, either by waiting for the ideal solution while losing their customers, or racing to issue ill-conceived, localized debit cards with even less geographical range than a check. Visa's staff continued to push the member banks to issue the debit card during the 1970s and 80s, but the lack of support from the issuers during this time period ultimately kept it out of the hands of consumers.

By resisting the debit card, the member banks attempted to establish limits on the role they thought Hock and the central organization should be playing. Of course, Hock continued to challenge these limits, attempting to expand the activities his organization coordinated, and redefining his own role as he saw fit. The tension this created between himself and the membership can be observed in the frustration he began to express in his annual conference speeches. He accused the bankers of being "highly suspicious of new structures ... historically successful at reaction rather than action ... [and] comfortable with the theology of centralized non-competitive

---

[60]Evans and Schmalensee (2005), pp. 206–211.

clearing of checks." He warned them that their stubborn adherence to existing structures and practices might soon turn them into an anachronism:

> Certainly the vast religion of electronic value exchange ought to be able to worship effectively in more than the temple of demand deposits, checks, Federal Reserve clearings and interest on loans, and without the priests requiring that all belong to the same sect. But I suppose that depends on whether it is the form or the substance of banking that we worship most. The congregation we call customers may remain for a time, since the temple is familiar, but other preachers with powerful messages are talking just outside.[61]

In another speech, he once again spelled out his vision of electronic value exchange, and warned the bankers that despite their better wishes, the world had changed, and it was now up to them to decide whether they would remain relevant:

> Above all else, a merchant wants to sell to the customers of all banks with a single, common, swift procedure at the point of sale, have a guaranteed transaction and use technology compatible with that required for his own pricing, inventory control and accounting. Merchants have time and again demonstrated willingness to pay well for such a service.
>
> Consumers want a secure place for their funds, a fair market return, and access to them 24 hours a day, 7 days a week from wherever they may be throughout the world. They too have demonstrated time and again willingness to pay well for such a service.
>
> There is no technological reason why such service should not be given. No law prevents it. No competitor can stop it. There is only lack of willingness among bankers to join together and do it... The battle to be won is not among traditional, regulated banks, but between banks as a whole and the unregulated predators...
>
> The situation facing baking can be synthesized in two sentences. The application of electronics to the exchange of value has irrevocably broken the banking oligopoly. The financial services business is being transformed into a low-cost, global industry, in which banks are high-cost, local providers.
>
> The consequences are obvious. The structure of banking will be radically altered. The unanswered question is, will it be altered by regulated bankers? If not, will they in the words of Omar Khayyam, eventually "go the way of yesterday's seven thousand years?"[62]

The debit card was only the first of these power conflicts between Hock and the member banks. In the next chapter, we will see how these conflicts continued to escalate, ultimately resulting in Hock's departure from the organization in 1984.

---

[61] 'Bank cards are real banking, too', American Banker (27 September 1974), p. 4.
[62] Hock (1984).

Chapter 9
Negotiating Roles: Controversies and the End of an Era

In the previous chapter, we reviewed the history of Visa's debit card, and saw that its relatively delayed adoption was due more to its complicated relationship with the member bank's electronic funds transfer (EFT) plans than it was to a concern over losing lucrative credit card profits. Visa's early debit card brought with it a particular technical and cooperative infrastructure that clashed with most banks' EFT plans, and the cultural divide between the consumer credit and deposit sides of the banks during the 1970s and 1980s kept Hock from reshaping those plans to more closely resemble his vision of electronic value exchange.

In this chapter, I will continue developing this theme, describing other such conflicts over what role Hock and the central organization should play, both in the Visa payment system and the banking industry as a whole. The central Visa organization was created to facilitate and coordinate those activities that members could not perform alone, but we should not assume that the boundaries of these activities were ever "natural" or obvious to all those involved. Indeed, different groups in the system had different understandings of what the central organization should do, and more importantly, should *not* do.

When NBI formed in 1970, most of the members assumed that the organization's role was solely to coordinate the interchange of credit card transactions: that is, fix the existing BankAmericard system. As we have seen, Hock's conception of his and NBI's roles was far larger. Hock was intent on creating the premier system for electronic value exchange, and credit cards were only an initial piece of that plan. Thus, the actual role Hock and the central organization ended up playing had to be "worked out" as the system evolved. This working-out was accomplished through various power struggles, some quiet and calm, others public and bitter.[1]

Although Hock and the members held different views about NBI's role, they were largely compatible for the first half of the 1970s. The establishment of the bylaws and operating regulations, the development of BASE I and II, and the formation of IBANCO could all be seen both as actions to fix the BankAmericard system *and*

---

[1]The idea that different actors in a network attempt to "enroll" one another comes from Actor–Network Theory. See Callon (1986a), Latour (1987, 2005), and Law (1987).

D.L. Stearns, *Electronic Value Exchange*, History of Computing,
DOI 10.1007/978-1-84996-139-4_9, © Springer-Verlag London Limited 2011

necessary building blocks for a larger electronic value exchange system. Both Hock and the members saw these developments as important, but they did so for different reasons.

All of this changed, however, in the mid-1970s, when, as we saw in the previous chapter, Hock introduced NBI's first signature-based debit card. For Hock, this was the next logical step in his electronic value exchange plan, but for the members, it was an unwelcome expansion of the role they had assigned the central organization. Throughout the later 1970s, Visa continued to challenge this limited role, and two incidents in particular give us a window into this negotiation process. The first was Visa's entry into the travelers cheque business in 1978, which the largest member banks interpreted as an encroachment upon their own proprietary travelers cheque programs.[2] The second came in 1979, when Hock signed a direct merchant agreement with JC Penny, one of the three largest US retail chains at the time, bypassing a merchant acquiring bank. In response, the members began to accuse Hock of empire building, and acting more like their *competitor* than their *coordinator*. As Hock and the members continued to struggle over their respective roles, tensions increased, Hock's power of persuasion began to fade, and he was ultimately forced out of the organization in 1984.

Visa Travelers Cheques

The first episode in which we can see the central organization negotiating its role was Visa's entry into the travelers cheque business beginning in 1978.[3] Travelers cheques were not an obvious business for Visa to consider, nor was the role Visa should play in the resulting program. As we shall see, their role had to be worked out with the largest of the member banks through a series of power struggles and compromises.

A Brief Background of Travelers Cheques

Before we discuss Visa's travelers cheque program in particular, it might be helpful to pause and explain what a travelers cheque is in general, as those born after 1990 may not have actually used or even seen one. The international expansion of electronic payment card networks such as Visa, as well as the worldwide ATM networks

---

[2]Because these instruments had worldwide acceptance, I will use the traditional international spelling for "cheque" instead of the American "check" in this chapter to avoid confusion.

[3]Information on Visa's travelers cheque program comes from interviews with Bill Powar and Tom Honey (both of whom played key roles in the program), as well as specific print sources cited below.

developed in the 1980s and 1990s, have now rendered travelers cheques nearly obsolete, but in the midst of the 1970s, travelers cheques were still the primary mechanism for those traveling abroad to transport and exchange the funds needed for their trip. This was especially true in areas of the world where credit and travel cards had not yet made significant penetration, such as the Middle East and Africa.

Travelers cheques are essentially prepaid, guaranteed, negotiable instruments, similar to a cashier's check. They are purchased from an issuing financial organization (or a licensed reseller) for fixed amounts of a given currency plus a service fee, and later redeemed for face value at another participating organization. Many merchants frequented by tourists also accept travelers cheques as payment for goods and services, and those merchants in turn redeem them for currency from a participating organization. Travelers cheques have been historically favored over cash while traveling primarily because most travelers cheque issuers would replace stolen or lost cheques within a relatively short amount of time, and in some cases, they were more readily accepted by foreign merchants than some lesser-known or less-trusted currencies. Their use has begun to dwindle in the first part of the twenty-first century, but they are still marketed by several issuers as a more disciplined and safe alternative to electronically-processed cards.

Although the original invention of travelers cheques is somewhat contested, it is generally acknowledged that the American Express Company (AmEx) developed the first large-scale travelers cheque network starting in 1891.[4] Over the course of the twentieth century, AmEx built a worldwide network of offices and agents each of whom helped establish acceptance of the cheques in particular and the AmEx brand in general. By the 1970s, AmEx travelers cheques were considered the safest and most accepted form of international currency, so it is not surprising that their cheque design and business model became the template for all those that followed.

Although American Express eventually operated offices worldwide, they sold most of their travelers cheques through the organizations most consumers would naturally think of visiting for money-related matters: their local banks.[5] AmEx licensed banks to resell the cheques, offering the bank part of the service fee as a commission. The AmEx service fee was traditionally around one percent of the purchased amount, and the commissions were negotiated to be anywhere between one and two thirds of this fee. The commission was not a large source of revenue for these banks; just like their early credit cards, they were less interested in making profit from the cheques themselves as they were in offering a service that they hoped would attract more customers and deposits. In fact, many banks paid the fees themselves (less their commission) for important customers, or as a promotion to attract new depositors.[6]

---

[4]Nilson (June 1978), Report No 190, p. 1. See also, 'Travelers checks: a far-flung banking business', Banking (September 1965), pp. 154–155.

[5]In the US, the largest reseller of AmEx travelers cheques in terms of sales volume was actually the Automobile Association of America, but the majority of their reselling agents were banks (Powar interview).

[6]'Travelers checks: a far-flung banking business', Banking (September 1965), p. 155.

Because their travelers cheques were replaceable, AmEx needed a way to authenticate the holder at the time of exchange so that a thief could not easily use stolen cheques. They employed a double-signature technique where the purchaser signed each cheque once at the time of purchase, and again at the time of use. Those accepting the checks (which often included hotels and other merchants frequented by tourists) were required to compare the signatures to verify a match, and consult a printed list of known stolen or invalidated cheque numbers if they suspected a forgery. Once authenticated, the travelers cheque became a guaranteed payment instrument; it was prepaid, so there was never the potential for insufficient funds, and in the case of undetected fraud, the AmEx absorbed the loss.

Travelers cheques became a highly successful enterprise for AmEx, but not due to the fees charged when purchasing the cheques. These fees were nominal, usually around one percent of the face value, so the fee barely covered the costs of printing and handling the cheques, much less the development and safekeeping of the original cheque printing dies, the operation of a worldwide network of offices, the replacement service, and fraud insurance. Instead, AmEx earned profits primarily by investing a portion of the funds not yet redeemed into short-term securities, just as a bank could do with a portion of its outstanding deposits. Furthermore, travelers cheques had another interesting and highly profitable property in practice: some were simply never redeemed. Purchasers who did not use all their cheques on a particular trip would often put the remainder in a drawer and completely forget about them. After the requisite period of time required by the relevant governmental power (typically four to seven years), American Express could then simply invalidate the cheque and escheat the funds behind it. ("Escheat" is a common-law term referring to the turning over of unclaimed property to a governmental authority. In most jurisdictions, AmEx could keep the funds from such unclaimed cheques, but still had to account for them as a liability on the balance sheet, as the original purchaser might file a claim with the government in the future. In practice, however, claims were rare and AmEx could continue to invest those funds, reaping significant returns.)

American Express has remained the top issuer of travelers cheques, but their success encouraged several other travel corporations, as well as a few large commercial banks, to start travelers cheque programs of their own during the early decades of the twentieth century. By the late 1970s, the top five travelers cheque issuers included two travel corporations (American Express and Thomas Cook, both of which were actually quasi-bank entities) and three commercial banks (Bank of America, Citibank, and Barclays).[7] Each of these organizations fought to license other banks and financial institutions to sell their particular brand of travelers cheques, and their primary competitive weapon was the seller's commission rate, which could be negotiated on a seller-by-seller basis.

Unfortunately, none of these issuers ever revealed their annual sales volumes nor their profits, but one journal in the mid 1960s estimated the *annual* sales volume of all issuers combined to be around $ 4 billion USD, and the *American Banker*

---

[7] Kutler (30 August 1979), p. 1.

newspaper estimated this had risen to \$12 billion USD by 1978.[8] It was also estimated that AmEx alone accounted for at least half of that volume. AmEx and BofA typically claimed that their profits were minimal due to handling and fraud prevention, but as we shall see, they also fought fiercely to retain their share of the market, suggesting that their profits were perhaps larger than they let on.[9]

Visa's Entry Into Travelers Cheques

By the mid 1970s, Visa had successfully competed with American Express in the credit card arena, but it was not at all obvious to either Visa's executives nor the member banks that it should compete with American Express on travelers cheques as well. After all, Visa had been formed to fix the BankAmericard system, and in many ways the internationally accepted Visa credit card of the late 1970s was a more flexible electronic *replacement* of the paper-based, currency-specific travelers cheque. Getting involved in travelers cheques would also mean competing not only with American Express, but also the proprietary travelers cheque programs of some Visa's largest member banks.

But there were some practical and strategic reasons why a Visa travelers cheque might make sense. Consumers in the 1970s still tended to trust that travelers cheques would be more readily accepted while traveling than a credit card, and Visa did not yet offer a speedy replacement service for lost or stolen cards like American Express did for travelers cheques. Getting local cash with a Visa card also required visiting a Visa member bank, as the international ATM networks did not yet exist, and many banks charged fees or immediate interest for cash advances. And perhaps most importantly, a Visa-branded travelers cheque might enable smaller banks to develop their own travelers cheque programs, benefiting from the worldwide recognition of the Visa mark. This would also allow them to enjoy the profits they were currently generating for American Express, a company they neither owned nor controlled. Hock in particular bristled at the idea of his member banks helping AmEx develop a brand the banks did not own, accusing AmEx of treating its licensee banks like "tenant farmers."[10]

In addition to these practical reasons, there was also a philosophical reason why a Visa travelers cheque might be appropriate. In Hock's vision of electronic value exchange, the device used to access funds did not necessarily need to be a plastic card. After all, the card was merely a historically-contingent artifact, a device to identify the cardholder as a member of the internationally-recognized and accepted Visa payment network. If the Visa mark appeared on a paper travelers cheque, it would still serve the same purpose. The refundable prepaid aspect of travelers cheques was

---

[8] 'Travelers checks: a far-flung banking business', Banking (September 1965), p. 154. 'Citicorp sues interbank over travel checks', American Banker (14 April 1978), p. 1.

[9] For example, see 'Travelers check plans disclaimed', American Banker (25 July 1978), p. 9.

[10] Kutler (10 July 1978), p. 1.

also not unlike a special deposit account from which the cheque holder could withdraw. In fact, a Visa travelers cheque would essentially act like a fixed-denomination debit card sales draft, and if it was eventually processed electronically, it would fit nicely into the overall vision.

Despite these reasons, a Visa travelers cheque still felt to some in the central organization like a step backward, and to the large member banks as a potential threat to the autonomy of their own proprietary travelers cheque programs. It also called into question the role Visa should play with respect to the member banks. Was its role simply to administrate credit and debit card interchange, or was it more generally to facilitate any payment-related endeavor that the individual member banks could not reasonably accomplish alone? Many of the larger issuers felt that it was strictly limited to the former, while Hock and most of his executive team understood it to be the latter.

The real catalyst for the Visa travelers cheque program, however, was the announcement in December of 1977 that the rival Interbank network would soon begin issuing Master Charge branded travelers cheques.[11] The recent institution of duality (discussed in Chap. 6) had made the existence of two separate systems owned by the same banks somewhat questionable, so Visa needed to offer a swift competitive response in order to retain its image as the technological leader in payments. In January 1978, Visa announced that it was "seriously studying the possibility of issuing travelers cheques," and Hock tasked two of his key executives, Tom Honey and Bill Powar, to formulate a plan.

Reactions and Negotiations

Meanwhile, Interbank began implementing their travelers cheque program. Following the design of American Express, Interbank formed a new subsidiary called MCTC Corporation, which acted as the sole issuer of Master Charge branded travelers cheques. Member banks were then recruited to resell the cheques, earning a slightly higher commission than they would for selling AmEx's cheques. This seemed to Interbank to be a good idea, as it would centralize issuance and the corresponding liability for redemption, replacement, and fraud. It would also provide Interbank with an additional source of revenue beyond their member and processing fees.

The distinction between *issuer* and *seller* is important here: the issuer is legally responsible for honoring the payment instrument when it is eventually redeemed, but the issuer also holds the outstandings and is able to earn most of the profits by investing the allowed portion of them in short-term securities. Sellers, on the other hand, merely resell the cheques to consumers, collecting a one-time commission for each sale. The Interbank model setup MCTC as the sole issuer, and all other member banks were simply resellers.

---

[11] 'Visa studies travelers checks', American Banker (25 January 1978), p. 1.

Unfortunately for Interbank, one of their largest members, Citibank, did not think this was such a good approach.[12] Citibank was one of the largest proprietary travelers cheque issuers at the time, with an estimated $2.4 billion in sales annually, and most of the 3,500 licensee banks that resold their cheques were also members of Interbank. Citibank objected that their own member fees would be used to pay for a competing program that those reselling banks would no doubt adopt, as they would then partially own it. The Board members from Citibank reportedly voted against Interbank's travelers cheque program, but were ultimately outnumbered, so Citibank then sued Interbank (which, strangely, they partially owned) for restraint of trade, asking for an immediate injunction against the program.

The Citibank suit clearly demonstrated that the large member banks would not allow Visa to play the role of sole issuer, as Interbank had done. To avoid being dragged into similar suits, Visa pursued an issuing model that more closely matched their existing credit and debit card programs. Although the travelers cheques would have a common visual design including the Visa mark, each member bank could become an issuer of the cheques if it chose to do so, and could feature its name prominently on the face. The issuers could then recruit other member banks to resell them, just as many of the card issuers did with their smaller correspondent banks.

Although each bank could become an issuer, Visa still underwrote the development and safeguarding of the original plates, operated the replacement service, and conducted the international advertising. These activities made sense to centralize, as they had very high initial costs that could be recouped only by operating at a significantly large scale. These were also the kind of activities smaller banks could not reasonably accomplish alone. Funding for these centralized services came from quarterly service fees paid by the travelers cheque issuers based on their sales volumes.

Because the Visa mark was on the cheques, Visa itself was also ultimately responsible for the instrument should the issuer become insolvent. This was one critical difference between the travelers cheque and credit card businesses: if a credit card issuer went bankrupt or was seized by the government, the card portfolio was an asset that could be sold relatively easily to another issuer, but travelers cheques were liabilities that purchasers would continue to redeem. To protect the system, Visa established different terms of membership for travelers cheque issuers; if the issuer started to show signs of instability, the issuer was required to establish an escrow account at a neutral bank, which could be used for travelers cheque redemption should the issuer become insolvent.

Visa's issuance model was certainly more attractive than Interbank's, but the Bank of America was still less than enthused about this expansion of Visa's role. BofA saw Visa's entry into the travelers cheque business as a form of competition to their own travelers cheque program, and communicated as much via the press: "Ironically, the Visa Travelers Cheque, assuming it is accepted by a sufficient number of financial institutions, will be competing against its former owning bank."[13]

---

[12] 'Citicorp sues interbank over travel checks', American Banker (14 April 1978), p. 1.

[13] Kutler (10 July 1978), p. 1.

The BofA also doubted the feasibility of the program, remarking that "banks opting for Visa or Master Charge travelers checks would need 'a lot of luck' to stay in the business."[14] Converting their own program over to a Visa-branded travelers cheque would have required BofA to pay fees to Visa, and the operating regulations would have constrained them in some ways, but those involved in the Visa travelers cheque program remarked that BofA's reluctance was primarily driven by a political opposition to Visa's expansion of its role.[15] In their minds, Visa existed to coordinate their credit card program, not compete with them in the travelers cheque business.

Visa also invited Citibank to join the program, but their response was to drag Visa into their suit with Interbank.[16] Tom Honey, the executive in charge of developing the Visa travelers cheque program, recalled that Citibank's intentions at the deposition were clear: encourage Visa to abandon their plans and stay out of the travelers cheque business.[17] Unfortunately for Citibank, Visa's decentralized issuing model made the complaints they had used against Interbank moot, and Citibank was eventually forced to drop Visa from the suit.

Launch

Despite the resistance from BofA and Citibank, the Visa International Board did vote to approve the travelers cheque program in September of 1978, and a few large commercial banks, including Wells Fargo and the First National Bank of Chicago, quickly signed up to issue them.[18] The program was approved with the condition that the initial development costs would be recouped through fees paid by the participating issuers within two years of the program's launch, a goal that required selling $1.5 billion USD of Visa travelers cheques.

Luckily for Visa, the fifth largest proprietary travelers cheque issuer was also one of the original international BankAmericard licensees: Barclays Bank of the UK. Barclays had found it difficult to sign resellers in the United States for their own cheques, and saw the Visa travelers cheque program as a way to expand their sales and gain market share from their competitors. Barclays agreed to convert their program in January of 1979, a move that virtually assured that Visa would reach their required sales volume goal. It was also a much needed validation of Visa's ability to administrate such an endeavor; as one reporter put it, "At least in Barclays' eyes, Visa is not an upstart travelers check program operator without appreciation of the complexities of the business, as has been alleged by its established competitors."[19]

---

[14]Brouillette (26 July 1978), p. 1.

[15]Powar and Honey interviews.

[16]'Citicorp sues interbank over travel checks', American Banker (14 April 1978), p. 2.

[17]Private correspondence with the author, July 2010.

[18]'FNB Chi, Wells first to announce Visa travel plans', American Banker (24 November 1978), p. 2.

[19]Kutler (4 January 1979), p. 1.

The set of participating members continued to grow, reaching 30 by the end of January, and when the first travelers cheques went on sale in November of 1979, Visa expected to sell over $3 billion in the first year alone, double the required amount in half the time. In May, Chase Manhattan Bank, the third largest commercial bank in America at that time, joined the program in order to enter the travelers cheque business for the first time, hoping to convert all their AmEx sales to their own Visa cheques.[20] By the end of 1980, $2.4 billion USD in Visa travelers cheques had been sold, and it was estimated that Visa had captured around eight percent of the worldwide travelers cheque market.[21]

Despite their initial success, Hock was still frustrated that many of the member banks continued to sell American Express travelers cheques instead of Visa-branded ones. In Hock's mind, this act essentially told customers that AmEx is a more trusted and accepted brand than Visa, a message that would not only threaten Visa's dominance in the credit card market, but also jeopardize Visa's leadership in the world of electronic value exchange in general. In a 1980 speech, he warned them by invoking a metaphor from his youth in rural Utah:

> My purpose is merely to suggest a question which it may be prudent to ask each time you put pen to contract with any organization you have no ownership or control over; Is this a company, or will it be bought by a company, that may, when the time is right, pounce on my deposits and loans like a duck on a June bug? If you don't think that will happen, then you haven't begun to understand how the world of electronic payments systems will function, or the first fundamental of corporate self-interest and responsibility to stockholders.[22]

The large member banks did eventually accept Visa's expansion into the travelers cheque business, but not without a fight. BofA competed with the Visa travelers cheque program for several years before ultimately deciding to join it in order to retain market share. Citibank eventually joined as well, but still continued to issue their own proprietary travelers cheques in addition (and in competition) to the Visa-branded ones.

Visa's travelers cheque volume continued to increase in the 1980s, but never rose to a level that would seriously threaten AmEx's dominance, nor displace AmEx from the member banks. Nevertheless, it did have one rather interesting effect on the relationship between AmEx and the member banks: in response to the competitive pressure created by the Visa travelers cheque program, AmEx was forced to raise their commission rates, which benefited nearly all of the Visa member banks, regardless of whether they participated in the Visa travelers cheque program or not. Bill Powar remarked that this helped him secure additional advertising funds to combat American Express as they began to compete with Visa's card products more aggressively in the late 1980s.

---

[20] Kutler (29 May 1980), p. 1.

[21] 'Visa intl's travel check sales surge; see 8% market share', American Banker (2 December 1980), p. 3.

[22] 'American Express no friend of ours, Hock Tells bankers', American Banker (18 September 1980), p. 1.

Visa eventually chose to deemphasize the travelers cheque program in favor of establishing a worldwide ATM network accessed by Visa-branded cards, and creating a new kind of prepaid card product known as "TravelMoney." This card was similar to Visa's debit card, except that it accessed a separate deposit account created and funded at the time of purchase. Like a travelers cheque, this limited the consumer's risk if the card was stolen, and it constrained the traveler to a pre-established budget.[23]

The JC Penney Deal

The Entrée card and the travelers cheque program certainly tested the boundaries of the central organization, but in terms of conflicts, these were relatively tame compared to Visa USA's infamous 1979 deal with JC Penney, one of the three largest American retail store chains at that time. This episode, more than any other, sparked extensive debates about what Visa's role should be, and whether Visa was now acting more like a competitor than a coordinator.

To understand this deal and the controversy it created, we must first review the context in which it took place. In the late 1970s, very few national retail chain stores accepted bank-issued credit cards. K-Mart and Fred Meyer did, and Macy's accepted American Express to attract tourists, but the largest stores—Sears, Montgomery Wards, and JC Penney—did not.[24] These stores had been offering their own, private charge or credit cards for many years, and by 1978, Sears alone had more cards in circulation than Visa and Interbank combined.[25] There was little economic incentive for these stores to accept bankcards: their own cards incurred no discount fees, and those that allowed customers to finance purchases generated additional interest revenue. Even if these revenues did not offset the costs of running their programs, they still considered them valuable, as they thought the cards engendered a sense of loyalty in their customers, one that they were reticent to give up by accepting bankcards.

The number of transactions these retailers generated was enormous compared to most of Visa's merchants, and Hock wanted Visa to process as many of them as possible. So far, the top three retailers had remained unified in their opposition to bankcards, but Hock also knew that large retailers are typically willing to break ranks if doing so can get them ahead of their competition. Sears was already the largest in terms of both sales and credit accounts, so Hock focused his efforts on one of their close competitors: JC Penney.[26] Penney had 2,000 stores across the nation, and 13.6 million cardholders. On average, 42 percent of their sales were done on their private credit card, comprising a total volume of $4.5 billion in 1978. Penney's credit volume alone was over 20 percent of Visa USA's entire volume for

---

[23]Powar interview.

[24]Kutler (5 April 1979), p. 1.

[25]Nilson (March 1978), Report No 182, p. 1.

[26]Various news reports listed Penney as either the second or the third largest retailer at that time.

the same period.[27] Capturing even a portion of that would result in a significant surge for Visa.

The Deal

After extensive negotiations with Hock, Penney agreed to accept Visa cards starting in the fall of 1979. But instead of signing an agreement with one of Visa's member banks, which all other merchants had done, Penney signed the agreement *directly with Visa USA*.[28] Thus, Penney became their own merchant acquirer, and would pay fees to Visa USA only.

Although the lack of merchant acquirer revenues was bad enough, the agreement also resulted in lower revenues for the issuers as well. To close the deal, Visa USA developed a special electronic interchange reimbursement fee (EIRF) rate that applied to any transaction authorized electronically and submitted to BASE II within three days. This was how Penney intended to operate, and the EIRF effectively gave them a 20-percent discount on the interchange fees they paid to issuers.[29]

To make matters even worse, Hock arranged the terms of the contract without first consulting the Board of Directors. He claimed that Penney required this for secrecy, but he must have also known that the Board was unlikely to agree to such terms in advance. At the end of a two-day Board meeting, Hock announced that there was one more item of business, and happily informed the Directors that he had convinced JC Penney to accept Visa cards.[30]

The Reactions

As one might imagine, when the Directors learned the *terms* of this deal, they did not react well. Although the inclusion of Penney would no doubt result in higher volumes, and ultimately lead to acceptance at the other national retailers, they all felt that Visa had cut them out of a very important and lucrative merchant contract.

Hock tried to justify the lack of a merchant discount by arguing that Penney did not need a merchant bank. They captured transactions electronically using their own equipment, authorized them directly with BASE I, and electronically submitted them for clearing to BASE II. All the services that a merchant bank typically provided were unnecessary for Penney, so why should they pay a merchant discount fee? Similarly, the EIRF was justified on the basis that Penney would be authorizing

---

[27] Kutler (5 April 1979), p. 1. Visa USA's volume was $22.1 billion in 1978.

[28] 'Usurpation feared in Visa, Penney Tie', American Banker (11 April 1979), p. 1.

[29] Kutler (27 June 1979), p. 1. This rate became the prototype for the two TIRF rates discussed in Chap. 7.

[30] Nocera (1994), p. 306. Confirmed in Russell interview.

every transaction, and the three-day clearing meant that issuers would see transactions much sooner, allowing them to detect and stem fraud more quickly.[31]

After a lengthy debate, the board reluctantly agreed to approve the contract. Chuck Russell described how it was finally settled:

> The deal was the subject of great controversy amongst the directors until Ken Larkin spoke up and said something like: "Look my fellow directors, none of you could have signed Penneys, as evidenced by the fact that none of you *have* signed Penneys. Let's take our victory, and enjoy the fruits of Dee's labor." The board finally calmed down, but contemporaneously adopted a resolution forbidding the signing of merchants by Visa management or staff.[32]

This resolution was of course another move to limit the scope of Hock's role, and firmly establish which activities should be done by the central organization, and which should be left to the member banks.

When news of the deal reached the general membership, they were livid. One officer of a regional merchant bank responded, "I don't like it. I intend to raise hell about it when I get the chance."[33] He asserted that Penney should be associated with a merchant bank, if only arbitrarily, so as "to preserve Visa's traditional standing as an association rather than a competitor with some of its more prominent members." In other words, this deal made it look like Visa was now becoming their competitor instead of their coordinator.

National Bankcard Corporation (NaBANCO), a large merchant processor in Florida, went so far as to file an antitrust lawsuit against Visa USA, part of which sought an immediate injunction of the Penney arrangement.[34] The NaBANCO suit is better known for its challenge of the interchange fee in general, but NaBANCO was also upset that Visa had denied them revenues they could have earned by acquiring Penney's transactions. They questioned whether Visa, as an association of competitors, had the right to compete with its members.

John Reynolds, the CEO of Interbank, whose sales volume by this time had slipped below Visa's, took advantage of the situation by declaring: "It appears they have begun to compete with their members."[35] He also attempted to establish a pattern of behavior by drawing a connection between this deal and Visa's recent travelers cheque program:

> Visa ventured into this territory once before, at least in the view of John J. Reynolds...
> He criticized Visa's approach to travelers checks because he saw Visa, unlike the Master Charge travelers cheque program, fashioning itself into a financial services entity of its own in potential competition with members.[36]

It should be noted that Reynold's comments are strangely ironic. It was the Master Charge travelers cheque program that fashioned itself into a separate entity in

---

[31] Streeter (1979).

[32] Russell correspondence.

[33] 'Usurpation feared in Visa, Penney Tie', American Banker (11 April 1979), p. 1.

[34] Kutler (27 June 1979), p. 1.

[35] Kutler (14 September 1979), p. 15.

[36] 'Usurpation feared in Visa, Penney Tie', American Banker (11 April 1979), p. 1.

competition with its members, and this was precisely the reason they were sued by Citibank. Visa's travelers cheque program worked just like the card: each bank could issue their own checks, and the Visa mark guaranteed acceptance at any Visa member bank. Although the BofA saw the Visa travelers cheques as competition to their own, it was the other issuing member banks that were competing with BofA, not Visa itself.

Frederick Hammer, Senior Vice President of Chase Manhattan Bank and a Visa USA Board member, responded by urging the membership to see the Penney deal as a necessary special case, and not a change in policy or a significant threat:

> It is clear this is a good thing. It is the most efficient way to handle authorizations and value transfer. Since his costs are lower, the merchant can price his products lower. And the banks in the system get their cards used more, and that is always their goal.[37]

He admitted that in this case, Visa USA was acting more like their competitor, but he urged the members not to be concerned about this in the long run:

> I personally wouldn't mind competing with a trade association. I haven't found one yet who could do anything as well as we do. It's a lot like competing with the government.[38]

Nevertheless, the controversy surrounding the deal continued to ferment "speculation and suspicion" amongst the members, and it was the "principal topic of conversation, both public and private, at the [1979] bank card convention."[39] Hock himself attempted to calm the situation by assuring the members that the contract was unique, and that Visa did not "intend to compete with banks for merchant business." Unfortunately, he also could not resist challenging their assumption that banks, as they currently existed, would continue to be necessary in the world of electronic value exchange:

> Little in the history of bank cards has aroused such diversity of opinion, or opinion more passionately held and emotionally conveyed. All we did was supply Penney with the ability to interface with the BASE (authorization and clearing) systems.... Penney has no need for a merchant bank and in fact, insists that it not have one. Many bankers refuse to realize that many large retailers can do everything a bank can do, and often better. Penney is more sophisticated in data capture and data communications than any bank I know of. Penney's computer system is three or four times more powerful than the entire BASE system. They don't want bankers to come in and train their clerks. They have the crazy idea that they can train their clerks better than bankers can.[40]

This was exactly the kind of statement that worried the member banks most. Visa was *their* association, and Hock was *their* employee. Why was he questioning the need for an acquiring bank? Why was he designing a system that could eventually make them unnecessary? Why was he continually enabling firms from competing

---

[37] Usurpation feared in Visa, Penney Tie', American Banker (11 April 1979), p. 1.

[38] Usurpation feared in Visa, Penney Tie', American Banker (11 April 1979), p. 1. This comment must have annoyed Hock considerably as he never wanted Visa to resemble a governmental bureaucracy.

[39] Kutler (17 September 1979), p. 3.

[40] Hock, quoted in Kutler (14 September 1979), p. 15.

industries, such as the new Merrill Lynch Cash Management Accounts, to participate in the system?[41] Whose side was he on?

Hock's Departure

In the minds of the members, the JC Penney deal, even more than the Entrée card
and the Visa travelers cheques, made it obvious that Hock had a very different view
of his role, and the role of the central organization, from theirs. From their perspective, NBI had been created to solve a very specific problem, and Hock was simply
their employee, a subordinate who existed to help them coordinate and make profits
on their credit card programs. But these events now made it seem that Hock was
following his own agenda, building his own empire that might someday threaten
their own.

The worries of the larger and more powerful member banks quickly turned into
open animosity toward Hock, often vented through the trade press. Hock responded
in kind, but always with his customary touch of wit. One exemplary exchange occurred in a 1980 *Business Week* article:

> "Visa was created for the limited purpose of licensing a trademark and serving as a clear-
> inghouse," says Hans H. Angermueller, senior vice-president of Citicorp... Now, Ange-
> mueller says, Visa is becoming a "Frankenstein" that is working against the best interests
> of the banks that gave it birth. Hock's response: "Citibank defines banking as Citibank. We
> don't."[42]

Hock's repartee might have quieted some of his critics, but he was still subject
to his Board of Directors. They controlled his salary and his budgets, and if they
felt he was following his own interests more than theirs, they could replace him.
So far, he had been able to maintain control over the Board by appealing to those
who shared his vision, and leveraging the credibility he earned by building BASE I
and II, creating IBANCO, and implementing the name change. But in the minds of
most Board members, the system was now "fixed," and even those who shared his
vision were beginning to resent his increasingly abrasive style.

Hock tried to reassure the Board and the membership that he was not building an
empire and had no ulterior motives. He would often say that "Visa is just a group
of ordinary people extraordinarily committed to banking."[43] Visa was simply their
coordinator and consultant, helping them cope with the radical changes occurring
in the US banking industry, and Hock was still their humble servant. Nevertheless,
a number of developments during the early 1980s made it appear that Hock was
indeed building a worldwide empire, and was more interested in his own agenda
than the needs of the US members.

---

[41] The Cash Management Account (CMA) offered consumers an investment account that functioned almost like a demand deposit account, complete with checks and a Visa card, but with the
potential for much higher rates of return than could be legally offered by a bank. For a history of
the CMA, see Nocera (1994), pp. 149–163.

[42] 'The iconoclast who made Visa No. 1', Business Week (22 December 1980), pp. 44–46.

[43] Nocera (1994), p. 314.

Signs of Empire Building

As discussed in Chap. 6, the Visa USA system experienced a period of explosive growth following duality and the name change, but by the late 1970s and early 1980s, the international system was also experiencing phenomenal expansion. By 1980, the Visa card was honored by more than 3 million merchants in 150 different countries, and several existing national systems had recently converted all their cards to Visa. The worldwide sales volume had climbed to $45.7 billion, nearly 40 percent of which came from issuers outside the US, and the 64 percent growth rate in Europe seemed paltry compared to Asia and Latin America, both of which were doubling their sales each year.[44]

Managing this rapid expansion was becoming difficult, as Visa International had only 500 employees, a mere 125 of which did something other than "clerical operations." By 1980, they had opened new offices in Miami (for Latin America), London (for Europe, the Middle East and Africa), and Singapore (for Asia/Pacific), but these were still rather small, with an average of ten employees each, so nearly all services were provided by the Visa USA staff. Although this allowed the US members to remain in control of the system's evolution, it also made the system seem more "American" than international. The leaders of Eurocheque and Eurocard, Visa's main competitors in Europe, often remarked that "Every time a Visa card is used in Europe, a cash register rings in the United States!"[45]

By this time, however, Hock was less concerned with the desires of the US members than he was with creating a new kind of decentralized "transnational" organization. In contrast to the approach taken by most multinational corporations, Hock wanted to divest power from the center, allowing each region to address their unique needs, create their own local policies, assess their own fees, and provide the specific services needed by their members. To achieve this, Hock re-organized Visa International in 1981 into five semi-autonomous regions, each of which had their own Board of Directors, bylaws, and operating regulations. The regions were then given seats on the International Board, which now handled inter-regional issues only, according to their percentage of the worldwide sales volume. Services such as financial analysis and product development were still provided by Visa USA's staff, but as these regions grew, those services would increasingly be provided by the regional offices.[46]

The re-organization required a bitter struggle between Hock and the US Board members, as it would effectively reduce direct power the American banks had over the worldwide system. The other regions were growing faster, and their sales would eventually overtake the US region, giving them more seats on the International Board. Hock saw it as a necessary move to make Visa a truly transnational system, and he was enamored with the idea of creating an organization with a stature

---

[44]Dougherty (1981), pp. 1–4.

[45]Cleveland (1999), p. 17, Dougherty (1981), p. 2.

[46]Dougherty (1981), pp. 5–9.

similar to the United Nations, with himself as its leader and spokesperson. The US members, however, saw it as yet another confirmation that he was pursuing his best interests and not theirs.

Signs of empire building were also evident on the technical side, particularly in what became known as the "long-range plan." Visa's switch to ACP and IBM hardware for BASE I had given them the necessary capacity to keep up with the growing worldwide volumes, but Hock wanted to expand the telecommunications network across the globe and build the greatest transaction processing system the financial services world had ever seen. He and the technical staff developed an extensive wish list, which went so far as to include a private communications satellite, totaling $150 million USD. Since Visa had no public stock, and no disposable capital or assets to speak of, they turned to their members, asking them to buy a series of special notes to be paid back over ten years with 11 percent interest. The members actually had little choice; those who elected not to buy the notes were forced to pay a special "Capital Fee" that amounted to the same price as buying the notes.[47]

Although the members did purchase the first round of notes totaling $62 million, Visa's CFO noted that they felt the whole process was "too cavalier," and that without a detailed prospectus regarding how the money would be spent, the notes amounted to "an enormous 'Trust me' which translated into something else for each member."[48] They feared that Hock would use this to further enlarge his growing empire, and their suspicions were confirmed when Hock began acquiring several member-owned processing organizations on the verge of collapse, as well as a manufacturer of POS transaction switching equipment.

The international re-organization and the long-range plan both became warning signs that Hock was beginning to formulate an empire and assume a role that went far beyond what the members had ever envisioned. But the most controversial sign of all came from something that normally draws little attention: office space.

101 California: Headquarters for an Empire

In 1980, a new sleek high-rise office building was being planned at one of the most prestigious locations in San Francisco's financial district. It would be at the intersection of Market and California streets, overlooking not only the Bay, but also all the other firms populating that powerful section of the West Coast's banking capital. Visa's CFO wrote that it perfectly "dovetailed with Dee's vision of the future for Visa International," and Hock signed a lease for the entire 44th floor. Unfortunately for him, he once again neglected to mention it to his Board.[49]

He spent the next three years turning the new space into a "showplace which included only 29 offices, enormous hallways and meeting rooms, and open sitting

---

[47]Cleveland (1999), p. 24.

[48]Cleveland (1999), p. 30.

[49]Cleveland (1999), pp. 33–36. See also Nocera (1994), pp. 312–313.

areas that communicated that Visa had 'arrived', and that it was a player in the world scheme of things."[50] Since the building was near-circular, Hock created a floor plan reflecting the four corners of the globe, with four sitting areas decorated to reflect each region's culture. He collected paintings, antiques, carpets, and even a bust of his most-adored leader, Marcus Aurelius, to adorn the offices. He designed a board room with state-of-the-art audio/visual equipment and integrated translation booths. It was a masterpiece of design, an office space fit for a major player in the worldwide banking industry, and that was exactly the problem.

In 1983, the Directors arrived for their first meeting in the new space, and they were aghast. Cleveland recalled their reactions:

> To them, the floor looked more like an opulent, antique showroom, not what they would have deemed proper for Visa. However, the boardroom and executive area at each Director's respective head office were just as plush, or in most cases more, than Dee's 101 creation. Unfortunately, the Directors did not share Dee's grand vision for Visa. Most had tired of Dee's methods for getting what he wanted from them. Each at some point had felt outsmarted, outwitted, outmaneuvered, and intellectually humiliated by Dee's unrelenting negotiating style. After all, most of them were lawyers, had gone to the finest schools, and had all manner of degrees and credentials, whereas Dee had merely attended junior college for a few quarters and a business career that in no way was comparable to theirs. In other words, they were tired of Dee's disrespect, and 101 California seemed to rub salt into some very old wounds.[51]

Although the Directors were upset over the money spent on this new space, they were even more upset about the *message* the space communicated about who Hock thought he was. Hock was their employee, but his offices made him look like their equal. The offices also looked like the headquarters of a major multinational holding company, not a simple switch for credit card transactions.

Furthermore, they realized that Hock had never sought their approval to build this new "pleasure palace in the sky," nor even to commit to the lease he had signed for the floor. They also wondered how much of the $62 million they recently loaned Visa for their long-range plan was used to build it. As Cleveland put it, "The proverbial straw was on the camels back, his front legs were buckled under, and the back legs were beginning to wobble."[52]

The King is Dead. Long Live the King

From that point on, Hock lost control over the board, and his detractors began to treat him with open disdain at Board meetings. Brian Ruder, one of Visa's technical staff, recalled one particular incident at a Board meeting he was asked to attend:

---

[50]Cleveland (1999), p. 34.

[51]Cleveland (1999), p. 34.

[52]Cleveland (1999), p. 36.

> I walked into the Board meeting and [Hock] is sitting there, and [a Director] was sitting next to him...they opened the meeting, and [the Director] opened the Wall Street Journal and lit a cigar, and I just couldn't believe it...it was just to say to Dee, "fuck you, I don't like you." Some of them had such disdain for Dee—they hated him.[53]

Even his stalwart supporters began to turn on him. At a Board meeting in early 1984, Hock was met with resistance at nearly every turn. Several times before he was able to break such resistance by threatening to resign if they did not follow his plans. He tried the tactic again, but this time it backfired. Here is how Visa's CFO, Tom Cleveland, described it:

> Bob Mitchell, the Chairman of the U.S. board and long-time Dee-supporter, paused and then responded to Dee's resignation proposal, "Thank you, Dee, for accepting the present circumstances and stepping down. We hereby accept your resignation, effective the day we appoint your successor, whom we would like your assistance in finding." Dee was momentarily in shock. The resignation tactic had failed. In fact, by all appearances, the decision to replace Dee had been a consensus decision reached well before the meetings had ever begun. An era was over.[54]

The exact sequence of events that led to Hock's departure are somewhat contested, but most agree that the Board was ready to see him go. Cleveland's account is based on what he heard after the scene, as he was not actually in the room. Joe Nocera, the financial journalist, provided a similar account based on interviews with the Directors, but he described Hock threatening to quit at a meeting in Greece over a denied raise in his salary.[55] Chuck Russell agreed with Nocera's account, but noted that the location was actually Venice. Visa's official corporate history claims that Hock decided to leave on his own accord, and that the Chairman "pleaded" with him to stay.[56] In his autobiography, Hock simply states that "in 1984, the curtain came down on my performance as CEO."[57]

Regardless of how it happened, Chuck Russell was soon appointed as the new President and CEO of Visa International and USA, and Dee Hock left the system he had nurtured for 14 years to tend his ranch on the California coast.[58] The long-range plan was cut back to fit within the funds already raised, and the 101 California lease was soon terminated, forcing the company to relocate their headquarters to the less-glamorous town of San Mateo. In true Dee Hock style, however, Visa was still able to keep a shred of their high-profile image by renting a post office box at the nearby San Francisco Airport, which allowed them to keep a more prestigious San Francisco mailing address.[59]

---

[53] Ruder interview. Russell also told a story of a Director reading the paper during Hock's speech, and a similar incident appears in Nocera (1994), p. 314.

[54] Cleveland (1999), p. 44.

[55] Nocera (1994), p. 314.

[56] Chutkow (2001), p. 234.

[57] Hock (2005), p. 251.

[58] Weinstein (25 May 1984), p. 3.

[59] Cleveland (1999), pp. 46–47.

Several sources remarked that the transition eventually needed to happen. Hock had pushed the members too far, too fast, and he was unwilling to wait for them to agree with him about such things as the asset card and electronic value exchange. Visa needed to evolve from a dynamic, entrepreneurial company to a more stable service organization that could dependably run an increasingly popular worldwide payment system. Electronic value exchange would come in time, but for now, the roles that Hock and Visa would play in the future of the payment system had been unequivocally redefined.

Hock's Legacy

Although the Board had grow tired of Hock, he was still highly respected by most of the membership, and many were sad to see him go. In just over a decade, he had turned what seemed like a lost cause into the world's largest electronic payment card network, and transformed most of the member bank's card programs from monetary sinkholes into highly profitable businesses. He more than anyone else set the agenda for Visa during these first 14 years, and his vision for ubiquitous electronic value exchange would continue to shape Visa's strategy in the years to come.

Of course, this is not to say that Hock was a lone inventor-hero. Hock may have cast the vision, but dozens of key Visa employees, many of whom were mentioned throughout this narrative, performed the hard work necessary to reshape and transform that vision into a practical reality. Without them, Hock's dreams would have remained wishful thinking, as he lacked not only the technical expertise to bring them to fruition, but also the other requisite marketing, financial, and administrative skills necessary to coordinate a system of that scope and scale.

Still, Hock's departure signaled the end of a significant era for Visa. The organization's first 14 years had certainly been extremely prolific in terms of innovation and expansion, and many were concerned that the organization might loose its focus and entrepreneurial edge. During Hock's last speech before the members, after which he received a standing ovation that lasted nearly a minute, he admonished them to remember the sacrifices that were made to create what they now enjoyed, as well as the responsibility they now had to improve it for the next generation:

Perhaps the oldest, most common tale throughout history is of those who after inheriting a great patrimony, chose the comfort and pleasure of spending it, rather than the sacrifice and labor of passing it on enhanced.

Through both success and failure, through good times and bad, I have grown to have abiding faith in the Visa concept. It is in harmony with where organizations are heading. It is already what others will take decades to achieve, what many will never accomplish. It has perhaps always been ahead of its time. Whether it will remain so is something I cannot answer, for that is now in your hands.

It is within your power to dissipate it by greed, diminish it by lack of vision, or destroy it by conscious design. And one or the other is the common fate of pioneering concepts, which after initial success are overwhelmed by reaction, only to be more successfully replicated when the minds of men are more receptive. And in the day to day struggle for position, power and profit, it is not difficult to drift into such smallness of mind, and meanness of spirit.

But it is equally within your power to perpetuate it and enhance it. And that is more difficult, for it requires vision, generosity and sacrifice, which are always hardest to sustain when success is already in hand. However, that is my greatest wish, for the thought that it should be otherwise is one which I do not care to embrace.[60]

---

[60]Dee Hock's Final Speech Before the Visa International Annual Meeting, May 1985 (transcribed from video).

Chapter 10
Conclusions: Toward a General Sociotechnical History of Payment Systems

The preceding chapters have been a rather long and detailed answer to the seemingly simple question posed in the introduction: how does my Visa card work? That is to say, how is it that I, living in Seattle, can use a small piece of plastic, issued by a bank in New York that I have never visited, to purchase goods and services from merchants I have never met, or obtain local currency from a machine owned by a completely different bank, in 170 different countries around the world? How is it that a merchant can accept this piece of plastic containing a particular logo, and within seconds obtain a guarantee of payment, regardless of where the issuer is located, what time it is there, or what currency unit is used for the account? How is it that the different institutions representing the merchant and the cardholder are able to coordinate their actions, even when they reside in different countries? And how has this come to feel so "normal," or even "natural?"

Although it may feel somewhat natural today, we have seen that the creation and development of the sociotechnical system that makes this all possible was anything but that. Any payment system, even simpler ones based on commodity money or specie, should be viewed as a particular *achievement* requiring an *explanation*. To borrow a phrase from Collins, a mature payment system is like a ship within a bottle: it is sometimes difficult for us to imagine that it was once simply a pile of sticks with no particular instructions on how to put it together.[1]

This book has recaptured and explained in detail how those metaphorical sticks became the payment network known today as Visa. We saw how Visa's roots stretch back to the disintegrated bank-issued credit cards of the 1960s, and how those programs were in turn influenced by the technological and business practices of the earlier charge card programs developed by Western Union, the department stores, the oil industry, and Diners Club. We observed how these bank-issued card programs affiliated in the mid 1960s to form regional, and eventually national, networks that facilitated not only the processing of interchange of transactions, but also the acceptance of the cards via common marks. We then looked at one of these networks in particular, the BankAmericard licensed by Bank of America (BofA), and we saw

---

[1]Collins (1975).

D.L. Stearns, *Electronic Value Exchange*, History of Computing,
DOI 10.1007/978-1-84996-139-4_10, © Springer-Verlag London Limited 2011

how an understanding of it as a sociotechnical system revealed that their operational problems could not be solved by additional technology, as they also suffered from serious organizational problems.

We then met Visa's founder, Dee Hock, who was an atypical banker with some fairly radical ideas about organizations and the future of payments in an electronically-networked world. We saw how his particular philosophy shaped the structure of the new organization that he proposed. This new organization replaced the existing licensing system, creating an effectively not-for-profit membership association that was initially called National BankAmericard Incorporated (NBI). We then analyzed how Hock and his early staff crafted the social dynamics of the organization to create a structure in which multiple competing financial institutions could compromise and trust each other, just enough, to build a payment system none could have realistically built alone.

After the organization was in pace, we observed how Hock and his staff set out to solve the various operational problems that were not only holding back the growth of the system, but also jeopardizing its continued existence. We noticed how various banks and processors automated the local authorization decision by replacing skilled humans with computerized logic, and how organizations such as Omniswitch demonstrated that interchange authorizations could be automated by switching electronic transactions across telecommunication networks. After a failed attempt at building a national joint authorization network, we followed NBI's creation of their own electronic authorization system, known primarily by its acronym BASE. I argued that it pushed the authorization process below the cardholders "threshold of indifference," making it "fast-enough" to be an reasonable alternative to other forms of payment, even when close to home. We also saw that during the development of BASE, Hock revealed some of his larger and more comprehensive ambitions for the system.

But authorization was only half the problem, and we next learned how NBI automated the clearing and settlement process by truncating the paper sales drafts, and processing them through a centralized electronic clearinghouse. Key to making this possible, however, was NBI's ability to "engineer" cardholder acceptance of descriptive billing, a process made easier by the use of "facsimile" drafts that looked like the original punched card. We then briefly reviewed NBI's attempt to provide general processing software for the member banks, an activity that was ultimately seen as a departure from their core coordinating mission, especially after the project spun out of control and had to be canceled.

With their core operational systems in place, NBI was then poised for a period of explosive growth, which I argued can only be understood completely when we keep the technological and organizational changes during that period in a dynamic tension. The creation of the international organization, the instigation of duality in response to antitrust investigations, and the name change to "Visa" touched off a rapid expansion of the organization, but we also saw how the switch to the Airline Control Program (ACP) on IBM hardware, the establishment of a second coordinated datacenter, the extension of the authorization network internationally, and multi-currency settlement allowed the system to handle the increased volume, and appear more attractive to new prospective members.

We then returned to the technological aspects of the system, reviewing how Visa helped to fully automate the point of sale. This was the first part of a larger vision Hock had for the system, one he started describing as "electronic value exchange." We discussed the controversies surrounding how account information should be encoded on the card, and whether security belonged more at the card or the system level. We then reviewed Visa's merchant dial terminal project, and how inexpensive electronic point-of-sale terminals altered not only the levels of fraud, but also the economics of acquiring business. This change in economics ultimately led to a rise of specialized acquiring banks and third-party processors.

In the final two chapters, we focused on the ways in which the central Visa organization had to "work out" its role with respect to the member banks through a series of power struggles, which were often touched off by the introduction of new kinds of technologies or services. We examined the case of Visa's signature-based debit card, initially known as Entrée, and saw how its delayed adoption by the issuing banks was due primarily to the ways in which the card's technical and cooperative requirements clashed with the banks' existing electronic funds transfer (EFT) plans. A card that accessed deposits was the next logical step in Hock's broader plan for electronic value exchange, but the member banks saw it as an unwanted departure from the role they had assigned the central organization.

We ended the narrative by discussing two other significant controversies surrounding Visa's role: the creation of a Visa-branded travelers cheque, which would compete not only with American Express, but also the proprietary travelers cheques issued by some of their largest member banks; and Visa USA's signing of a direct merchant agreement with the national retail giant JC Penney, bypassing a merchant acquiring bank. In response, many of the member banks began to wonder if Visa was now acting as their competitor instead of their coordinator, and if Hock was beginning to pursue his own interests above those of the member banks. The reorganization of Visa International into a "transnational" structure, the ambitiously expensive long-range technology plan, and the opulent new Visa headquarters all appeared to the membership as signs of empire building, and we saw how this ultimately led to Hock being forced out of the organization.

Contribution to Grand Themes

This detailed narrative provides us with a rich empirical case study of the origins of an everyday sociotechnical system, as well as its transition from paper-based information processing to computerization. As such, it has also given us ample opportunity to interact with two grand themes from the study of technological systems in general.

The first is the ways in which technological systems are often shaped by social dynamics, and the ways in which those systems, once adopted, begin to reshape those social relations in return.[2] Engineers are often frustrated when design

---

[2]MacKenzie and Wajcman (1999).

decisions become "political," or when products deemed to be technologically "inferior" dominate the market, but a detailed historical examination typically reveals that technological artifacts and systems are *always* shaped by social forces: economics, politics, legislation, regulation, and general cultural preferences. In the Visa case, we saw this social-shaping of technology at work in several instances. Electronic authorization messages were switched between autonomous centers instead of processed centrally due in part to political considerations. Delays were also added to early authorization services to mimic a more human-scale speed. A personal feud between Hock and IBM influenced the initial hardware used for BASE I, as well as the process of switching it to IBM after the scale increased. The shift to electronic clearing and descriptive billing had to be eased with the use of facsimile drafts. The design of multi-currency settlement was not surprisingly shaped by economic considerations. Both economics and politics were at play in the debates surrounding the encoding of account information on the card, as well as the widespread adoption of point-of-sale terminals. And the delayed adoption of the debit card was highly influenced by the cultural tensions within the banks, as well as interbank politics and business strategy.

We also observed the reshaping of social relations due to technological adoption. Hock's main point about electronic value exchange was that the adoption of computers and telecommunications had fundamentally altered what it meant to be a "bank," and that several organizations outside the banking industry were better suited to provide electronically-based financial services to consumers. Electronic authorization and the widespread adoption of inexpensive point-of-sale terminals also shifted fraud liability away from the merchants, and began to restructure the economics of the acquiring business, leading to specialization and the rise of third-party processors. Lastly, Visa's debit card challenged the deep cultural divides between the deposit and consumer credit sides of the banks, and although this challenge was initially resisted in many cases, it did contribute to the eventual removal of such barriers.

Another location in which this mutual shaping of technology and social relations occurred in the Visa case was in the adoption of payment cards by consumers, a process often referred to as "domestication."[3] We saw how consumers and professional societies created specific categories of goods and services that were appropriate to purchase using credit cards, and others, such as groceries or health care, that were not. Visa attempted to reshape these categories through national advertising campaigns, urging consumers to think of their BankAmericards not solely as a vehicle for consumer credit, but also as a new kind of global currency, suitable for routine purchases. Through advertising, debit cards, widespread merchant acceptance, and various air-mile/point/cash-back benefits, Visa and the large issuers were eventually successful in redefining the payment card in consumers' minds, transforming it into a more convenient and more flexible replacement for cash and checks.

The second grand theme is the influence that earlier information processing practices often have on the way firms adopt electronic computers and telecommuni-

---

[3] Hartmann et al. (2005), Mackay and Gillespie (1992).

cations.[4] Yates showed in her book that most insurance firms followed a path of "incremental migration," initially favoring the use of their familiar tabulator applications on simpler computers rather than the more disruptive but flexible integrated applications on the UNIVAC. In the Visa case, we saw some evidence that supports this theme, and other evidence that seems to run counter to it. For example, the existing dual-message processing for transactions (one for authorization and one for clearing) was retained in the shift to computer processing (as opposed to the single-message approach used by ATMs), but the choice of a realtime-processing DEC minicomputer for BASE I was a significant departure from the hardware customarily used by the banking industry. Even when Visa switched to IBM hardware to handle the increased scale, they adopted the more obscure but highly efficient Airline Control Program (ACP) instead of the banking industry's more traditional platform of OS/370 and the Customer Information Control System (CICS).

Using punch cards for the bottom later of the sales drafts is another mixed example. Banks were already standardizing on Magnetic Ink Character Recognition (MICR) for automated check processing, but the early credit card programs adopted more powerful and flexible punch-card-reading computers instead. This would seem to be a fairly radical departure from the banks' existing check processing practices, but I think this would be the wrong way to see it. As we saw in Chap. 8, there was a deep cultural divide between the consumer credit and deposit sides of the banks at this time, so the technology decisions made by the credit card programs would likely have been influenced more by the practices of the consumer loan and credit reporting firms of the day than those of the banks or the Federal Reserve check clearing system. In other words, existing practices from other industries might sometimes hold more sway than those of the host firm, especially when the department in question is more culturally akin to those other industries than it is to its own.

But there other instances where support for this theme was perhaps more obvious. For example, issuers outside the US were accustomed to using a telex to obtain authorizations, and Visa's "auto-telex" interface allowed them to continue this practice even after the central switch and many of the issuers had converted to entirely automated processing. Facsimile drafts also allowed some banks to continue the practice of country-club billing for a time, even though the sales draft had been truncated at the acquiring bank. Finally, we saw that many banks supported an EFT strategy that was a simple electronic analog to the existing check clearing system run by the Federal Reserve instead Hock's more radical approach of electronic value exchange.

Some New General Dynamics in Payment Systems and Cooperative Networks

The Visa case not only helps us understand more fully these grand themes from the history of technology, but also suggests some new general dynamics that I think may

---

[4] Yates (2005).

apply to other kinds of payment systems, or transactional networks more broadly. The first concerns the interplay between authorities, their marks, and trust in the payment devices they issue. The second concerns the interaction between transactional networks and established social boundaries.

Value Flows According to a Mark

During my interviews with Visa's pioneers, I was struck by how often they spoke about the importance of Visa's marks: the blue-white-and-gold bands design; and the name "Visa." They considered the marks to be not only key contributors to Visa's success, but also the most important asset Visa owned, even more important than the BASE I and II software. The regional Visa organizations spend vast amounts each year developing awareness of, and goodwill toward, those marks, which have subsequently become some of the most recognized in the world.[5] We have long been accustomed to products and services being branded, but it may seem odd at first that the *way we pay* for those has become seemingly branded as well. But this is not a new phenomenon: marks have played an important role in payment systems throughout history, and will likely continue to do so in the future.

Marks

Marks, as I will define them, first appear in the shift from commodity money to coins. In a commodity money payment system, a particular raw material, such as shells, beads, pelts, or gold, is used as a primary trading currency. This commodity money (sometimes referred to as "full-bodied money"), still typically has some kind of intrinsic value for the participants, though that value may be more symbolic than practical. More importantly, the commodity money is not issued, marked, or guaranteed by any kind of authority. It is simply a commodity that is plentiful enough to enable trade, but scarce enough to maintain sufficient value.[6]

For example, in a commodity money system, a buyer might offer a lump of gold in exchange for goods or services, but that lump would not bear any seal or mark that attested to its weight or fineness. It is simply a lump of metal ore, and no authority guarantees it or stands behind it. Thus, the transaction implies some amount of risk for the seller: the lump may not be of sufficient weight, the gold might be impure, or it might not be gold at all, just some metal that merely looks like it.

Risk is endemic to all economic transactions, but a seller will typically seek to reduce that risk as much as possible by leveraging some source of knowledge the seller already trusts. One source might be the buyer himself; if the seller knows and trusts the buyer through some other social link, the seller may accept the buyer's

---

[5]Chutkow (2001).

[6]Humphrey (1995), Richardson (1970), Chandler (1986).

claims as to the weight and fineness, especially if the social link affords the potential of retribution. If the buyer is unknown, however, the seller might consult the testimony of an authority, such as an expert skilled in weighing and assaying. Alternatively, the seller might perform those experiments herself using technologies developed by those skilled experts.

As early as the seventh century BCE, the Lydians began transforming the lumps of electrum they used as commodity money into something new: a *coin*. What made these "coins," as opposed to uniform lumps of metal, was the presence of a *mark*, the Lydian State seal, which attested to the ingot's weight and fineness.[7] Through the use of their mark, the Lydian State was, in essence, guaranteeing these properties of the coin, providing a new and presumably trusted source of knowledge for participants in the payment system. Because the mark belonged to a commonly-recognized and trusted authority, the participants could treat the coins as conceptual black boxes: things that could be simply counted instead of weighed and assayed.[8]

But this black-boxing was a two-edged sword: it did not eliminate the risks as much as shift them to new locations. Participants may trust the authority and its mark, but the coin could be shaved after it was marked, the mark could be forged, or the authority itself may be corrupt. Indeed, authorities often systematically reduced the fineness of their coins in order to generate a *seignorage*, that is, a profit based on the difference between the metal content and face value of the coin. If those administering the payment system do not develop techniques to mitigate these risks, participants may quickly lose trust in the authority and its mark, rendering its guarantees or assurances essentially meaningless. Without trust, sellers and buyers will cease to participate in the payment system, and without continued exchanges, the payment system will quickly collapse. Following Latour, we might say that a payment system is essentially a performance, in which each value exchange recreates and sustains it. When trust fails and exchanges cease, the social links dissolve, and the system evaporates.[9]

Marks and Value Exchange Rules

Notes, like coins, also typically bear the marks of a commonly-recognized authority, which could be the State or some other reputable organization. This is most commonly a bank, but other organizations can issue more limited-use notes as well. For example, the Walt Disney Company began issuing their own private currency called "Disney Dollars" in 1987, which are still accepted in most domains controlled by the Disney company. What makes a note different from an ordinary piece of paper is not the shape, color, or sign of denomination: it is the set of marks, the authority behind them, and the trust participants place in that authority.

---

[7] Einzig (1966), p. 217.

[8] Einzig notes that there is some disagreement as to whether the Lydian merchants accepted the coins by tally only, but that seems to have been the intent of the issuer.

[9] Strum and Latour (1987), Latour (2005).

In the case of notes, however, the authority guarantees something different than in the case of coins: the particular *rules of value exchange*. Recall that representative notes are only claims upon another substance (usually specie) the issuing authority currently uses to represent value. To redeem that other substance, the note must be presented to the issuer in a certain manner. The rules for how that is accomplished are tied up with the issuer's mark, and are often printed on the note itself. Incidentally, value-exchange rules are also included on notes in a fiat money system (where the notes themselves are the direct representation of value) through a performative declaration such as these notes are "legal tender for all debts public or private." Thus, a set of marks often represents a corresponding set of rules that govern final value exchange, and it is those rules that the authority "stands behind" or guarantees. If the participants within the payment system trust that authority, and believe those rules to be enforceable, the rules and their corresponding marks can provide a significant source of trust during a transaction.

Rules and Guarantees

It should now be easier to see why personal checks, especially those issued in America, engender little trust. There are two principal reasons. First, although a check may bear the marks of the issuing bank, it does not have to. Anything can be a check, including a hastily-scribbled piece of paper, provided it contains the necessary information and the words "pay to the order of." Even if it does bear the marks of an issuer, those marks are known only within a limited geographic area. Merchants outside the area do not typically recognize the issuing bank as an authority, and thus have no way of knowing if the check is even drawn on a valid or extant bank. Second, even when the mark is present and recognized, it cannot act as a source of trusted knowledge, because the value-exchange rules that govern checks are actually defined by a different authority (common law, or the Universal Commercial Code) and they guarantee nothing for the depositor. A check is only a *tentative* claim on funds, subject to inspection of the document and the account to which it is supposedly tied. Thus, the seller is limited to the same sources of knowledge discussed in the commodity money example: the seller's social links with the buyer; or the testimony of a trusted authority, which in this case would be a check authorization or guarantee system, if one is available.

Travelers cheques provide an interesting counter-example. They also bear the marks of a non-governmental issuing organization, but that organization typically goes to great lengths to establish itself as an authority amongst its network of recipients. Furthermore, the value-exchange rules represented by the issuer's marks actually *guarantee* payment, primarily because a travelers cheque is closer to a representative note than a conventional check. Recipients typically believe those rules to be enforceable, as they are written into formal business contracts subject to contract law. In an interesting twist, the retribution that was previously offered by the seller's social link to the buyer is now transferred to the recipient's social link with the issuer. Even if the travelers cheque was a forgery, the recipient can still seek restitution from the issuer, provided the recipient can demonstrate that the authentication rules were followed.

Marks and Payment Cards

As we come to payment cards, our analytical framework should now help us understand how the marks played a fundamental and powerful role in the adoption and development of these systems. Like other payment devices, the cards also bear the marks of an issuing organization, and in the Visa case, this issuer was initially the Bank of America (BofA). As discussed in Chap. 1, the BofA was widely recognized as a trusted authority within California, but in order to expand the system nationally, it needed to enlist the help of other banks that were already established as authorities in their local areas. In contrast to checks, the BofA required that all cards use the same, consistent marks, and since the marks consumed the entire face of the card, all cards effectively looked alike. Because the local authority had introduced those marks to their merchants, the merchants would readily accept any card bearing those marks, regardless of issuer. Similarly, because the local authority had "trained" its cardholders to look for the marks on merchant signs, cardholders could easily identify participating merchants, regardless of acquirer. This enabled the BankAmericard system to expand geographically in a way that eluded the nascent Interbank system, whose common "i" mark was barely noticeable next to the issuer's more-dominant marks.

Because cardholders and merchants were introduced to these marks by a trusted, local authority, they were able to transfer the trust in that authority to the marks themselves, as well as the system that stood behind them. These local bankers became what Giddens terms "access points" to an abstract system.[10] Giddens argues that in the majority of cases, users are typically unable to develop the requisite trust in an abstract system itself without some kind of contact with a human representative of that system. The interpersonal trust users develop with these human representatives is then transferred to the impersonal system itself, allowing the users to feel comfortable relying on a system that they know little to nothing about.

Furthermore, like travelers cheques, the value-exchange rules represented by the BankAmericard (and eventually Visa) marks guaranteed payment, provided the merchants followed their part of the rules. Electronic communications and the eventual replacement of human authorizers with programmed logic were the key to offering this guarantee of payment, which completely eliminated the merchant's risk. Merchants no longer needed to seek trust through their social links with cardholders, because the cardholder was no longer the "buyer." From the merchant's perspective, the "buyer" of a Visa transaction is actually the acquiring member bank, and ultimately the Visa system itself. Indeed, before the widespread adoption of point-of-sale terminals, the member banks would speak of "buying paper" from merchants, as opposed to processing their transactions.[11] Thus, merchants can confidently accept Visa cards from customers they have never met, regardless of the customer's nationality, native language, or native currency unit.

---

[10]Giddens (1990), p. 83.

[11]For example, see Larkin (1970), p. 32.

This becomes most evident when we consider what the marks say about the card-holder. Just as the mark on the Lydian coin attested to the metal's weight and fine-ness, the mark on your Visa card attests to your creditworthiness.[12] Even if the issuer did not perform an adequate credit check on you, the merchant can still consider you as such, because Visa is the actual "buyer." When you are issued a Visa card, Visa "stands behind" you in a very real sense, because any transaction processed under the mark is ultimately guaranteed by the Visa system, even if you default or over-draw, and even if the issuing organization becomes insolvent.

Even if Visa is not the ultimate buyer, the marks on your Visa card may still attest to your general trustworthiness. For example, before the widespread use of check guarantee systems, American merchants commonly asked those paying with a check to provide a major credit card as a secondary proof of identity. What made that piece of plastic an acceptable form of economic identification was not the embossed account number or expiration date: it was the marks, the authority behind them, and the trust the merchants placed in that authority.

Lastly, trust in the authority behind a payment card system, its corresponding marks, and the value-exchange rules represented by those marks, can falter just as easily as it can with other kinds of payment devices. Network and processing out-ages, billing errors, security breaches, financial organization failures, or excessive (or well-publicized) fraud can quickly erode participants' trust in the system. As we saw in Chap. 4, the BASE I authorization system was designed from the beginning to deliver a reliable service, and the capacity enhancements discussed in Chap. 6 en-abled BASE I to remain dependable throughout Visa's period of explosive growth. These are only a small part of Visa's overall focus on dependability, which I have discussed in detail elsewhere.[13]

Application

In summary, *value always flows according to a mark*.[14] The mark (or set of marks) is established by an authority, and only those who recognize and trust that authority will continue to participate in the payment system. Through the mark, the authority attests to or guarantees something, which can be properties of the instrument, or the rules by which the instrument can be exchanged for value. If those rules guarantee payment, and if participants believe them to be enforceable, they can provide a sig-nificant source of trust that can offset many of the risks merchants face in accepting payments, or at least shift them to other parties, where they can be addressed in a consolidated manner.

---

[12]Or, your ability to pay in general. The mark on your debit card might not be related to a credit line, but from the merchant's perspective, it attests to a guarantee of payment.

[13]Stearns (2006).

[14]This phrase comes from the insights of Tom Honey, who took the time to explain the importance of Visa's marks during our interviews.

There is one important implication of this lesson that should be briefly mentioned here: *payment systems are not neutral conduits through which value flows*. Rather, value flows according to a mark, which represents certain rules that govern not only how the value is exchanged, but also who pays for the service, who pays for fraud, how disputes are resolved, and who gets to alter and interpret the rules.[15] In most cases, those rules will favor one group over another, and occasionally may be designed to restrict access. Although we rarely think about these things when paying for goods and services, payment systems have real and often profound effects upon the ways in which value is exchanged.

Networks, Boundaries, and Gateways

The second general dynamic I want to highlight is the ways in which transactional networks can reinforce or undermine established social boundaries, both within and between organizations.

Making Value Flow

As opposed to other kinds of digitized content, such as audio files, value does not "flow" across a communications network like water flows through a pipe. There are no electronic pennies that stream across the wire from one node to another. Instead, value is exchanged by offsetting the balances of accounts that are linked together into a hierarchical network in response to standardized instructional messages. Let us build this up, step by step.

A single bank is perhaps the simplest example of a network of accounts. All the accounts maintained by a given bank are in effect linked together. When one account holder wishes to transfer money to another, the payer does so by sending some sort of standardized message indicating at least the source, target, and amount. The funds are then transferred by simply debiting the payer's account and crediting the payee's.

The banks themselves are also linked together through complex networks of accounts. Smaller banks often maintain accounts with a correspondent bank in a larger money center. Some of those larger banks also maintain correspondent accounts with banks in other countries to enable foreign exchange. Banks belonging to a cooperative clearinghouse typically maintain accounts with a common clearing bank. In the US, members of the Federal Reserve System are also required to maintain accounts with their respective district bank. This complex network of accounts allows

---

[15]This is similar to the point made in Howells and Hine (1993). Their focus was on the process of designing a new electronic funds transfer system, but this corollary suggests that all past or existing payment systems also have inherent politics. Winner has also discussed the possibility of inherently political technologies in Winner (1980).

the banks to move value quickly and safely over long distances by simply sending standardized messages that instruct the recipient to debit one account and credit another. Value still "flows," but only in a metaphorical sense.

A check or a payment card sales draft is actually a similar kind of standardized message: it instructs the issuer to debit the payer's account and credit the bearer's account upon presentment. If the bearer is a different bank, the paying bank merely sends another standardized message to the clearing bank to debit its account and credit the other bank's account.

Interestingly, all of this existed long before the banks adopted digital computers. The standardized messages were encoded onto paper, which naturally limited the speed at which they could travel, but once they were received, value moved through simple bookkeeping entries. Thus, the "revolution" in payment systems that occurred in the 1960s and 1970s was not solely enabled by the digitization of *accounts*, for those were already stored in an easily-manipulable form and never left the domain of the bank. Rather, it was primarily enabled by the digitization of those *standardized messages*.

When Visa truncated the paper sales drafts and began clearing transactions electronically through BASE II, those messages could now travel anywhere in the world almost instantly. This enabled Visa to clear and settle transactions for the entire system overnight, greatly accelerating the flow of value, as well as reducing the handling and float costs incurred by the slow movement and difficult reconciliation of paper drafts.

But this also introduced a new possibility. From a technical perspective, any organization that maintained accounts could become a node on this network, regardless of geographic location or industry. In addition to banks, this could include investment brokers, national retail chains, universities, telecommunications providers, transit systems, utility companies, and a host of others. In other words, many different kinds of organizations could now suddenly act like a "bank," accepting deposits and providing electronic payment services.

This was a frightening potential for most bankers, who had grown accustomed to the protections afforded by the strict regulatory boundaries that separated them from other industries. The question then became, will the Visa network be extended in a way that respects these existing boundaries, or transgresses them? Would these other types of organizations be allowed to participate in the payment system, and if so, on what terms?

Boundaries

I should pause at this point to define what I mean by a "boundary." Boundaries, as I am using them here, are conceptual demarcations erected by actors to define a given social world. They might define the extent of a workgroup, a discipline, an organization, an industry, or a political state. In some cases, these boundaries remain strictly conceptual, but in others, they are also made incarnate in the form of regulations, policies, or even physical barriers. Boundaries establish who is inside and who is outside, and as such, designate who is allowed to participate in certain activities, who is allowed to access or contribute resources, and who is allowed to influence policy decisions. They can be crossed, but not without effort or cost.

Nevertheless, it is important to realize that these boundaries are neither natural nor static: they are actively erected and defended, and often challenged or transgressed, especially when there is money or power to be gained or lost. New boundaries may appear, existing ones may shift, or established ones may disappear altogether. These boundary shifts may then become mechanisms by which larger, industry-wide changes occur.[16]

The central claim I am making here is that transactional networks are one mechanism by which these boundary changes may occur. Transactional networks link various actors together to perform work, often on behalf of an external user, and when those networks cross established social boundaries, they can begin to undermine them in subtle ways, making them more porous, and eventually rendering them more cosmetic than restrictive. Often, this causes actors to question those boundaries and ultimately remove them. Of course, this does not always occur. Powerful actors may defend existing boundaries and limit or control the ways in which networks are allowed to cross over them, especially when those boundaries provide a significant political or economic advantage.

Physical and Logical Structure

When discussing networks and boundaries, it is also important to make the distinction between a network's *physical* and *logical* structure. The physical structure refers to the arrangement of nodes and how they are connected to one another. Any given node has one or more direct connections to other nodes, but those nodes may also connect to still other nodes, creating indirect paths between nodes that are not directly connected.

A *gateway* is a special kind of node that allows a network's physical structure to respect established social boundaries. A gateway stands between two networks, each of which can be controlled by different parties. The gateway is responsible for bridging the two networks, forwarding messages between them and translating the protocols if necessary.[17] The key point is that in order to get to the other network, one must go through the gateway, and *submit to its terms*. In this way, the gateway functions like Callon's "obligatory passage point," a node in the network that has made itself the funnel through which all activity must flow.[18]

In contrast to the physical structure, the logical structure of a network refers to the way in which *the user conceives it*. The degree to which the physical and logical structures differ is largely determined by how visible or noticeable the gateways are.

---

[16]For the concept of boundary-working, see Gieryn (1983), and MacKenzie (1990), pp. 413–417.

[17]In computer networking, the node is called a "gateway" if it translates protocols, or a "router" if it merely forwards the messages without conversion. Since I am dealing more with questions of boundaries than communication, I will simplify the discussion by using the term gateway only.

[18]Callon (1986b).

For example, on the Internet, a message may route through several nodes and across several gateways before reaching its destination, but the connections are entirely seamless. From the user's perspective, the source and destination nodes appear to be connected *directly* without any significant barriers in between. In contrast, when one uses an ATM in the US that is owned by a bank other than the one that holds the source account, the gateways are made quite visible through the warning and levy of additional "foreign" transaction fees.

Thus, gateways are rarely neutral, and their configuration may become a point of serious contention. Those actors that wish to defend or reinforce the boundaries will typically seek to make the gateways very noticeable and costly to cross, while those that wish to undermine the boundaries will strive to make the gateways as seamless and transparent as possible. Noticeable gateways will tend to reinforce the existing social boundaries, reminding participants that there is a clear *distinction of kind* between those inside and those outside. In contrast, transparent gateways tend to diminish the conceptual power of existing social boundaries, causing participants to eventually think of them as merely cosmetic, annoying, or even unnecessary. Undermined boundaries change the distinction from one of kind to one of degree; those inside and outside now become viable alternatives, and the consumers choice will now be made based on other competitive factors (e.g., price, service, etc.). Once these conceptual boundaries begin erode, their physical manifestations often start to change as well, leading to even larger-scale changes in the industry.

Transgressing and Defending Boundaries

The Visa case provides us with a few examples of how this might work out in practice. As we have seen, enabling connections to any organization that held value was at the heart of Hock's vision of electronic value exchange. He wanted to allow cardholders to access not only a line of credit issued by a bank, but also any pool of value they might possess, including demand deposits and investments. The question was not *if* the network should be extended to include these types of accounts, but *how*.

Boundaries Within the Banks: Debit Cards

As we saw in Chap. 8, the boundary between deposit and credit accounts within most banks was actively defended when NBI introduced the asset card. NBI was essentially proposing that banks extend their internal BankAmericard network to include the demand deposit accounts in addition to the credit accounts. This challenged the boundary that the deposit bankers had erected to keep this strange unsecured consumer credit device away from the "real banking." In banks where this boundary was strong, the card was not adopted, and thus the networks remained unlinked.

Eventually, this boundary was breached at most banks, but not until a generation of bank management had retired. By that time, many other changes, both within the banking industry and the Visa system, had made the boundary less important, and the deposit bankers of the 1990s were less interested in defending it. Once the boundary was crossed, it began to be questioned, and in many banks today it has been completely removed. At most banks, customers can link their debit and credit accounts together, and use the latter to cover transactions when there are insufficient funds in the former.

Boundaries Between Types of Banks: the Thrifts

Although NBI was initially unsuccessful at crossing boundaries within the banks, they were successful at transgressing some of the categorical boundaries within the banking industry. When NBI formed in 1970, the initial bylaws restricted membership to commercial banks only, primarily because all the existing BankAmericard licensees were commercial banks. Shortly thereafter, Hock began pushing to open the membership to mutual savings banks, savings and loan associations, and credit unions as well. These other types of banks, collectively referred to as "the thrifts," were more restricted in their activities than commercial banks, and some types were organized as not-for-profit. They primarily accepted savings deposits and made relatively safe loans, such as mortgages. As such, they were not subject to the same regulations as the commercial banks, and most importantly, could offer higher rates of interest on deposits.

The commercial banks, however, could offer their customers a key service that the thrifts could not: third-party payment instruments.[19] One could deposit money into a thrift, but getting it back out again required a trip to the branch to obtain cash. It was far more convenient for customers to put their money into a commercial bank account, where they could write checks against it, or use a credit line attached to their BankAmericard.

As discussed in Chap. 8, many thrifts began to eliminate this advantage in the early 1970s by offering what became known as "Negotiable Order of Withdrawal" (NOW) accounts. These were interest-bearing savings accounts that acted like demand deposit accounts, complete with a negotiable payment instrument that looked and acted just like a traditional check. If the thrifts were allowed to join NBI, they could then issue BankAmericards as well. This would undermine the boundaries between commercial and thrift banks, especially in the depositor's mind, making them simply cosmetic.

Hock eventually got his way, and the thrifts were allowed to join NBI provided their state charters allowed it.[20] The physical structure of the transactional network was then extended over the existing boundaries separating the various types of

---

[19]Third-party payment instruments can be transferred from the account holder to a party other than the source bank, such as a merchant. See Nielsen (1989).

[20]'NBI amends by-laws to permit membership by savings banks', American Banker (18 October 1973), p. 1. Russell noted that this was partially due to fears of antitrust litigation. If they had denied membership to the thrifts, they could have been sued for being exclusive.

banks, destroying them completely. There was still a legal distinction between the various types, but from the depositor's point of view, the boundary was no longer restrictive. Thrift accounts could now participate in the check and BankAmericard payment systems just as well as commercial bank accounts could.

Boundaries Between Financial Organizations: CMAs

A similar story can be told about the boundaries between different kinds of financial organizations, particularly those between banks and investment brokerages. Prior to the 1970s, the distinction between commercial bank accounts and investment brokerages in the minds of consumers was one of kind, not degree. Although an investor could maintain a balance of un-invested cash in a brokerage account, that investor could not access those funds via a third-party payment instrument, such as a check or payment card. Excluding investment brokerages from the national payment systems was one way in which commercial banks were able to defend the social boundary of banking, keeping the investment brokerages *outside*.

In the early 1970s, however, this distinction began to blur somewhat. Starting in 1972, several investment firms began offering what became known as "money market funds," which pooled together customer deposits and invested them into relatively safe, short-term securities, such as Treasury bills. Unlike ordinary investments, customers could withdraw their capital incrementally, on demand, similar to a demand deposit account at a commercial bank. When Fidelity introduced their version in 1974, they completed the service by issuing a check-like payment instrument, known as a "Negotiable Order of Withdrawal" (NOW), which had been pioneered by the thrifts earlier in the decade.

In 1977, Merrill Lynch took this one step further when they unveiled their new "Cash Management Account" (CMA).[21] This rather creative service combined a traditional investment portfolio with a money market account. Investment dividends and sale proceeds were automatically "swept" into the money market account where they began earning market-rate interest immediately. But the most interesting aspect of the CMA was that it came not only with checks, but also *a Visa card*. Visa transactions debited the cash in the money market fund, or an automatically funded margin account secured by the investments if not enough cash was available. It was exactly what Hock had been advocating with his asset card concept, except it was being provided by an investment broker and not a commercial bank.

Although the member banks agreed to let the thrifts join, they were not about to let investment brokers become members. In 1977, the US economy was experiencing a high rate of inflation, and observant consumers noticed that the interest rates on their commercial savings accounts were actually *less* than the rate of inflation. The buying power of their money was evaporating, but the commercial banks were prohibited by law from offering a higher rate, or any interest at all on demand deposits. The CMA offered consumers something that looked and acted just like a

---

[21]Nocera (1994), pp. 155–164.

commercial bank account, but provided a rate of return that would not only preserve their money's buying power, but also increase it.

Since Merrill could not join Visa as a member, it contracted with City National Bank and Trust (CNBT) of Columbus, Ohio, to act as their gateway into the network. CNBT built software to bridge the two networks, forwarding both BASE I authorization messages as well as cleared transactions from BASE II. From the perspective of the Visa system, CNBT was the issuer and thus responsible for settling the transactions, but once the Visa settlement was complete, CNBT's computer systems immediately settled again with Merrill.

The member banks won the battle to make the physical structure respect the existing boundaries, but they eventually lost the war because the logical structure did not. CNBT made the gateway completely seamless, and as such, made it appear to cardholders that Merrill was directly connected to Visa's transactional network. A Merrill CMA customer had no idea that CNBT was involved, nor did they need to. From the depositor's point of view, the boundaries between commercial banks and CMA-style accounts became so porous that they began to question why the boundaries existed at all.

The key point here is that the seamless gateway changed consumers' perceptions of the boundary claims between commercial banks and investment brokerages. The difference between a commercial bank and CMA-style account was transformed from one of kind to one of degree. They were no longer two completely distinct things: a "demand deposit account" versus an "investment account." Rather, they had both become "accounts" for cash management, and viable alternatives to one another. Depositors would now choose where to put their money based on other competitive factors such as minimum balance requirements, fees, and time-place convenience.

As consumers' perceptions of the boundary began to crumble, most of the commercial banks wisely abandoned their defense of it, and instead lobbied heavily for deregulation that would allow them to offer the same kinds of services. Today, the regulatory boundaries between commercial banks and investment brokers in the United States no longer exist, but Visa USA's bylaws still prohibit the brokers from becoming members. To gain access to Visa, most brokers have since purchased some type of bank (commonly an Industrial Loan Company), which can become a Visa member, and provide a seamless gateway between Visa and their own account networks. The physical structure of the Visa network still respects the boundaries that have been defended by the member bankers, but the logical structure has rendered them mostly meaningless for the consumer.

Boundaries Between Industries: JC Penney

For a final example, let us consider the JC Penney deal that was already discussed at length in Chap. 9. In order to get JC Penney to accept Visa cards, which would eventually force the other large national retailers to accept them as well, Visa had to allow JC Penney to connect directly into the transactional network, bypassing an acquiring bank. This was not simply a direct technological connection for submitting transactions: JC Penney was setup with a bank identification number and settlement account, just like any other member bank. Thus the network was physically extended over the existing boundary that separated banks from large retailers.

As we saw, the Board reluctantly agreed to honor this deal, but JC Penney remained the only US retailer ever to participate directly in the settlement network. After signing the deal, the Board amended the bylaws to prohibit this kind of incursion from ever happening again. Thus, they effectively defended the boundary between banks and retail organizations, which still exists to this day. All other retailers must go through a member bank, which acts as a gateway to the settlement networks. As opposed to the gateways used by the investment brokers, these are not seamless. The discount fee keeps the gateway noticeable, reminding the merchants that the boundary is restrictive and actively defended.

Application

In summary, the networks that make value move in the Visa system were sometimes designed to respect existing social boundaries, and other times to transgress them. In the case of the asset card, the deposit bankers defended their boundaries for a time, keeping the network away from their accounts. In the case of the thrifts, the physical structure of the network punctured the boundaries between the different kinds of banks, eventually rendering them cosmetic. In the case of the CMA, the physical structure respected the boundaries, but because the gateway was so seamless, the logical structure eventually undermined them. In the case of JC Penney, the bankers successfully defended the boundary, forcing other large retail merchants to go through an acquirer, which is essentially a noticeable gateway.

This interaction between network structure and boundaries should apply to the study of other of cases as well. Whenever a transactional network is created to link disparate actors together across existing social boundaries, the designers will necessarily have to decide if the physical structure will respect those boundaries or not. If gateways are used, they can be configured to be seamless, or noticeable and costly to traverse, and that will have profound effects on how the users of the network perceive those boundaries. Powerful actors may seek to defend their boundaries by limiting traffic through the gateway, or using it to extract fees. On the other hand, seamless connections will tend to undermine those boundaries, calling them into question, and jeopardizing their future existence.

Epilogue

In this final chapter, we have seen how the Visa case not only informs two of the grand themes from the history of technology, but also suggests two new dynamics that may be applicable to other cases. I discussed how value always flows according to a mark, and how those marks can mitigate risk when they guarantee something, such as value-exchange rules that are backed by a commonly-recognized and trusted authority. I also described how transactional networks can be designed to either respect or transgress existing social boundaries, and the ways in which seamless gateways can eventually undermine and call those boundaries into question.

These general dynamics build upon the rich and detailed history that makes up the bulk of this book, and it is about this history that I wish to make my concluding remarks. Part of what attracted me to this case in the first place was the way in which Visa has become such an integral yet unexamined part of our daily lives. Visa may be one of the best known brands in the world, but few have any idea what Visa is, how it is structured, or how it functions. Most of us think of our Visa cards the same way we think of a water faucet, a light switch, or a telephone. We no longer notice the systems lying behind these access devices because they have faded into the background, blended in with the task itself, and effectively become invisible.

When we hand our Visa card to a merchant, we rarely think about the magnetic stripes, integrated circuits, terminals, telecommunications, computers, and software programs that make electronic value exchange possible. Nor do we think about the people who determined how to make those cards machine-readable, how to build inexpensive point-of-sale terminals, how to connect merchants and banks throughout the world, how to authorize thousands of transactions each second, and clear and settle hundreds of millions of dollars worth of purchases each night in multiple currencies. Nor do we think about those who labored to standardize magnetic stripe and transaction formats so that devices and computer systems could exchange information easily and efficiently. Nor do we think about the organizational structures that allow the 20,000 Visa members around the world to cooperate just enough to coordinate their work, resolve their disputes, and determine future policy. We rarely think about this because, at least most of the time, it simply "works."

Forty years ago, Californians would crowd around the checkout to see someone pay with a BankAmericard. Today, it has become so commonplace that we are shocked and somewhat annoyed when the person in front of us at the grocery store begins the agonizingly slow process of writing a paper check. The first time I put my Visa card into an ATM in a foreign country and received local currency, it seemed like magic. Now I rarely think twice before boarding an international flight with nothing but a plastic card for payment. We are no longer amazed when a merchant far from home swipes our card through a terminal and receives an authorization, a *guarantee of payment*, a few seconds later. We have just come to expect it, as we have with countless other technological innovations.

But this is precisely the reason we historians of technology do what we do. We tell the stories of how technological systems came to be so that we can not only see them anew, but also recapture how they have altered the ways in which we think and act. In essence, our job is to make the invisible technologies visible again, if only for a moment.

Appendix
Core System Statistics

As was mentioned in Chap. 3, Visa began gathering system-level statistics in 1971. Because Visa was not a stock-issuing corporation during this period, they did not issue an annual report to stock holders with these data. Instead, these statistics were typically included in press releases, portions of which were reprinted in various banking industry publications such as the *American Banker* or *The Nilson Report*. Often these were corrected slightly in later articles, and the table below includes those revisions.

During the period covered by this book, Visa published four key measures with consistency. The first was commonly called "sales volume," which was the total dollar amount (in US Dollars) of all transactions (credit and debit) from all member banks. Typically, this included both cash advances and direct merchant purchases, but this was not always made explicit. The second was commonly labeled "number of cardholders," but this was actually the *number of cards issued*, not the number of *distinct cardholders*, which would typically be less, as many consumers had multiple cards. The third was the number of "accepting merchants," but this was somewhat ambiguous as to whether it counted each merchant location, or just each distinct business. Whether ATMs were eventually included in this number was also not specified. The last was the number of member institutions, which was relatively straightforward, and reflects the number of members as of the last day of the calendar year.

Visa did not typically report on the *number of transactions* processed by their systems, but Dougherty included statistics on the average transaction dollar value, which increased steadily from $17 in 1971 to $40 in 1980. This may be used to roughly estimate the number of transactions processed by the *system as a whole*, but it cannot be used to estimate the transaction volume passing through BASE II, as that system processed only *interchange* transactions; local transactions involving merchants and cardholders represented by the same bank would not be submitted to BASE II. It also has little bearing on the volume passing through BASE I at this time, as authorizations did not always result in clearing transactions (e.g., hotels and car rental agencies authorize a deposit that is not actually charged unless theft or damage occurs).

D.L. Stearns, *Electronic Value Exchange*, History of Computing,
DOI 10.1007/978-1-84996-139-4, © Springer-Verlag London Limited 2011

Table A.1 Core worldwide statistics

Year	Sales volume (billions USD)	Cards issued (millions)	Accepting merchants (millions)	Member institutions
1971	$4.06	25.7	1.07	3,978
1972	$5.48	29.1	1.29	4,525
1973	$7.68	33.3	1.42	5,226
1974	$10.27	38.1	1.59	6,076
1975	$12.28	41.4	1.81	6,752
1976	$15.22	45.2	1.95	7,889
1977	$20.15	58.7	2.40	9,707
1978	$24.50	66.6	2.40	10,836
1979	$34.00	79.6	2.90	11,385
1980	$45.70	94.8	3.10	11,930
1981	$51.80	93.6	3.40	13,072
1982	$59.40	98.2	3.70	13,683
1983	$70.00	106.2	3.90	15,485
1984	$85.00	121.0	4.30	16,724
1985	$107.00	136.0	5.00	17,700

Source: Various articles in the *American Banker* and *Business Wire*, and Dougherty (1981)

Since Visa was a non-stock membership association during this period, it also did not report on revenues the central organization received from member and transaction fees. Since Visa's members were also their owners, all revenues were applied to the operations of the core organization, so there was no net profit to report.

Finally, Visa also did not typically disclose its number of employees during this period, but this number would likely be misleading anyway for two important reasons. First, the employees working for the central organization were only a small fraction of the total number of people working on the system as a whole. Each member bank had some portion of their staff working on their particular card program, and these member bank employees were the ones contributing to system growth by recruiting new merchants and cardholders, responding to authorization calls, and processing transactions. After duality, the employees of many of the member banks would also have been doing these tasks for both the Visa and Interbank systems, making a full accounting of contributing employees quite difficult. Second, most of Visa's technical system development work in the 1970s was actually done by a mix of employees, consultant, contractors, and outside firms, most of whom would not be considered "employees."

Visa's chief rival during this period was the Interbank network. When NBI formed in 1970, it held a minority market share, both in terms of sales volume and member banks, but this relationship reversed over the course of the decade. The following table reports the relative market shares of NBI/Visa and Interbank during the second half of the decade. It was during this time that Visa began to overtake Interbank in the United States, and Visa's international growth in the early 1980s

Table A.2 Comparative US sales volumes for NBI/Visa and Interbank, 1975–1980

Year	Visa volume (billions)	Relative share	Interbank volume (billions)	Relative share
1975	$8.99	44.21%	$11.30	55.69%
1976	$11.11	44.78%	$13.70	55.22%
1977	$13.90	45.40%	$16.71	54.60%
1978	$22.07	49.65%	$22.38	50.35%
1979	$27.87	50.16%	$27.69	49.84%
1980	$28.32	53.48%	$24.63	46.52%

Source: Various issues of the *Nilson Report*

cemented their lead worldwide (see Chap. 6). Note that the sales volume numbers in this table are for the United States only.

References

25 Colorado banks will start offering Entree. American Banker, p. 2 (23 April 1976)

ABA adds to guides for magnetic card coding. American Banker, p. 1 (18 March 1971)

ABA issues credit card criteria, reaffirms support of magnetic stripe. American Banker, p. 1 (14 November 1973)

Abbate, J.: Inventing the Internet. MIT Press, Cambridge (1999)

Alvesson, M., Berg, P.O.: Corporate Culture and Organizational Symbolism: An Overview. Walter de Gruyter, Berlin (1992)

American express no friend of ours, Hock Tells bankers. American Banker, p. 1 (18 September 1980)

Arthur, B.W.: Competing technologies and economic prediction. In: MacKenzie, D., Wajcman, J. (eds.) The Social Shaping of Technology, 2nd edn., pp. 106–112. Open University Press, Maidenhead (1999)

Baker, D.: Shared ATM networks: the antitrust dimension. Federal Reserve Bank of St. Louis Review, pp. 5–17 (November/December 1995)

Bank cards are real banking, too. American Banker, p. 4 (27 September 1974)

Bank cards push for the big stores. Business Week, pp. 107–108 (27 September 1976)

Bank cards take over the country. Business Week, pp. 44–54 (4 August 1975)

Bank credit-card and check-credit plans. Federal reserve system report. Federal Reserve System (July 1968)

BankAmericard sales. American Banker, p. 2 (1 February 1973)

BankAmericard starting ad campaign urging public to think of card as money. American Banker, p. 1 (10 March 1971)

The Banker's EFT Handbook. American Bankers Association, Washington (1975)

Banking at the chain store—closer that you think. US News and World Report, pp. 77–80 (16 September 1974)

Banking lacks national structures to deal adequately with change. American Banker, p. 1 (25 September 1974)

Barnes, B., Bloor, D., Henry, J.: Scientific Knowledge: a Sociological Analysis. University of Chicago Press, Chicago (1996)

BASE is a system of people. BankAmericard World, p. 2 (June 1973)

BASE unveiled in S.F. BankAmericard World, p. 1 (June 1973)

Bátiz-Lazo, B., Maixé-Altés, J.-C., Thomes, P. (eds.): Technological Innovation in Retail Finance: International Historical Perspectives. Routledge, London (2011)

Baxter, W.F.: Bank interchange of transactional paper: legal and economic perspectives. Journal of Law and Economics 26(3), 541–588 (1983)

Beamish, P.W., Killing, J.P. (eds.) Cooperative Strategies: North American Perspectives. New Lexington Press, San Francisco (1997)

Beating the new credit cards. Business Week, pp. 120–122 (11 August 1973)

Becker, H.S.: Culture: a sociological view. Yale Review **71**, 513–527 (1982)

Bernard, J.: New directions in bankcard competition. Catholic University Law Review **30**, 65–102 (1980)

Berry, H.V.: The credit card and the debit card. In: Critical Issues in Bank Cards, pp. 102–123. American Bankers Association, Washington (1980)

Besnard, D., Baxter, G.: Human compensations for undependable systems. Technical Report CS-TR-819, School of Computing Science, University of Newcastle upon Tyne, November 2003

Bezroukov, N.: Open source software development as a special type of academic research (critique of vulgar Raymondism). First Monday **4**(10) (1999)

The big-name credit cards and how they compare. Changing Times **27**, 25–28 (1973)

Bloch, M.: The watermill and feudal authority. In: MacKenzie, D., Wajcman, J. (eds.) The Social Shaping of Technology, 2nd edn., pp. 152–155. Open University Press, Maidenhead (1999)

Bodnar, J.: Power and memory in oral history: workers and managers at Studebaker. Journal of American History **75**(4), 1201–1221 (1989)

Borland, K.: "That's not what I said": interpretive conflict in oral narrative research. In: Perks, R., Thomson, A. (eds.) The Oral History Reader, pp. 320–332. Routledge, London (1998)

Bradford, T., Weiner, S.E.: Who's processing your payments? Payments system research briefing, Federal Reserve Bank of Kansas City, August 2005. http://www.kc.frb.org/FRFS/PSR/PSR-BriefingAug05.pdf—visited on 6 October 2005

Brandel, R.E., Terraciano, J.E.: Legal and regulatory environment. In: Critical Issues in Bank Cards, pp. 124–152. American Bankers Association, Washington (1980)

Brooke, P.: MAPS planners, in final report, urge payments system free of fed control. American Banker, p. 1 (3 May 1971)

Brooke, P.: Banks reappraise cards as losses mount. American Banker, p. 1 (18 May 1971)

Brooke, P.: Public opposes shift to electronic payments. American Banker, p. 1 (9 July 1971)

Brooke, P.: City NB&T, columbus, to test point-of-sale card authorization, data capture in suburbs. American Banker, p. 1 (14 July 1971)

Brooke, P.: National BankAmericard requires banks data for analysis of card profits, losses. American Banker, p. 1 (6 August 1971)

Brooke, P.: Quigley describes operation of omniswitch; urges cooperation in national development. American Banker, pp. 6–7 (11 August 1971)

Brooke, P.: ABA defends card stripe against fraud ease charge. American Banker, p. 1 (3 November 1971)

Brooke, P.: ABA magnetic stripe highly vulnerable to fraud. American Banker, p. 6 (3 November 1971)

Brooke, P.: NBI plans to sign pact for nationwide authorization system by year's end. American Banker, p. 1 (4 November 1971)

Brooke, P.: Omniswitch, national data joining system. American Banker, p. 1 (4 January 1972)

Brooke, P.: Bank, shopper, stores like electronic funds transfer in ohio test. American Banker, p. 1 (28 January 1972)

Brooke, P.: Bankamericard schedules April start for 24-hour national card authorization. American Banker, p. 1 (21 August 1972)

Brooke, P.: Magnetic stripe credit card encoding nears worldwide test. American Banker, p. 1 (18 October 1972)

Brooke, P.: Citicorp says students find cheap, easy ways to defraud magnetic stripe cards. American Banker, p. 1 (9 April 1973)

Brooke, P.: Bank credit card leaders back magnetic stripe. American Banker, p. 1 (13 April 1973)

Brooke, P.: Electronic data transmission net linking all US BankAmericard centers is operative. American Banker, p. 1 (11 May 1973)

Brooke, P.: In past year, EFTS concepts shift from theory to action. American Banker, p. 13 (4 June 1973)

Brooke, P.: NBI hires Centurex to design software system for member banks. American Banker, p. 1 (1 August 1973)

Brooke, P.: NBI moves toward electronic interchange of bank card sales drafts to reduce costs. American Banker, p. 1 (29 August 1973)

Brooke, P.: Completion of standards for thrifts seen spurring conflict over magnetic stripes. American Banker, p. 1 (14 September 1973)

Brooke, P.: National licensing of citicard planned. American Banker, p. 1 (11 September 1974)

Brooke, P.: IBANCO, Ltd., organized to manage worldwide BankAmericard program. American Banker, p. 1 (20 September 1974)

Brooke, P.: BankAmericard begins electronic interchange of drafts. American Banker, p. 1 (6 November 1974)

Brooke, P.: NBI moves to reinstate contested ban of dual membership. American Banker, p. 1 (20 November 1974)

Brooke, P.: TTI: Citicorp's own EFT Think Tank. American Banker, p. 1 (8 May 1975)

Brooke, P.: New NBI debit card is named ENTREE. American Banker, p. 1 (22 August 1975)

Brooks, F.P.: The Mythical Man Month: Essays on Software Engineering, anniversary edn., reprint of 1975. Addison-Wesley, Reading (1995)

Brouillette, G.: NBI set to launch debit card plan as early as october. American Banker, p. 1 (28 April 1975)

Brouillette, G.: BankAmerica girds for more travelers check competition. American Banker, p. 1 (26 July 1978)

Buchan, J.: Frozen Desire: the Meaning of Money. Farrar, Straus and Giroux, New York (1997)

Buchanan, R.A.: Theory and narrative in the history of technology. Technology and Culture **32**(2), 365–376 (1991)

Burns, A.F.: The ongoing revolution in American banking. American Enterprise Institute for Public Policy Research, Washington (1988)

Burns, T., Stalker, G.M.: The Management of Innovation. Tavistock, London (1961)

Calder, L.: Financing the American Dream: a Cultural History of Consumer Credit. Princeton University Press, Princeton (1999)

Callon, M.: Some elements of a sociology of translation: domestication of the scallops and the fishermen of St Brieuc bay. In: Law, J. (ed.) Power, Action and Belief: a New Sociology of Knowledge, pp. 196–233. Routledge, London (1986b)

Callon, M.: The sociology of an actor-network: the case of the electric vehicle. In: Callon, M., Law, J., Rip, A. (eds.) Mapping the Dynamics of Science and Technology: Sociology of Science in the Real World, pp. 19–34. MacMillan, Basingstoke (1986a)

Callon, M.: Society in the making: the study of technology as a tool for sociological analysis. In: Bijker, W.E., Hughes, T.P., Pinch, T. (eds.) The Social Construction of Technological Systems: New Directions in the Sociology and History of Technology, pp. 83–107. MIT Press, Cambridge (1987)

Campbell-Kelly, M.: From Airline Reservations to Sonic the Hedgehog: a History of the Software Industry. MIT Press, Cambridge (2003)

Campbell-Kelly, M., Aspray, W.: Computer: a History of the Information Machine. Basic Books, New York (1996)

Can the stores trump bank credit cards? Business Week, pp. 62–64 (30 January 1971)

Card groups take own authorization paths. American Banker, p. 1 (29 June 1971)

Card may be solution to unpaid doctor's bills. American Banker, p. 1 (26 January 1971)

Card plans show big gains. Burroughs Clearing House **52**(5), 15–16 (1968)

Carr, E.H.: What is History? Penguin Books, New York (1961)

Carrington, M., Langguth, P.W., Steiner, T.D.: The Banking Revolution: Salvation or Slaughter? How Technology is Creating Winner and Losers. Pitman Publishing, London (1997)

Carter, N.H.: A different view of the checkless society. Banking **59**(8), 119–121 (1967)

Ceruzzi, P.E.: A History of Modern Computing. MIT Press, Cambridge (1998)

Chandler, L.V.: The Economics of Money and Banking, 9th edn., reprint of 1948. Harper and Row, New York (1986)

Chandler, A.D.: The Visible Hand: The Managerial Revolution in American Business. Harvard University Press, Cambridge (1997)

The charge-it plan that really took off. Business Week, pp. 58–63 (27 February 1965)

Cheney, J., Rhine, S.: How effective were the financial safety nets in the aftermath of Katrina? Discussion paper, Payment Cards Center of the Federal Reserve Bank of Philadelphia, January 2006. http://www.philadelphiafed.org/pcc/HurricaneKatrinaJan06.pdf—visited on 2 February 2006

Chown, J.: A History of Money: From Ad 800. Routledge, London (1994)

Chutkow, P.: Visa: the Power of an Idea. Harcourt, Chicago (2001)

Citicorp sues interbank over travel checks. American Banker, p. 1 (14 April 1978)

Clark, B.R.: The organizational saga in higher education. Administrative Science Quarterly **17**, 178–184 (1972)

Cleveland, T.: The Visa history: Tom Cleveland's perspective. Unpublished compilation of personal stories by Tom Cleveland, former CFO of Visa International (April 1999)

Coghlan, R.: The Theory of Money and Finance. Macmillan, London (1980)

Collins, H.: The TEA set: tacit knowledge and scientific networks. Social Studies of Science **4**(2), 165–186 (1974)

Collins, H.M.: The seven sexes: a study in the sociology of a phenomenon. Sociology **9**(2), 205–224 (1975)

Collins, H.M.: In praise of futile gestures: how scientific is the sociology of scientific knowledge? Social Studies of Science **26**, 229–244 (1996)

Colton, K.W., Kraemer, K.L. (eds.): Computers and Banking: Electronic Funds Transfer Systems and Public Policy. Plenum Press, New York (1980)

Competition and innovation in the credit card industry at the consumer and network level. Hearings before the Subcommittee on Financial Institutions of the Committee on Banking, Housing, and Urban Affairs, United States Senate, 106th Congress (25 May 2000)

The Consumer Credit Protection Act Ammendments of 1977. Hearings on HR 8753 before the Subcommittee on Consumer Affairs of the Committee on Banking, Finance, and Urban Affairs, United States House of Representatives, 95th Congress, First Session (March 1977)

Copeland, D.G., Mason, R.O., McKenney, J.L.: Sabre: the development of information-based competence and execution of information-based competition. IEEE Annal of the History of Computing **17**(3), 30–57 (1995)

Court upsets ruling against NBI dual card ban. American Banker, p. 1 (25 September 1973)

Credit Cards: A study of consumer attitudes and usage, survey conducted for National BankAmericard Incorporated by Market Facts Incorporated (1975)

Critical Issues in Bank Cards. American Bankers Association, Washington (1980)

A data stripe puts speed in credit cards. Business Week, pp. 68–69 (16 September 1972)

David, P.A.: Path dependence and the quest for historical economics: one more chorus of the ballad of QWERTY. Discussion Papers in Economic and Social History 20, University of Oxford, November 1997

Davies, G.: A History of Money: from Ancient Times to the Present Day. University of Wales Press, Cardiff (1994)

Desmonde, W.H.: Magic, Myth, and Money: the Origin of Money in Religious Ritual. Free Press of Glencoe, New York (1962)

Debit card volume rises 187% at Visa: American Banker, p. 9 (14 December 1981)

Digital and Banking: Promotional brochure produced by Digital Equipment Corporation (1976)

Don't just pay that charge account bill. Read it! Changing Times, pp. 37–40 (February 1973)

Dosi, G.: Technological paradigms and technological trajectories: a suggested interpretation of the determinants and directions of technical change. Research Policy **11**(3), 147–162 (1982)

Dougherty, J.S.: Visa International: the Management of Change. Harvard Business School Case Study. Prepared under the supervision of Robert G. Eccles, Jr. (1981)

Douglas, M.: Risk Acceptability According to the Social Sciences. Routledge and Kegan Paul, London (1985)

Drury, T., Ferrier, C.W.: Credit Cards. Butterworths, London (1984)

Dryer, D.: The limits of technology transfer: civil systems at TRW, 1965–1975. In: Hughes, A.C., Hughes, T.P. (eds.) Systems, Experts, and Computers: The Systems Approach in Management and Engineering, World War II and After. MIT Press, Cambridge, pp. 359–384 (2000)

Dyer, D.: TRW: Pioneering Technology and Innovation Since 1900. Harvard Business School Press, Boston (1998)

Ederer, R.J.: The Evolution of Money. Public Affairs Press, Washington (1964)

Egleton, C., Williams, J.: Money: A History. Firefly Books, Buffalo (2007)

Einzig, P.: Primitive Money in Its Ethnological, Historical and Economic Aspects, 2nd edn., reprint of 1949. Pergamon, Oxford (1966)

Electronic funds transfer test announced by City NB&T. Payment Systems Newsletter, p. 5 (July 1971)

Essinger, J.: Electronic Payment Systems: Winning New Customers. Chapman and Hall, London (1992)

Essinger, J.: The Virtual Banking Revolution: the Customer, the Bank and the Future. International Thomson Business Press, London (1999)

Evans, D.S.: Bank interchange fees balance dual demand. American Banker **166**(18), 17 (2001)

Evans, D.S.: Will retailers stampede to drop signature debit? American Banker **169**(1), 10 (2004)

Evans, D., Schmalensee, R.: Paying with Plastic: the Digital Revolution in Buying and Borrowing, 2nd edn. MIT Press, Cambridge (2005)

Evans, D., Schmalensee, R.: Catalyst Code: the Strategies Behind the World's Most Dynamic Companies. Harvard Business School Press, Boston (2007)

Facts about BankAmericard. National BankAmericard Incorporated Booklet (October 1975)

Fast credit card authorization is offered to banks and merchants by CSI. American Banker, p. 8 (6 January 1971)

Fazar, W.: The origin of PERT. The Controller, pp. 598–602, 618–621 (December 1962)

Federal legislation is introduced to establish electronic fund transfer systems commission and study. Payment Systems Newsletter, p. 1 (April 1974)

Fee income spurs new debit strategies. Banking, pp. 92–94 (September 1991)

Felgran, S.D.: From ATM to POS networks: branching, access, and pricing. New England Economic Review, pp. 44–61 (May/June 1985)

Felgran, S.D.: Shared ATM networks: market structure and public policy. New England Economic Review, pp. 23–38 (January/February 1984)

Fenstermaker, J. Van, Perry, D.: An examination of a charge card system. Journal of Bank Research **2**(1), 9–13 (1971)

Ferguson, N.: The Ascent of Money: a Financial History of the World. Penguin, London (2008)

Fernelius, L.W., Fettig, D.: The Dichotomy Becomes Reality: Ten Years of the Federal Reserve as Regulator and Competitor. http://minneapolisfed.org/pubs/ar/ar1991.cfm—visited on 26 August 2006

Fisher, J., et al.: Bank Cards. American Bankers Association, Washington (1980)

FNB Chi, Wells first to announce Visa travel plans. American Banker, p. 2 (24 November 1978)

For Everything. Time (23 March 1959)

Francis, G.J., Siegel, S.M.: Principles of Banking: an Overview of the Financial Services Industry, 7th edn. American Bankers Association, Washington (2001)

Frazer, P.: Plastic and Electronic Money: New Payment Systems and Their Implications. Woodhead-Faulkner, Cambridge (1985)

Friedlander, P.: Theory, method and oral history. In: Perks, R., Thomson, A. (eds.) The Oral History Reader, pp. 311–319. Routledge, London (1998)

Friedman, A.L.: Computer Systems Development: History Organization and Implementation. John Wiley and Sons, New York (1989)

Fry, M.J., Kilato, I., Roger, S., Senderowicz, K., Sheppard, D., Solis, F., Trundle, J.: Payment Systems in Global Perspective. Routledge, London (1999)

Gaddis, J.L.: The Landscape of History: How Historians Map the Past. Oxford University Press, Oxford (2002)

Galanoy, T.: Charge It: Inside the Credit Card Conspiracy. GP Putnam's Sons, New York (1980)

Galbraith, J.K.: Money: Whence it Came, Where it Went, revised edn., reprint of 1975. Houghton Mifflin, Boston (1995)

Gerdes, G.R., Walton, J.K.: The use of checks and other noncash payment instruments in the United States. Federal Reserve Bulletin (2002). www.federalreserve.gov/pubs/bulletin/2002/0802_2nd.pdf—visited on 12 November 2010

Gerson, E.M.: Reach, Bracket, and the Limits of Rationalized Coordination: Some Challenges for CSCW. In: Ackerman, et al. (ed.) Resources, Co-Evolution, and Artifacts: Theory in CSCW, pp. 193–220. Springer, London (2008)

Giddens, A.: The Consequences of Modernity. Stanford University Press, Stanford (1990)

Gieryn, T.F.: Boundary-work and the demarcation of science from non-science: strains and interests in professional ideologies of scientists. American Sociological Review **48**(6), 781–795 (1983)

Goldberg, L.G.: The effect of state banking regulations on bank credit card use. Journal of Money, Credit and Banking **7**(1), 105–112 (1975)

Good, B.A.: The Changing Face of Money: Will Electronic Money be Adopted in the United States? Garland, New York (2000)

Great Wolf Lodge Rides the RFID Wristband Wave. http://www.pdcorp.com/crowd-control/case-study-great-wolf.html—visited on 13 September 2006

Grele, R.J.: Movement without aim: methodological and theoretical problems in oral history. In: Perks, R., Thomson, A. (eds.) The Oral History Reader, pp. 38–52. Routledge, London (1998)

Gulati, R.: Alliances and networks. Strategic Management Journal **19**, 293–317 (1998)

Gunn, J.V.: Autobiography: Towards a Poetics of Experience. University of Pennsylvania Press, Philadelphia (1982)

Guseva, A.: Into the Red: the Birth of the Credit Card Market in Postcommunist Russia. Stanford University Press, Stanford (2008)

Hagiu, A.: Cash, Credit, or Car? http://www.marketplatforms.com/payingwithplastic/mpdperspectives/—visited on 7 September 2006

Hardstone, G., D'Adderio, L., Williams, R.: Standardization, Trust and Dependability (2004). Unpublished chapter

Hartmann, M., Berker, T., Punie, Y., Ward, K. (eds.): Domestication of Media and Technology. Open University Press, Maidenhead (2005)

Hashagen, U., Keil-Slawik, R., Norberg, A. (eds.): History of Computing: Software Issues. Springer, Berlin (2002)

Hayashi, F., Sullivan, R., Weiner, S.E.: A Guide to the ATM and Debit Card Industry. Payment Systems Research Department, Federal Reserve Bank of Kansas City, Kansas City (2003)

Head, R.V.: Getting Sabre off the ground. IEEE Annal of the History of Computing **24**(4), 32–39 (2002)

High court refuses Worthen-NBI review. American Banker, p. 1 (20 February 1974)

Hock, D.: Birth of the Chaordic Age. Berrett-Koehler, San Francisco (1999)

Hock, D.: One from Many: Visa and the Rise of Chaordic Organization. Berrett-Koehler, San Francisco (2005). 2nd edn. of *Birth of the Chaordic Age*

Hock, D.: Bank cards: today's popular song or an unfinished symphony? Speech given at the American Bankers Association Bank Card Conference, San Francisco (14 September 1976)

Hock, D.: Bank card industry must press for legislation on national level. American Banker, p. 4 (3 October 1973)

Hock, D.: Electronic funds transfer or electronic value exchange? Paper presented at the Federal Reserve Bank of Boston Conference, Melvin Village, New Hampshire (October 1974)

Hock, D.: Competition for financial services in an electronic banking environment. Speech given to the National Marketing Conference of the American Bankers Association, Chicago (March 1975)

Hock, D.: Address Before the American Bankers Association 1984 Telecommunications and Financial Networks Conference (February 1984)

Hopton, D.: Payment Systems: a Case for Consensus. Bank for International Settlements (1983)

Hosemann, M.J.: The rationale for electronic banking. In: Critical Issues in Bank Cards, pp. 60–101. American Bankers Association, Washington (1980)

How banking tames its paper tiger. Business Review of the Federal Reserve Bank of Philadelphia, pp. 2–11 (May 1960)

Howells, J., Hine, J. (eds.): Innovative Banking: Competition and the Management of a New Networks Technology. Routledge, London (1993)

Hughes, T.P.: Networks of Power: Electrification in Western Society, 1880–1930. Johns Hopkins University Press, Baltimore (1983)

Hughes, T.P.: The seamless web: technology, science, etcetera, etcetera. Social Studies of Science 16(2), 281–292 (1986)

Hughes, T.P.: The evolution of large technological systems. In: Bijker, W.E., Hughes, T.P., Pinch, T. (eds.) The Social Construction of Technological Systems: New Directions in the Sociology and History of Technology, pp. 51–82. MIT Press, Cambridge (1987)

Humphrey, D.B.: Payment Systems: Principles, Practice and Improvements. The World Bank, Washington (1995)

The iconoclast who made Visa No. 1. Business Week, pp. 44–46 (22 December 1980)

Introduction to Entrée: Brochure on the new Entrée card produced by National BankAmericard Incorporated for its members (1975)

Jelliffe, C.G.: President of CNBT, quoted in the Payment Systems Newsletter, p. 6. (July 1971)

Jevons, W.S.: Money and the Mechanism of Exchange. Twentieth Century, London (1875)

Johnson, R.W., Sullivan, A.C.: Statistical analysis of bank card usage. In: Critical Issues in Bank Cards, pp. 1–59. American Bankers Association, Washington (1980)

Jutilla, D.: Fundamentals of Bank Credit Cards. American Institute of Banking, Tacoma Chapter, Tacoma (1973)

Katz, M.L., Shapiro, C.: Network externalities, competition, and compatibility. American Economic Review 75(3), 424–440 (1985)

Kent, R.P.: Money and Banking, 4th edn., reprint of 1947. Holt, Rinehart and Winston, New York (1961)

Kirkman, P.: Electronic Funds Transfer Systems: the Revolution in Cashless Banking and Payment Methods. Basil Blackwell, Oxford (1987)

Klebaner, B.J.: Commercial Banking in the United States: a History. Dryden Press, Hinsdale (1974)

Kling, R.: Value conflicts and social choice in electronic funds transfer system developments. Communications of the ACM 21(8), 642–657 (1978)

Knight, J.R.: A case study: airlines reservations systems. Proceedings of the IEEE 60(11), 1423–1431 (1972)

Kraft, P.: Programmers and Managers: the Routinization of Computer Programming in the United States. Springer, New York (1977)

Kuhn, S.: The limits to industrialization: computer software development in a large commercial bank. In: Wood, S. (ed.) The Transformation of Work? Skill Flexibility and the Labour Process. Unwin Hyman, London (1989)

Kuhn, T.S.: The Structure of Scientific Revolutions, 3rd edn., reprint of 1962. University of Chicago Press, Chicago (1996)

Kunda, G.: Engineering Culture: Control and Commitment in a High-Tech Corporation. Temple University Press, Philadelphia (1992)

Kutler, J.: Phoenix merchant fights Visa debit fee. American Banker, p. 1 (9 June 1977)

Kutler, J.: Visa enters travel check field in challenge to Master Charge. American Banker, p. 1 (10 July 1978)

Kutler, J.: Barclays to switch travel checks operations to Visa. American Banker, p. 1 (4 January 1979)

Kutler, J.: Visa international plans magnetic stripe for all cards. American Banker, p. 1 (6 February 1979)

Kutler, J.: Penney to honor Visa; 1st big retailer to accept bank cards. American Banker, p. 1 (5 April 1979)

Kutler, J.: Visa approves interchange stripes. American Banker, p. 3 (12 June 1979)

Kutler, J.: Visa sued on price fixing, Penney Tie. American Banker, p. 1 (27 June 1979)

Kutler, F.: Former cook exec sees little room for new travel checks. American Banker, p. 1 (30 August 1979)

Kutler, J.: Interbank's Reynolds calls Visa, Penney Tie harmful to banking. American Banker, p. 15 (14 September 1979)

Kutler, J.: Visa, Penney Tie seen unique, not threat. American Banker, p. 3 (17 September 1979)

Kutler, J.: Chase becomes biggest of 31 banks in Visa's travelers check program. American Banker, p. 1 (29 May 1980)

Kutler, J.: Age of the debit card is coming. American Banker, p. 1 (9 March 1981)

Kutler, J.: Metal plates to duality: the shaping of an industry. American Banker, pp. 30–36 (September 1994). Special insert

Laprie, J. (ed.): Dependability: Basic Concepts and Terminology in English, French, German, Italian and Japanese. Springer, Vienna (1992)

Larkin, K.V.: Dealer paper in the age of the consumer. Banking 63(4), 32–33 (1970)

Latour, B.: Science in Action: How to Follow Scientists and Engineers Through Society. Harvard University Press, Cambridge (1987)

Latour, B.: Ethnography of a high-tech case: about Aramis. In: Lemonnier, P. (ed.) Technological Choices: Transformation in Material Cultures Since the Neolithic, pp. 372–397. Routledge, London (1993)

Latour, B.: Aramis, or, the Love of Technology. Harvard University Press, Cambridge (1996)

Latour, B.: Give me a laboratory and I will raise the world. In: Biagioli, M. (ed.) The Science Studies Reader, pp. 258–275. Routledge, New York (1999a)

Latour, B.: On recalling ANT. In: Law, J., Hassard, J. (eds.) Actor Network Theory and After, pp. 15–25. Blackwell, Oxford (1999b)

Latour, B.: Reassembling the Social: an Introduction to Actor-network-theory. Oxford University Press, Oxford (2005)

Law, J.: Technology and heterogeneous engineering: the case of Portuguese expansion. In: Bijker, W.E., Hughes, T.P., Pinch, T. (eds.) The Social Construction of Technological Systems: New Directions in the Sociology and History of Technology, pp. 111–134. MIT Press, Cambridge (1987)

Lee, W.: Visa debit card volume tops credit worldwide. American Banker, p. 11 (21 April 2004)

Lejeune, P.: On Autobiography. Translated by Leary, K., edited by Eakin, P.J. University of Minnesota Press, Minneapolis (1989)

Leveson, N.G.: Safeware: System Safety and Computers. Addison-Wesley, Reading (1995)

Levinson, M.: The Box: How the Shipping Container Made the World Smaller and the World Economy Bigger. Princeton University Press, Princeton (2006)

Liebowitz, S.J., Margolis, S.E.: Path dependence, lock-in, and history. Journal of Law, Economics, and Organization 11(1), 205–226 (1995)

Losowsky, A.: I've got you under my skin. The Guardian (10 June 2004). http://technology. guardian.co.uk/online/story/0,3605,1234827,00.html—visited on 13 September 2006

Lummis, T.: Structure and validity in oral evidence. In: Perks, R., Thomson, A. (eds.) The Oral History Reader, pp. 273–283. Routledge, London (1998)

Mackay, H., Gillespie, G.: Extending the social shaping of technology approach: ideology and appropriation. Social Studies of Science 22(4), 685–716 (1992)

MacKenzie, D.: Missile accuracy: a case study in the social process of technological change. In: Bijker, W.E., Hughes, T.P., Pinch, T. (eds.) The Social Construction of Technological Systems: New Directions in the Sociology and History of Technology, pp. 195–222. MIT Press, Cambridge (1987)

MacKenzie, D.: Inventing Accuracy: a Historical Sociology of Nuclear Missile Guidance. MIT Press, Cambridge (1990)

MacKenzie, D.: How do we know the properties of artefacts? Applying the sociology of knowledge to technology. In: Fox, R. (ed.) Technological Change: Methods and Themes in the History of Technology, pp. 247–263. Harwood, Amsterdam (1996)

MacKenzie, D.: Mechanizing Proof: Computing Risk and Trust. MIT Press, Cambridge (2001)

MacKenzie, D.: A view from the Sonnenbichl: on the historical sociology of software and system dependability. In: Hashagen, U., Keil-Slawik, R., Norberg, A. (eds.) History of Computing: Software Issues, pp. 97–122. Springer, Berlin (2002)

MacKenzie, D., Wajcman, J. (eds.): The Social Shaping of Technology, 2nd edn., reprint of 1985. Open University Press, Maidenhead (1999)

Magnetic stripe for credit cards urged by ABA unit. American Banker, p. 1 (16 February 1971)

Magnis, N.E.: Descriptive billing—a solution to the paperwork problem. ABA Banking Journal **62**(10) (1970)

Makino, S., Beamish, P.W.: Performance and survival of joint ventures with non-conventional ownership structures. Journal of International Business Studies **29**(4), 797–818 (1998)

Mandell, L.: Credit Card Use in the United States. University of Michigan Institute for Social Research, Ann Arbor (1972)

Mandell, L.: The Credit Card Industry: a History. Twayne, Boston (1990)

Mandell, L., Murphy, N.B.: Bank Cards. American Institute of Banking and American Bankers Association, Washington (1976)

Mann, R.J.: Charging Ahead: the Growth and Regulation of Payment Card Markets. Cambridge University Press, Cambridge (2006)

Manning, R.D.: Credit Card Nation: the Consequences of America's Addiction to Credit. Basic Books, New York (2000)

Marti, J., Zeilinger, A.: Micros and Money: New Technology in Banking and Shopping. Policy Studies Institute, London (1982)

Martin, B.: The critique of science becomes academic. Science Technology and Human Values **18**(2), 247–259 (1994)

Martin, B.: Sticking a needle into science: the case of Polio vaccines and the origin of AIDS. Social Studies of Science **26**, 245–276 (1996)

Mason, J.E.: The Transformation of Commercial Banking in the United States, 1956–1991. Garland, New York (1997)

Mathews, H.L., Slucum, J.W. Jr.: Correlatives of commercial bank credit card use. Journal of Bank Research **2**(4), 21–27 (1972)

Mayer, M.: The Bankers: The Next Generation. Truman Talley, New York (1997)

McAndrews, J.J.: The evolution of shared ATM networks. Federal Reserve Bank of Philadelphia Business Review, pp. 3–16 (May/June 1991)

McKenna, K.: Banks find credit cards are useful… and costly. American Banker, p. 3 (19 June 1971)

McLeod, R.W.: Bank Credit Cards for Efts: a Cost-benefit Analysis. University Microfilms International, Ann Arbor (1979)

Meyer, A.D., Starbuck, W.H.: Interactions between ideologies and politics in strategy formation. In: Roberts, K.H. (ed.) New Challenges to Understanding Organizations, pp. 99–116. Macmillan, New York (1993)

Millard, S.: The foundations of money, payments and central banking: a review essay. http://d.repec.org/n?u=RePEc:mmf:mmfc06:106&r=his

Mitchell, G.: Governor Mitchell considers tomorrow's banking. Banking **59**(6), 33–34 (1966)

Modi, M.: POS Microcosm. Banking, pp. 68–72 (October 1987)

Money goes electronic in the 1970s. Business Week, pp. 54–76 (13 January 1968)

Murmann, J.P.: Knowledge and Competitive Advantage: the Coevolution of Firms, Technology, and National Institutions. Cambridge University Press, Cambridge (2003)

Nashville Banks Cautious on EFT. American Banker, p. 1 (11 December 1975)

National Authorization Joint Feasibility Study Final Report (29 January 1971). Provided by member of committee

NBI amends by-laws to permit membership by savings banks. American Banker, p. 1 (18 October 1973)

NBI announces Entree card. Payment Systems Newsletter, p. 1 (September 1975)

NBI buys Centurex on-line card system. American Banker, p. 5 (2 January 1974)

NBI finds no major problems with facsimile drafts. American Banker, p. 81 (10 October 1973)

NBI maps new rules banning dual membership. American Banker, p. 1 (17 September 1974)

NBI planning paperless card drafts. American Banker, p. 1 (18 December 1973)

NCNB to become biggest bank in Visa debit card program. American Banker, p. 3 (8 March 1979)

NDC credit authorization pilot underway. Payment Systems Newsletter, p. 7 (July 1971)

Newlyn, W.T.: Theory of Money, 2nd edn., reprint of 1962. Clarendon, Oxford (1971)

Nielsen, J.F.: Banking Terminology, 3rd edn. American Bankers Association, Washington (1989)

Nilson, S.: The Nilson Report. HSN Consultants, Oxnard (1970 to present). A twice-monthly newsletter on the payment card industry

Noble, D.: Forces of Production: a Social History of Industrial Automation. Knopf, New York (1984)

Nocera, J.: A Piece of the Action: How the Middle Class Joined the Money Class. Simon and Schuster, New York (1994)

O'Brien, J.A.: The Impact of Computers on Banking. Bankers, Boston (1968)

Omniswitch tests merchant-to-bank authorization system. Payment Systems Newsletter, p. 4 (July 1971)

Omniswitch: A Cornerstone for National Authorization Through Interbank (December 1971). Description of the Omniswitch system prepared for a meeting in Atlanta, GA. Provided by Tom Schramm, VP of operations for Omniswitch

O'Neil, P.: A little gift from your friendly banker. Life **68**, 48–50 (1970)

O'Neil, M.: Charge-card networks are working. ABA Banking Journal **66**(3), 116 ff (1973)

Operations and systems notes. American Banker, p. 6 (16 February 1972)

Orr, J.: Talking About Machines: an Ethnography of a Modern Job. Cornell University Press, Ithaca (1996)

Parker, M.: Organizational Culture and Identity: Unity and Division at Work. SAGE, London (2000)

Payment Systems Newsletter, p. 5 (July 1971)

Penick, E.M.: Quoted in Worthen B&T offers debit card service. American Banker, p. 1 (12 September 1975)

Perks, R., Thomson, A. (eds.): The Oral History Reader. Routledge, London (1998)

Perrow, C.: Normal Accidents: Living with High-risk Technologies. Basic Books, New York (1984)

Peters, T.J., Waterman, R.H.: In Search of Excellence: Lessons from America's Best-run Companies. Harper and Row, New York (1982)

Petroski, H.: The Evolution of Useful Things. Vintage Books, New York (1994)

Pettigrew, A.M.: On studying organizational cultures. Administrative Science Quarterly **24**, 570–581 (1979)

Pinch, T.J., Bijker, W.E.: The social construction of facts and artefacts: or how the sociology of science and the sociology of technology might benefit each other. Social Studies of Science **14**(3), 399–441 (1984)

Pinch, T.J., Bijker, W.E.: The social construction of facts and artefacts: or how the sociology of science and the sociology of technology might benefit each other. In: Bijker, W.E., Hughes, T.P., Pinch, T. (eds.) The Social Construction of Technological Systems: New Directions in the Sociology and History of Technology, pp. 17–50. MIT Press, Cambridge (1987)

Pittsburgh NB will offer Entree card. American Banker, p. 6 (3 March 1976)

Plea for new hearing by Worthen is denied. American Banker, p. 1 (25 October 1973)

Poitevent, J.L.: OCR for credit card processing. Datamation **15**(7), 49–52 (1969)

Pollock, N., Cornford, J.: ERP systems and the university as an 'unique' organisation. Information Technology and People **17**(1), 31–52 (2004)

Portelli, A.: What makes oral history different? In: Perks, R., Thomson, A. (eds.) The Oral History Reader, pp. 63–74. Routledge, London (1998)

Powell, W.W.: Neither market nor hierarchy: network forms of organization. Research in Organizational Behavior **12**, 295–336 (1990)

The Public Appraises Bank Cards: A National Survey of Public Attitudes Toward and Use of Bank Cards (1971). Survey conducted for National BankAmericard Incorporated by Field Research Corporation

Quigley, D.: Omniswitch system described as reality, not concept. American Banker, p. 8A (1 December 1971)

Raymond, E.S.: The Cathedral and the Bazaar: Musings on Linux and Open Source by an Accidental Revolutionary, revised edn. O'Reilly, Sebastopol (2001)

Reason, J.: Human Error. Cambridge University Press, Cambridge (1990)

Reason, J.: Human error: models and management. British Medical Journal **320**, 768–770 (2000)

The recession catches up with credit cards. Business Week, p. 47 (17 February 1975)

Reed, J.: The case for own-your-own. Banking, p. 20+ (October 1972)

The republican's bold credit card campaign. Business Week, pp. 33–34 (4 December 1978)

Richardson, D.W.: Electric Money: Evolution of an Electronic Funds-transfer System. MIT Press, Cambridge (1970)

Riday, J.W.: The checkless society. Banking **61**(3), 49–50 (1968)

Roberts, K.H.: Some characteristics of one type of high reliability organization. Organization Science **1**(2), 160–176 (1990)

Roberts, K.H. (ed.): New Challenges to Understanding Organizations. Macmillan, New York (1993)

Robertson, F.: The aesthetics of authenticity: printed banknotes as industrial currency. Technology and Culture **46**, 31–50 (2005)

Rochet, J.-C., Tirole, J.: Cooperation among competitors: some economics of payment card associations. RAND Journal of Economics **33**(4), 549–570 (2002)

Rochlin, G.I.: Defining 'high reliability' organizations in practice: a taxonomic prologue. In: Roberts, K.H. (ed.) New Challenges to Understanding Organizations, pp. 11–32. Macmillan, New York (1993)

Ross, I.: The credit card's painful coming-of-age. Fortune **84**(4), 108–111, 150–156 (1971)

Rothbard, M.N.: A History of Money and Banking in the United States: the Colonial Era to World War II. Ludwig von Mises Institute, Auburn (2002)

Rowlingson, K., Kempson, E.: Paying with Plastic: a Study of Credit Card Debt. Policy Studies Institute, London (1994)

Russell, T.: The Economics of Bank Credit Cards. Praeger, New York (1975)

Sapolsky, H.M.: The Polaris System Development: Bureaucratic and Programmatic Success in Government. Harvard University Press, Cambridge (1972)

Schantz, H.F.: The History of OCR: Optical Character Recognition. Recognition Technologies Users Association, Manchester Center, VT (1982)

Schreft, S.L.: How and Why Do Consumers Choose Their Payment Methods? (October 2005), Prepared for the Federal Reserve Bank of Boston's Consumer Behavior and Payment Choice Conference, October 2005

Schulman, P.: The analysis of high reliability organizations: a comparative framework. In: Roberts, K.H. (ed.) New Challenges to Understanding Organizations, pp. 33–53. Macmillan, New York (1993)

Scrutchin, T.W. Jr.: TPF: performance, capacity, availability. In: IEEE Compcon 1987 Digest of Papers, pp. 158–160. IEEE Computer Society, Washington (1987)

A second card in your future? ABA Banking Journal, p. 54 (August 1976)

Security Pacific, California, contracts for POS system for merchants. American Banker, p. 2 (7 October 1976)

Simmel, G.: The Philosophy of Money, 3rd, enlarged edn., reprint of 1978. Routledge, London (2004)

Simmons, M.: The Credit Card Catastrophe: the 20th Century Phenomenon That Changed the World. Barricade Books, New York (1995)

Simon, H.A.: Administrative Behavior: a Study of Decision-Making Processes in Administrative Organization, 3rd edn. The Free Press, New York (1976)

Siu, L.: Octopus and Mondex: the social shaping of money, technology and consensus (April 2002), http://www.sociology.ed.ac.uk/finance/Papers/Siu_Octopus.pdf—visited on 4 September 2006, Social Studies of Finance working paper

Siwieć, J.E.: A high-performance DB/DC system. IBM Systems Journal **16**(2), 169–195 (1977)

Smith, S., Watson, J. (eds.): Getting a Life: Everyday Uses of Autobiography. University of Minnesota Press, Minneapolis (1996)

Smith, S., Watson, J.: Reading Autobiography: a Guide for Interpreting Life Narratives. University of Minnesota Press, Minneapolis (2001)

Spengemann, W.C.: The Forms of Autobiography: Episodes in the History of a Literary Genre. Yale University Press, New Haven (1980)

Stallwitz, J.F.: A market research study of the attitudes and reactions of member and non-member merchants to bank credit card plans. Masters thesis, University of California Berkeley (December 1968)

Standards are the glue. Payment Systems Newsletter, p. 1 (July 1972)

Stanley, L.: The Auto/biographical I: the Theory and Practice of Feminist Auto/biography. Manchester University Press, Manchester (1992)

Stanley, L.: On auto/biography in sociology. Sociology 27(1), 41–52 (1993)

Starr, C.: Social benefit versus technological risk. Science 165(3899), 1232–1238 (1969)

Staudenmaier, J.M.: Technology's Storytellers: Reweaving the Human Fabric. MIT Press, Cambridge (1985)

Stearns, D.L.: In plastic we trust: dependability and the Visa payment system. http://www.sociology.ed.ac.uk/finance/Papers/StearnsDIRC06.pdf—visited on 17 August 2010. Paper presented at the DIRCshop Conference, 10–11 April 2006, Newcastle, UK

Stigler, G.J.: The division of labor is limited by the extent of the market. Journal of Political Economy 59(3), 185–193 (1951)

Streeter, B.: Let's stop using EFT jargon, and start offering new services. ABA Banking Journal 71(7), 69–75 (1979). Interview with Dee Hock

Struble, F.M.: Bank credit cards and check credit plans in the nation and the district. Monthly Review of the Tenth Federal Reserve District, pp. 3–9 (July–August 1969)

Strum, S., Latour, B.: Redefining the social link: from baboon to humans. Social Science Information 26(4), 783–802 (1987)

Swindells, J. (ed.): The Uses of Autobiography. Taylor and Francis, London (1995)

Thompson, P.: The Voices of the Past: Oral History, 3rd edn. Oxford University Press, Oxford (2000)

Thomson, A.: Anzac memories: putting popular memory theory into practice in Australia. In: Perks, R., Thomson, A. (eds.) The Oral History Reader, pp. 300–310. Routledge, London (1998)

Travelers check plans disclaimed. American Banker, p. 9 (25 July 1978)

Travelers checks: a far-flung banking business. Banking, pp. 154–155 (September 1965)

Tyson, D.O.: Citibank introduces check card different from others. American Banker, p. 1 (25 October 1973)

Unsolicited bank credit cards. Hearings before the Committee on Banking and Currency, United States House of Representatives, 19th Congress, First Session (8 and 9 November 1967)

Using Credit Cards to Buy the Groceries. Business Week, p. 50 (9 November 1974)

Usurpation feared in Visa, Penney Tie. American Banker, p. 1 (11 April 1979)

Vansina, J.: Oral Tradition: a Study in Historical Methodology. Translated by H.M. Wright. Routledge, London (1965)

Vaughan, D.: The Challenger Launch Decision: Risky Technology, Culture and Deviance at NASA. University of Chicago Press, Chicago (1996)

A Visa-card offensive angers the opposition. Business Week, p. 31 (5 September 1977)

Visa Debit Card Service: a Digest of Key Research Findings (March 1977). Produced by National BankAmericard Incorporated

Visa Debit Card Services (1977). Brochure on the Visa debit card produced by Visa USA

Visa dial terminal pilot project final report (April 1982). Produced by Visa USA

Visa intl's travel check sales surge; see 8% market share. American Banker, p. 3 (2 December 1980)

Visa seeks decentralized issuance of its travelers checks. American Banker, p. 2 (14 July 1978)

Visa studies travelers checks. American Banker, p. 1 (25 January 1978)

Visa verification net reaches UK, Canada. American Banker, p. 1 (22 July 1977)

Visa, Visa International Annual Report http://corporate.visa.com/av/reports/corp_report.jsp. (2006)—visited on 2007

Visa, Visanet Fact Sheet. http://corporate.visa.com/md/fs/corporate/visanet.jsp—visited on 26 June 2007

Visa's climb to No. 1 in cards. Business Week, pp. 26–27 (16 July 1978)

Visa's climb to No. 1 in cards. Business Week, p. 26 (17 July 1978)

von Bertalanffy, L.: General System Theory: Foundations, Development, Applications. George Braziller, New York (1968)

Wade, W.: President to Sign Check 21 Today. American Banker, p. 23 (28 October 2003)

Weatherford, J.: The History of Money. Three Rivers, New York (1997)

Weick, K.E.: The Social Psychology of Organizing, 2nd edn. Random House, New York (1969)

Weick, K.E.: Organizational culture as a source of high reliability. California Management Review **29**(2), 112–127 (1987)

Weick, K.E.: Sensemaking in Organizations. SAGE, Thousand Oaks (1995)

Weinberg, G.M.: An Introduction to General Systems Thinking. John Wiley and Sons, New York (1975)

Weinberg, A.: Payments 2004: The merchant perspective: exploring the payments acceptance landscape. Technical report, Glenbrook Partners (August 2004). http://www.glenbrook.com/opinions/merchant-perspective-2004.html—visited on 6 October 2005

Weiner, S.E.: Electronic payments in the U.S. economy: an overview. Federal Reserve Bank of Kansas City Economic Review **84**(4) (1999)

Weinstein, M.: Visa elects Russell as President, chief executive. American Banker, p. 3 (25 May 1984)

When we achieve a nationwide electronic funds transfer system. Banking, pp. 29–32 (May 1974)

Why big stores are taking outside credit cards. Business Week, pp. 132–134 (3 September 1979)

Wiegold, C.F.: Worthen suit against NBI's ban needs full trial. American Banker, p. 1 (12 July 1973)

Wiegold, C.F.: Omniswitch tests system of merchant-to-bank authorization to aid card use, reduce fraud. American Banker, p. 1 (18 June 1971)

Wiegold, C.F.: NBI appeals to court for chance to prove dual membership ban is not group boycott. American Banker, p. 1 (2 January 1973)

Winner, L.: Do artifacts have politics? Daedalus **109**, 121–136 (1980)

Witt, U.: Firms as realizations of entrepreneurial visions. Papers on Economics and Evolution 0510 (Max Planck Institute of Economics, Jena, 2005). https://papers.econ.mpg.de/evo/discussionpapers/2005-10.pdf—visited on 2 Feb 2006

Wittgenstein, L.: Philosophical Investigations, Translated by G.E.M. Anscombe, 3rd edn. Blackwell, Oxford (1958)

Wonglimpiyarat, J.: Strategies of Competition in the Bank Card Business: Innovation Management in a Complex Economic Environment. Sussex Academic Press, Brighton (2004)

Word bankamericard volume sets record. American Banker, p. 3 (2 May 1973)

Worthen asks high court to review reversal. American Banker, p. 1 (11 December 1973)

Worthen opposes call for full trial. American Banker, p. 1 (23 July 1973)

Worthington, S.: Retailer aspirations in plastic cards and payment systems. Journal of Retailing and Consumer Services **1**(1), 30–39 (1994)

Yates, J.: Structuring the Information Age: Life Insurance and Technology in the Twentieth Century. Johns Hopkins University Press, Baltimore (2005)

Zelizer, V.A.: The Social Meaning of Money: Pin Money, Paychecks, Poor Relief and Other Currencies. Basic Books, New York (1994)

Index

101 California, 194

A

ABA, 74
ABA Monetary and Payments System (MAPS)
    planning committee, 78
Access points, 207
Addressograph-Multigraph, 139
Addressograph, 74
Advisor groups, 49, 56
Airline Control Program (ACP), xv, 127
Alta Mira hotel, 46
American Airlines, 11, 127
American Bankers Association (ABA), 140
American Express (AmEx), 16, 20, 78
American Express Company, 181
American Medical Association (AMA), 169
Angermueller, Hans H., 192
Antitrust, xiv, 113, 190
Arthur Andersen, 62, 101
Asset card, 165, 212, 214
At par, 2, 5, 168
AT&T, 82, 86, 101, 130
ATM, 148, 159, 173
Authorization, xiv, 30, 33, 58, 71, 124, 132,
    150, 167
Autobiographies, xiii
Automated clearinghouse (ACH), 96, 159

B

Bank of America (BofA), xiv, 19, 54, 118,
    182, 185
Bank of California, 119
Bank Service Corporation (BSC), 50
BankAmericard Authorization System
    Experimental (BASE), 71, 80
BankAmericard licensing program (system),
    29, 37

BankAmericard Service Corporation (BASC),
    26, 36, 54, 110
BankAmericard, xiv, 20, 29, 30, 43, 56, 117
Barclaycard, 118
Barclays, 182, 186
Barclays Bank, 27, 110, 134
BASC, 39, 44, 45, 113
BASE, 95
BASE I, xiv, 95, 124
BASE II, xiv, 35, 91, 92, 143
BASE III, xiv, 103
BASE IV, 136
Bloomingdale, Alfred, 15
Blue-white-and-gold (BWG) bands design, 57,
    117, 167, 168
BofA, 38, 45, 47, 50
Boundaries, 179, 210
Burroughs, 143

C

California Institute of Technology (Cal Tech),
    145
Capacity, 125
Carte Blanche, 16
Carte Bleue, 118
Cash Management Account (CMA), 164, 214
Cashless-checkless society, 26, 157, 159
Centurex, 104, 105
Century Airlines, 11
Certificate of sales, 61
Chaordic, 43, 51, 88
Charg-It, 18
Charga-plate, 8
Charge card, 6
Chargeback, 33, 62
Chargex, 118